# Trade, Reputation, and Child Labor in Twentieth-Century Egypt

# Trade, Reputation, and Child Labor in Twentieth-Century Egypt

*Ellis Goldberg*

First published 2004 by
PALGRAVE MACMILLAN™
175 Fifth Avenue, New York, N.Y. 10010 and
Houndmills, Basingstoke, Hampshire, England RG21 6XS
Companies and representatives throughout the world

PALGRAVE MACMILLAN is the global academic imprint of the Palgrave Macmillan division of St. Martin's Press, LLC and of Palgrave Macmillan Ltd. Macmillan® is a registered trademark in the United States, United Kingdom and other countries. Palgrave is a registered trademark in the European Union and other countries.

ISBN 0–312–29629–0 hardback

Library of Congress Cataloging-in-Publication Data

Goldberg, Ellis
    Trade, reputation, and child labor in twentieth-century Egypt /
Ellis Goldberg.
        p. cm.
    Includes bibliographical references and index.
    ISBN 0–312–29629–0 (alk. paper)
        1. Cotton trade—Egypt. 2. Trade regulation—Egypt. 3. Child labor—
Egypt. 4. Egypt—Economic policy. I. Title.

HD9087.E42G65 2004
331.3' 18—dc22                                          2004040006

A catalogue record for this book is available from the British Library.

Design by Newgen Imaging Systems (P) Ltd., Chennai, India.

First edition: September, 2004
10 9 8 7 6 5 4 3 2 1

Printed in the United States of America.

*For Peg, Louis, Sofia and Abraham*

# Contents

*Acknowledgments*     ix

*Note on Transliteration*     xi

Chapter 1    Introduction     1

Chapter 2    Reputation, Regulation, and Trade     11

Chapter 3    Growing the World's Best Cotton: Colonial
Crisis or Business as Usual     33

Chapter 4    Regulation for Reputation in the Egyptian Delta     63

Chapter 5    Economics, Development, and Egyptian Economists     89

Chapter 6    Labor Regulation in Egypt After 1952     119

Chapter 7    Efficiency Wages, Moral Economies, and Involution     143

Chapter 8    Conclusion     163

*Notes*     175

*Bibliography*     189

*Index*     207

# Acknowledgments

I began work on the themes this book addresses a decade ago. The unacknowledged debts I have accumulated are not many but they are large. They fall into two categories: those who encouraged or aided me in the production of the book, its argument, and its substance directly and those who have provided me with a sense of community. Abdellah Hammoudi was more than generous as the director of the Transregional Center for the Study of the Middle East, North Africa, and Central Asia at Princeton University. He invited me to spend the 1997–1998 academic year at Princeton as a resident fellow for which I will always be grateful. It was in essence the kind of sabbatical my own institution cannot afford to provide. Avrom Udovitch arranged for me to spend the 1999–2000 academic year in the Near Eastern Studies Department at Princeton where I was able to pursue further the research for this book in the Firestone Library at Princeton.

Bob Vitalis has undoubtedly read far more of this book in draft form than anyone should have to. His comments have always been intelligent, encouraging, witty, and incisive. My intellectual and moral debt to him is great. I have also benefited greatly from Roger Owen's comments and encouragement as well as from comments by Israel Gershoni, Steve Heydeman, and Juan Cole. Audiences at colloquia at the School of Oriental and African Studies, Princeton, Harvard Law School, Bogazici University, and the University of Pennsylvania were gracious in hearing parts of the argument and providing cogent comments. So were the members of the 1999–2000 Princeton discussion group that met faithfully at the home of Beth Baron and Yitzhak Nakash. Jere Bacharach read, commented, and even fetched documents for me.

Another group of people provided indirect but equally great influence on the writing of this book. Writing about the politics and history of the Arab world is an especially contentious issue today. In substance I have benefited greatly from reading the writing of Kanan Makiya, Mai Ghoussoub, and

Hazem Saghie, but I have benefited even more from discussions with them over the past several years on many topics. This is an academic book but if it addresses important issues including the exploitation of children and what actually happened during the imperial era more forthrightly than I would have a decade ago, it is due in large part to their influence. There are four people whose influence endures but who I greatly regret will never see this work in its final form. Bent Hansen and Charles Issawi were erudite economists and profound humanists; Ahmad Sadiq Saᶜd was a politically active intellectual of uncommon honesty. I regret that I will not be able to share this book with these three students of Egyptian history with whose work nearly every page of this book is in dialogue. My father, who died as I was completing this manuscript, will also never see this book although my mother will.

Raising three children, Louis, Sofia, and Abraham, has made the situation of children in the world we live in far more real to me than when I was engaged in earlier studies of the Egyptian political economy. Their impact on this book is substantial as is that of my wife, Peg Benson. When we met nearly two decades ago I promised that my next book would be dedicated to her.

# Note on Transliteration

Transliterations in the text are based on the system used by the *International Journal of Middle East Studies* but without reference to macrons or other symbols to differentiate long vowels. Where an established transliteration exists (as in Abdel Nasser) or where an author chose how to transliterate his own name for publication in a European language I have used those forms.

# CHAPTER 1

## Introduction

Specialization, we are told, is good because it promotes efficiency, which in turn makes everybody better off. Everywhere, that is, except in international trade where high degrees of specialization by countries in particular products seem to be associated with poverty, tyranny, corruption, or all three. Why do some countries specialize in the production of some goods to the degree that they become so intimately connected that we can speak of banana republics and petro-states? Nature clearly has something to do with it: Saudi Arabia has lots of oil and little arable land whereas Argentina has lots of grass land (and cows) and little oil. Although the gifts of nature are rarely as specific as in the South American pampas or the Ghawar oil field, countries specialize despite the dangers of doing so. Why this should be so is something of a mystery and the volume of advice to political leaders to diversify their country's economies is only exceeded by the volume of academic studies attempting to explain why they fail to do so. Without claiming to resolve the mystery I can shed light on a largely ignored aspect of specialization. Simply put, factor endowments matter but human agency matters too and one of the most important drivers of specialization is human agency in the form of a search by economic policy makers to segment global markets to gain a premium price for products with a reputation for quality. States, in short, create brands to promote exports.

If agency matters, its appearance will be in the form of politics and politics matters to political scientists at least as much as it matters to the world's rich and the world's poor, a large fraction of whom happen to be children. Politics matters in the world at large because formal institutions that structure the lives of the rich and the poor are directly affected by the state. Without the state such institutions (even when considered as private bodies) could not exist although states cannot effectively replace many of them. Politics matters in the academic discipline because its working promotes important, albeit intellectual, conflicts about how human life can be made better or at least how human beings can be made better off. Political scientists live intellectually in the shadow of the claim that economic growth does not just happen; it requires the constant adjustment of policy makers utilizing the instruments of the state to massage, transform, and affect the underlying structures of the economy.

What is quality? It is an unexamined truism of contemporary life that the finest products are made from the finest ingredients and that the finest of all products are in such demand everywhere that they may be categorized with the appellation "world-class." Contrarily to this truism, to appreciate the role of quality and reputation in global trade is to upset much of our current conventional wisdom and to resuscitate debates about trade and growth that dominated much of the early twentieth century. Quality is not a thing in itself but a product that appeals to a particular segment of consumers because it meets highly specialized needs. When this truth was more commonly recognized it was understood, even if not advertised, that some of the highest quality goods in international trade were (and still are) themselves produced by employing some of the lowest quality inputs imaginable. Egyptian cotton, French wine, and Persian carpets were highly prized goods in global trade whose production depended on the intensive use of illiterate and poorly paid labor and most particularly on the labor of children.

Certainly in Egypt the labor of children was the single largest input for the production of a high-quality good in international trade for at least two-thirds of the twentieth century. Egypt is not the only country where unskilled workers, especially children, have produced high-quality goods for export but it is an exceptionally revealing place to examine theories of trade, government regulation, and development. Given the ubiquity of children in the markets for wage labor for hundreds of years, it is surprising how rarely children appear in studies of development, political economy, or social change. What few studies there are of child labor usually approach it as a slightly shameful condition and because children are highly unskilled the product of their labor is treated as if it were derisory and of little economic consequence. Yet children are not simply very small and very weak adults; profound social consequences result from the myriad individual decisions to employ children rather than to educate them.

Important as the consequences of child labor were, so too were its causes, although to be more precise we might speak instead of the factors that conduced to the employment of children and made it possible to ensure that the good they produced was of truly high quality. The choice to hire children was invariably due to the cheapness of their wages, but then the labor of weak, illiterate, poorly motivated, and easily distracted workers ought to be cheap. How was it possible to utilize vast quantities of such labor effectively? It could be achieved through the use of public and private regulatory institutions that provided adults with incentives and information to ensure that Egyptian cotton was truly of high quality. Political scientists tend to consider regulation as institutions through which society is disciplined by an external body, the state. Regulatory institutions work most effectively, however, when it arises from and reinforces the incentives that bind very disparate actors into networks of cooperation. I propose to call these networks bound by regulatory institutions "coalitions." I draw this use of the word from the work of Avner Greif but where he employs it to refer to institutions I use it to discuss social groups bound together through institutions that affect implicit (and explicit) contractual relations, expectations, and specific mechanisms for the collection and transmission of information (Greif 526).

The institutions and policies that brought together a coalition stretching from the Egyptian countryside to the English factory were sophisticated and effective. Extending Greif's definition emphasizes the causal role of institutions in aligning what are often called social coalitions and also brings out in relief that their membership crossed international boundaries. The more common use of the term coalition is grounded in the assertion of common interests aligned by economic structure and relationship to factors of production (Gourevitch [1977] 308–309, Katzenstein 890, Mares 696, Rogowski 7). Ultimately such an understanding turns our attention away from the contingent and political ways in which social coalitions are formed to its opposite, an assertion of social cleavage that structures individual preferences about trade. To argue that such coalitions are contingent and based in institutions requires us to investigate agency both through the examination of specific institutions and through the discussion of specific policies that inform their work.

Egyptians in the early twentieth century understood that they produced a product—highly uniform bales of extra-long staple cotton—whose high quality was embodied in its internationally known reputation and they understood that its production required prodigious political as well as physical investments. Thus, in 1927 when the annual meeting of the International Cotton Congress was held in Cairo, an Egyptian economist, Dr. Joseph Nahas, rose to present a paper. Somewhat annoyed that he was repeating early arguments about why the price of Egyptian cotton remained high, he nevertheless reminded an audience of European spinners that Egyptian farmers had made great efforts to produce a fiber that commanded a premium over American produce. "The privilege of producing high-grade cotton, of which Egypt has almost the monopoly is not the gift of Nature only. Much work and great expense are involved which have to be recouped." What his listeners would have understood immediately was that Nahas had neatly elided and criticized Herodotus's observation that Egypt was the gift of the Nile and a then-dominant belief that international trade was wholly determined by natural endowments.

Nahas never tired of reminding his audiences at international meetings that he was himself a landowner and part of the Egyptian social and political elite. He was also the first Egyptian to earn a doctoral degree in economics. The landowning elite prospered as it resolved recurrent conflicts among its members about how a small, open economy such as that of Egypt fit into a global market given its specific resource endowments. If the elite spent hugely on themselves and their farms (but not on those who labored in their fields), men like Nahas also spent prodigious amounts of energy on making policy, immersed in the institutional minutia that governed the production of high-quality cotton and its marketing as well as lobbying government officials about policy implementation. They were phenomenally successful in centering the Egyptian economy on the production and export of cotton for half a century.

Unfortunately their success also rested on the degree to which one particular factor of production, the unskilled labor of children, could be employed to produce a high-quality good. There was a heavy price for the successful use of this factor of production: the widespread employment of children in the countryside retarded the growth of literacy. If literacy is, in the modern world, a fundamental necessity for autonomy, then many Egyptians paid dearly in terms of individual human well-being for the country's success in global trade. Literacy is more than a personal good and the persistence of widespread illiteracy made slowed the transition to industrialization.

The existence of a coalition structured around the production of high-quality cotton, did not preclude the emergence of other coalitions. The Great Depression engendered dramatic change around the world both in institutions and in economic theory (Hall, Gourevitch [1977]). By the 1930s urban entrepreneurs, government officials, and academic economists in Egypt, as in many other agricultural countries, turned their attention to reshaping an economy that had been battered by the collapse of agricultural prices and where the old social coalition of cotton export had been severely shaken. The creation of an industrial sector whether for home consumption or export required new institutions, the formation of new factor endowments through policies of public investment, and consequently a very different coalition of actors. If the labor of children was the crucial factor endowment for the production of high-quality cotton, the labor of moderately literature adults was, along with physical capital in the form of machinery, the crucial factor endowment for industry. To transform the economy required the creation of new regulatory institutions to insure that literate adults could find and keep jobs in the new sector of the economy. When a new government came to power in 1952 committed to industrialization it undertook a variety of measures to reshape the labor market so as to limit the competition to adult employment from children in the new sector of the economy as well as to increase the supply of literate adults.

This book is about the trajectory of an agricultural economy from an open exporter of staples into the early stages of what was to be called import-substituting industrialization. This is not a new story, but telling through a focus on the production of a high-quality good, provides three original and important insights into economic development. First, the success of open economies under free trade requires institutions as rich and complex as those of more developed market economies as well as of the closed or socialist economies. Egypt had created many public and private regulatory institutions, from import control legislation to sophisticated financial markets, that are rarely the subject of investigation by political scientists or historians. One remarkable indication of the power of this analysis is that it reveals that, contrary to the standard account of the Egyptian political economy (Richards; Hansen [1991]; Beinin [1999]; Mitchell [2002]), Egypt did not experience ecological crisis in the first third of the twentieth century. What has been narrated as ecological crisis was a rapid response by Egyptian growers to global shifts in demand for a highly reputable primary good. Second, as Egyptian officials and entrepreneurs invested in technological innovation and reputation they developed a demand for unskilled labor that was met by children. As poor families supplied children to markets for wage labor, they also decreased their demand for education. Consequently the existence of an active market for child labor inhibited investment in education and literacy and Egypt continued to be a country well endowed with unskilled and illiterate labor. With only limited supplies of an important factor of production—literate labor—Egyptian industry remained noncompetitive locally and globally. Third, Egyptian history demonstrates that standard accounts of economic development and industrialization pay insufficient attention to how institutional choices linked investments in product reputation to child labor, high levels of illiteracy, and low levels of economic development. Standard accounts usually focus on the high costs of local raw materials and the absence of sufficient capital but assume that labor was abundant. On the contrary, the trajectory of Egyptian economic development in the 1940s and 1950s was, I argue, inhibited by the absence of a large reserve of educated adults, especially women. Egypt was not abundant in the semiskilled labor that drives light industrial development. Consequently the workforce engaged in such economic sectors responded very favorably to the closure of local labor markets and to the closure of the national economy. This resolves a long-standing puzzle about Egyptian labor law and the policies of the new government after 1952: why did a government that seemed committed to industrialization under the leadership of the private sector enact labor legislation that appeared remarkably favorable to trade unions? Because it hoped that rising wages and trade union power would not only expel children from the urban workforce but "bootstrap" the economy to a new equilibrium.

These insights emerge from the power of using a new theoretical tool to examine an old story while also paying careful attention to contemporary accounts by local (Egyptian) actors and intellectuals. This argument therefore looks like two new stories: a story of the staples economy told through the economics of imperfect information (reputation) and a story about import-substitution industrialization told through expectations about increasing returns, which is short-circuited through inadequate levels of human capital formation and labor market competition. Because both the new information economics and import substitution theories have roots in the work of John Maynard Keynes and diverge significantly from the approach of neoclassical economics, I call this a Keynesian story. Egyptians were, to some degree, aware of these stories. It will become apparent that when Egyptians in the first half of the twentieth century discussed economic policy they themselves frequently referred to reputation and returns to scale. The technical advances in understanding the economics of reputation and scale effects make it easier to understand those old debates. They also let us recapture debates about the role of the state in terms Egyptian elites themselves understood (Vitalis [1995]; Davis [1983]).

What is striking about Egyptian debates on industrialization and even the early years of policymaking is their contrary course. Government economists, advisers, and other influential figures clearly shared the expectation that the new policies would more closely connect the Egyptian and the global economies. Early proposals about industrialization were Keynesian insofar as they presumed that Egypt possessed unemployed or underemployed resources that could easily expand production. Many later ones were explicitly framed on the then cutting-edge models later formalized as "new trade theory" and sound remarkably similar to contemporary explanations for the successful industrialization of the "tigers" of East Asia.

The link between early agricultural regulation and later regulation for industrialization lies in 50 years of disciplinary debates conducted by Egyptian economists. Egyptian economists sustained lengthy debates about the implications of Ricardian, Keynesian, and new trade theories for economic policy. My presentation of those debates is the first sustained account of them and the first to propose an explicit argument about how they miscarried.

There are many detailed studies of the Egyptian political economy in the nineteenth century and the second half of the twentieth century (Owen [1969]; Tignor [1995]; Waterbury; Hansen and Nashashibi). Apart from the work of Bent Hansen and a few specialized studies, however, we know remarkably little about what Egyptian landowners or businessmen did in the first half of the twentieth century (Vitalis [1995]; Tignor [1984]; Hansen [1990]). There are no complete biographies in Arabic or other languages of the key leaders in government or business in the first half of the century. There are no studies of economic policy-making or studies of conflicts over economic theory in a country with a century of engagement by professional economists. Nahas, landlord and economist, was followed by an increasingly large number of Egyptian economists who wrote in Arabic, French, and English about the economic policies. Any study of policy making must therefore be, at least in part, a study of some of the arguments Egyptians had about trade, investment, and development. Nahas opened the debate of determined intervention in the economy as a necessary aspect of free trade, but others responded by mid-century urging limitations on trade and what are now called development policies.

How the Egyptian elite constructed economic and political institutions to segment a global market for a staple good sheds light on the working of a free-trade regime. It illuminates the ways national governments enhance sectoral interests in global markets and it therefore allows us to see more clearly how state regulation in poorer economies worked. The persistence of the legal and institutional foundations of regulation also allows us to see the difficulties of turning a regulatory regime into one for direct control of the economy. The dependency literature once proposed that national governments in Asia, Africa, and Latin America participated with domestic and foreign investors in supplying raw inputs for industrial producers centered in the United States and Europe. Entrepreneurs and government officials certainly played aggressive roles in shaping their own societies to fit into an emergent international division of labor. What the dependency literature never provided was a mechanism linking investment decisions in countries that produced primary commodities with those of the countries in which they were sold. As Nahas implied, however, Egyptian growers had developed their own economic strategies and had carried them out at significant expense. The missing link is the recognition that dependent elites developed policies designed to enable them to wield monopoly power within those markets. The analytic weakness of dependency theory became evident when investment decisions and freer trade in the 1960s led to explosive growth and economic development in countries in East Asia. Strategic economic policies carried out by powerful regulatory agencies were often said to be at the core of that explosive growth. What I am proposing is that economic growth was not constrained by state weakness as much as it was by the interaction of factor endowments and the import policies of the wealthy countries of Europe and the United States.

To segment the global market for fiber, Egyptian growers influenced the foreign policy of their own government and also engaged in an ongoing private commercial diplomacy. Private diplomacy resembled the kind of international economic bargaining, which is today formally carried on by states. This diplomacy was conducted through international associations of producers and consumers and was especially important because of the heterogeneous nature of elite interests in Egypt and the semicolonial nature of the state in which foreign citizens played important roles in administrative and judicial institutions.

Britain had occupied Egypt in 1882 and British officials heavily influenced Egypt's government. The absence of any prolonged discussion of colonial rule will strike many readers as perplexing at best if not completely wrongheaded. However, in order to focus on the Egyptian elite and their contribution to policymaking I have made the decision generally not to address the role of British officials in Egypt. The British were notorious for running empire on the cheap. The implications of this are obvious: empire was a network sustained largely by an indirect collaboration among a global assortment of local elites none of whom had any ties with each other. Thus British policy was in some ways as constrained by the preferences of local elites as the preferences of local elites were by British policy. Colonizing Egypt was therefore a collaborative effort accomplished neither by gazing at Egyptians nor by incarcerating them.

The quest for political autonomy was important in many ways and at crucial moments it will impinge on the themes of this book. Joseph Nahas, for example, had a long and close personal relation with the nationalist leader, Sa'd Zaghlul, joined the nationalist delegation in Paris in 1919, and ardently desired complete independence for Egypt. He was a patriot but not quite a nationalist in the way we have come to understand the word today. That there was a cultural and political boundary between Egypt and Europe was clear to him but the sharpness of that boundary was less clear and the difficulty of crossing it less apparent than it has since become.

For the landowners to influence policy about the supply of fiber was, of course, not as hard as developing a policy of industrial growth that required addressing problems of investment in physical capital and in labor supply. In the mid-twentieth century important academic economists and policy makers frequently claimed that the crucial ingredient for growth was the utilization of supposedly unemployed labor. There is no doubt the military government after 1952 reshaped the economy in accord with some of these theories by reshaping the labor market to win political support from industrial workers and their organizations. Two crucial features of the Egyptian political economy came together after the coup: low-labor productivity in industry and a government able to employ regulatory policy to create a new social coalition. The emergence of "socialist" policies in which the state used a variety of mechanisms to protect local industry is surprising. Both the new government and the local labor force ought to have welcomed foreign investment. The army leaders, many of whom were vocal supporters of private property, undertook policies that were supposed to encourage such investment and institutions representing labor, an abundant factor of production, ought to have favored free trade and even increased investment (Rogowski). Labor, however, was far from a homogenous factor of production: it was strongly split into relatively highly skilled and almost completely unskilled sectors. The relatively skilled workers whose interests were dominant in the trade union movement were an extremely scarce factor of production and the army officers had many reasons to fear a coalition centered on foreign or domestic investors. Therefore when the dust settled a new coalition was formed whose core members no longer desired an open economy. As I shall show, the development policies of the new government, centered largely on what later came to be called "manpower development," reinforced the segmentation of Egypt's labor force and provided continuing support for policies of limiting free trade.

Under that new government, Egyptian economic policy-making was successful in detaching Egypt from the free trade relationships that had dominated it for nearly a century and has long remained so. I believe that this was, like the experience of the elite that dominated the cotton export economy, a costly success. The precise causal sequence of this exercise in policy making is frankly ambiguous because in 1956 an exogenous shock—war over the Suez Canal—occurred. Nevertheless, the new policies that were negatively perceived by foreign investors were popular with many workers in domestic industry. Government regulation cannot be successful if it takes society as an externally given constant because the coordination of behavior and interests that underlies successful regulation requires constant effort to adjust the coordination of incentives and expectations.

That the government cannot take society as a given and that regulation requires the coordination of expectations and incentives for successful implementation is the last, and perhaps most novel, conclusion of this book. In place of regulation as an indicator of the strength of the state relative to society, regulation is more properly seen as the creation of a coalition. Like all coalitions, a regulatory coalition will only last as long as it provides incentives compatible with the interests of its members.

The concepts that will guide this study are drawn from several economic literatures, which are likely to be unfamiliar to students of comparative politics and even more so to students of Egypt. They have not even found their way into much work by specialists in comparative political economy on development, governance, and growth. Before I can use the concepts of reputation and regulatory coalitions, I need to explain what they are. I also need to show why they are necessary if we are to resolve the long debate about the relationship of states to markets, development, and dependence and to these tasks I turn my attention in chapter 2.

# CHAPTER 2

# Reputation, Regulation, and Trade

T aking the reputation of agricultural or indeed any primary goods seriously is a break with an entire disciplinary tradition of comparative politics and political economy because it places collective agency at the heart of the analysis. Doing so requires and allows us to understand the political economy of trade and the role of regulatory institutions, especially in less developed countries, more clearly. It also allows us to understand many of the debates about economic policy in Egypt and elsewhere more clearly and it provides us with an exceptionally good vantage point to see a way out of the dilemma inherent in the Weberian concept of state bureaucracy as a rule-enforcing mechanism that seems so at odds with the actual functioning of state institutions in countries like Egypt. Employing the concept of reputation allows us to understand what happens when the assumption of perfect information that underlies both neoclassical economic analysis and the Weberian concept of the state are undone. The very fact that some goods have a reputation reveals profound problems in the economic theory that informs our understanding of global trade and the creation of reputations is so frequently connected to the creation of regulatory institutions that it reveals the need to revisit in a fundamental way the understanding of governing institutions in the discipline of political science.

## What is Reputation and Why Does It Exist?

In common use since the thirteenth century, the word reputation has, in English, been connected with a common or general estimate of the quality of a person or thing. In contemporary economic theory, reputation refers more narrowly to estimates formed by consumers of the present or future quality of goods produced by firms based on their past experience with the same goods (Shapiro [1983] 659). Reputation has value and, like other assets, is produced by investment. Producers invest in reputation because information is imperfect; if information were perfect consumers would always know rather than estimate the quality of goods they buy and match their needs perfectly. Although investment in reputation plays little role in the literature of international political economy (see Falvey for one of the rare accounts), it is a well-developed aspect of the literature on firms, domestic markets, regulation, and policy making (Spulber; Dixit; Vietor). Information is imperfect for two important reasons. First, it is impossible to know everything if only because the cost of obtaining and storing such knowledge would be too great. Even if we could know everything, there remains the cost of holding large amounts of irrelevant information; we cannot match the information we might need with the information we can obtain.

Aside from cost, information may also be strategically imperfect: one party to a contract knows something about itself that is advantageous to withhold from the other. The classic examples of this problem are associated with writing insurance contracts, but the concept has a more general application. An insured person may engage in riskier behavior than the insurer expects simply because an insurance contract has been signed. This so-called moral hazard appears in many settings where one party to an agreement may change his or her behavior simply because of the existence of the agreement or completed contract or purchase. Because the quality of many goods— from the raw cotton used by spinners to a shot of bourbon purchased in a bar—cannot be evaluated until after it is consumed, buyers often prefer a highly reputable producer to one unknown but cheaper.

Insurers also discover that if they set their rates sufficiently high they actually exclude those less likely to engage in risky behavior from their pool of purchasers and that the purchasers therefore include an unexpectedly large proportion of people who will file claims. This, so-called adverse selection, also occurs in other settings where prices do not simply provide information and clear markets but affect the behavior of parties to a contract. Another classic example of adverse selection is interest rates that are sufficiently high to exclude viable investments but there are other similar examples. It is not uncommon that when firms offer employees job security to induce highly skilled or highly motivated to stay that they end up retaining more of the less skilled or less motivated than they expected.

The relevance of these concepts to the production of goods is straightforward. Providing a guarantee to purchase may be necessary to induce producers to invest in the production of goods of a desired quality but it may also induce them to make goods of less than the desired quality. When purchasers set a price that is too low they may not be able to find suppliers of goods of the quality they desire, but when they set a price that is too high they may find themselves encouraging the production of substandard goods.

Moral hazard and adverse selection can only arise, of course, in a world of imperfect markets. If there were a very large number of suppliers and consumers for all goods, none of whose decisions affected price, then it would always be possible to match supply and demand for any kind of good at an equilibrium price. Many goods and certainly many services obviously are not traded in perfect markets. What is surprising, however, is to realize that, although many agricultural goods appear to provide paradigmatic examples of perfect market, they are not inherently so. Raw agricultural goods are not inherently shaped for trading in perfect markets. Goods that are produced in nature (as opposed to in factories) are inherently highly uneven in terms of quality and the dimensions of quality on which they differ are many, complex, and difficult to regulate. This being so, purchasers of raw materials must, in the unexpectedly colorful language of economists, induce some producers to differentiate themselves from "fly by night" entrepreneurs. They must induce some producers (sellers) to provide information about the quality of the goods they produce and they must also induce producers to provide products of the desired rather than substandard quality.

## Reputation as an Asset

In modern economic theory assets are frequently defined as being tangible or intangible, but the underlying concept is that an asset is formed by ownership of a specific instance of a factor of production or a claim over such a specific instance. The factors of production are land, labor, and capital. In the modern world individuals own only their own labor but they can contract the use of their labor-power to others. The factors of land and capital, however, can be held in shared ownership or subject to complex contractual relationships. Financial assets such as money, loans, shares of stock, or credit are probably the assets that first come to mind as intangible assets, but they are not the only kind. Information is also clearly a valuable resource and although it can be assimilated to labor under the concept of human capital or to capital under the concept of intellectual property, it is more useful for the purposes of this study to treat it as a distinct kind of asset in an analytic framework introduced later.

What is a reputation and how is reputation produced? Reputations provide information to buyers. To acquire reputations, producers must make significant investments in the production of goods of appropriate quality. Reputations are, at least in this sense, nearly ubiquitous. Many producers, for example, provide goods of higher quality than they are legally required to and sometimes producers provide goods of far higher quality than consumers actually desire. Examples include the old telephone handsets provided by Western Electric and kitchen appliances that outlast their warranties. In this sense investment in reputation requires investments in physical capital and labor to ensure that goods of appropriate quality are produced (Dixit) although it is apparent that there are many dimensions of quality and therefore quite distinct kinds of reputations.

Reputations not only provide information; they are also valuable, paradoxically, because they allow buyers to punish sellers. They can be described as the "trigger mechanism" of a weapon the producer points at his or her own head. Through reputation, private firms commit to investments that form a wedge in an open market between price and the cost of production. What is initially a loss becomes a premium over time as consumers are willing to pay for quality and provides consumers with a way to influence the quality of production over time (Shapiro). Should consumers notice that quality declines they can cease their purchases of goods to which a producer has committed an investment and thereby cause the producer significant harm. When sellers have routinely begun to produce goods above minimal quality, they can induce buyers to enter into implicit contracts that are not (and probably could not be) guaranteed by third-party public institutions (Shapiro; Klein and Leffler).

Reputation facilitates a transaction whenever a purchaser cannot fully determine the quality of goods at the time of sale (Shapiro). Such a world of imperfect information is more than a step away from the conventional models of neoclassical economics (also conventionally referred to as the rational choice world by political scientists) in which all actors have perfect information and in which, therefore, reputations are irrelevant.

Up to this point reputation and quality may appear to refer only to a small fraction of goods: those composed of the finest ingredients and made with the most care. This is not accurate. In addition to the level of quality exhibited by particular examples goods, there is also an aggregate kind of quality: producing nearly identical items even if they are all of average quality. In such a case, standardizing a product whose quality is variable and unobservable falls under the rubric of investing in a reputation for high-quality production.[1] This kind of quality is so deeply embedded in industrial production that we almost completely ignore it although, for example, automobile manufacturers try to avoid gaining a reputation as producers of "lemons," that is, having a disproportionate number of cars be of less than average quality. Many, if not most, raw materials more obviously fall into this category if for no other reason than that buyers (e.g., canners or spinners who will transform the raw materials into other goods) cannot easily tell before the season is finished what quality of goods they will be provided but who do require standard inputs to minimize the expense of providing standard outputs. The rise of franchise businesses in the contemporary world indicates that a concern with this dimension of quality affects a wide range of service providers as well—whether at McDonald's or Starbucks. Thus although what is often in business referred to as "quality control" is a nearly ubiquitous part of economic production, it is almost wholly overlooked in discussions of comparative or international political economy.

If reputations are produced and have value they are clearly an asset for those who produce them. Those who own economic assets are usually concerned to protect their value and to deploy them in the search for an economic return. There is little problem with understanding that those who own land or capital will, if necessary, resort to politics to protect the value of their assets and to ensure their continued profitable deployment. There are good theoretical reasons for believing that the fundamental conceptual framework in understanding the political implications of asset ownership is between specific and nonspecific assets rather than between tangible and intangible assets. The continuum between specific and nonspecific assets, however, is easier to define than is the measurement of the specificity of any given asset. Highly specific assets are those that are so devoted to the production of a particular commodity that they have no value outside its production. Common examples have been the production of automobile nameplates or chassis although an oil field in Saudi Arabia and a baseball team in Chicago are also highly specific assets. Nonspecific assets are those that can be easily removed from the production of one good and deployed in the production of another. Common examples are highly liquid assets such as money or financial instruments but so too are assets such as a river or commercial buildings. This idea of asset specificity is therefore clearly closely linked to the idea of factor mobility. The more specific the assets in which factors are embodied the less mobile are the factors themselves.

Despite an unresolved debate about how asset specificity affects the decisions of asset owners to engage in politics, a few implications of the theoretical distinction are clear. Holders of highly specific assets are more likely to engage in political action to preserve their values when faced with challenges to their market position or their property rights than are holders of nonspecific assets (Frieden). Holders of highly specific assets, after all, face ruin if they cannot continue to employ them because, by definition, they have no value other than as scrap. Per contra, there is good reason to believe that holders of nonspecific assets can far more easily threaten politicians with their redeployment (including redeployment outside the polity) than can holders of specific assets (Bates and Lien). Consequently political leaders might be far more responsive to the desires of holders of such assets. Of course, just because owners of less specific assets can redeploy the underlying factors of production more easily they may be less affected by the political or administrative decisions.

Succeeding chapters deal directly with the kinds of assets economic actors in Egypt and their trading partners abroad possessed. The basic factor inputs for cotton production in Egypt, land and unskilled labor, appear at first glance to be highly nonspecific. Fertile soil and children's hands can produce many crops besides cotton. They can shift to the production of other goods more easily, it would seem, than metal-stamping machines or tool-and-die makers can shift from the production of automobiles to radios or trolley cars. To focus so narrowly, in this case, on plots of land or skill sets, is misleading. To some degree the infrastructural investment in cotton was somewhat specific although less so than often maintained in sectoral analysis. There was an entire structure of social investment in very particular institutions—from irrigation systems through model farms to financial markets effectively denominated in cotton—that were sufficiently specific to be difficult to deploy to other uses. Without the production of cotton these institutions, especially the financial markets (because they were denominated in cotton) had no other value. More important, it must also be apparent that, to the degree that many Egyptians profited from the investment in the reputation of their cotton, they shared the benefit of a highly specific asset. The reputation for the production of high-quality cotton has no value whatsoever if the production of cotton itself ends. It is therefore an asset whose holders we can expect will engage in tenacious political activity to defend and those who hold the assets will be a coalition made up of all those engaged in its production. This is rather different from the commonly held idea that the government had only poor information about how to develop sectors of the economy other than cotton; it is to assert that a relatively large coalition of Egyptians can be considered as joint holders of a highly specific asset whose value, in the absence of the cotton trade, would immediately plummet to zero.

## Imperfect Information and Theories of Trade

Because international trade occurs in a world of imperfect information, the reputation of traded goods matters globally as much as it does domestically although it has rarely been considered in the theoretical literature. The absence of attention, in theories of international exchange, to a real problem of staples trade cannot be due to their relative unimportance in generating economic theory. Considerations of primary goods—among the most famous of which are studies of the market for hogs (Coase and Fowler [1935]; Coase and Fowler [1937]) and the reception of new technologies in corn production (Griliches)—have provided many important instances for the development of economic theory apart from international trade.

To understand better how reputation affects international trade, it is necessary first to look at existing theories of trade, which almost invariably avoid any discussion of the possibility that imperfect information plays a role in it. For more than a hundred and fifty years, economists from Adam Smith to Alfred Marshall struggled to analyze the sources of the gains from trade and their distributive effects. Modern economic analysis began with Adam Smith's *The Wealth of Nations* and Smith's concern with both domestic and international exchange continues to play a profound role in the study of economics. Smith was aware that trade could "inflame the violence of national animosity" (Smith 522), but he argued that exchange, more generally, increased the wealth of both partners. What Smith meant by domestic exchange, as evidenced in his parable of the making of nails, was a social process of specialization and the consequent improvement of labor (Smith 8–9). Anything that made exchange easier thereby increased the size of the market for a good that, in turn, expanded the division of labor and made goods yet cheaper. Whether particular national economies had natural advantages in world trade or had simply acquired an advantage through the division of labor was, for Smith irrelevant (Smith 480). In Smith's world, there does not appear to be any sharp difference in quality between producers for as the parable of the nail also suggests implicitly, production is of identical goods all produced by the greatest possible skill. Smith, writing in the eighteenth century when the mechanization of production was rudimentary and when agriculture was still a dominant economic sector, viewed agricultural products favorably. Nevertheless he noted that processed goods were more valuable than "rude" products, but he naturally attributed the difference in value to the greater specialization that processed goods necessarily required.

Not long after Smith wrote of labor-process specialization as the source of gains from trade, David Ricardo analyzed the gains themselves more generally. Ricardo clearly enunciated the idea of trade based on comparative advantage in a famous quantitative example that explained why England should specialize in the production of textiles and Portugal of wine even if

England could produce both goods more cheaply than could Portugal. Not all the implications of Ricardo's "magic numbers" were fully understood at the time and the idea is still frequently misunderstood. In distilling a concept of comparative advantage Ricardo made it clear that Portugal does not, it must be emphasized, need to produce wine more cheaply than England does. Portugal only needs to produce wine less inefficiently than it produces textiles. Ricardo's crisp arithmetic provided the necessary framework for conceptualizing international free-trade policies and it has been subject to continuous (and frequently skeptical) review down to the present (Irwin; Maneschi 3). For literary, mathematical, and political reasons, Ricardian analysis makes it appear as if the goods each country produces are identical (a single type of wine or textiles or utensils) and as if each country produced only one good using only one factor of production (land, labor, or capital). With more goods and more factors of production, the model becomes technically intractable and an elegant analysis turns into detailed description.

Rhetoric and analytic tractability aside, early discussions of international trade were necessarily rooted in concerns about the sovereignty of states and the well-being of their inhabitants. The empirical problem was that although the logic of comparative advantage worked in theory to make both parties to trade better off, economies that specialized in the production of rude goods appeared to enjoy living standards well below those of economies that specialized in industrial production. Trade did not, it appeared, lead to higher standards of living or higher levels of consumption. Besides a concern with human well-being, politicians and state officials were necessarily cautious about foregoing the advantages of having an industrial base that included not simply higher incomes but higher military capabilities as well. Those were already the prevailing concerns among mercantilist theorists of trade and among policy makers. An apt description is that "mercantilism followed two different methods: the first consisted in deflecting economic activity directly towards the particular ends demanded by political, and more especially military, power; the second in creating a kind of reservoir of economic resources generally, from which the policy of power could draw what it required" (Heckscher, I, 31). Mercantilist thinkers were not concerned to maximize total world income, but with the division of wealth and power in the world. Mercantilist policies therefore sought to maximize the production of strategic goods whose production could never be fully justified by a mere economic analysis of citizen well-being.

The main line of theoretical analysis of trade through the logic of comparative advantage was further developed in two models: the so-called Heckscher–Ohlin–Vanik and the Stolper–Samuelson models. For purposes of the analysis here, what matters is that both these theories analyzed the global trade in goods as a trade in the use of productive factors. With admirable brevity it can be said, "factor services are being exchanged through trade. Commodities serve only as a bundle within which factor services are wrapped" (Leamer [1984] 15). These theories of trade are exercises in static relationships with important implications for what might happen as the assumptions are relaxed (Leamer [1984] 11–35). For the theory to work, it was necessarily assumed that factors of production were immobile globally but perfectly mobile domestically, that global markets for products cleared and that technology was available without cost to all producers.[2] To assume that the factors of production domestically are highly mobile is also to assume that they are not highly specific. If all factors of production were embodied in highly specific instances (machines that produce nameplates to use the earlier example), then switching to new forms of production would necessarily require the complete scrapping of a country's capital stock.

The theory here helps to explain how Ricardo's arithmetic might work because it suggests that countries (or national economies) have different amounts of productive factors, or, more formally, that they are characterized by different factor abundances. Some countries have more than the world's average of capital; others have more than the world's average of fertile land; still others have more than the world's average of unskilled labor. Under free-trade countries (or more properly firms within countries) will choose to specialize in the production of goods that maximize use of the abundant factor of production. A political implication of this theory is that owners of the abundant factor will welcome free trade because demand for its employment will bid up its price and that owners of a scarce factor will be in the reverse situation (Rogowski). Rogowski's analysis of political coalitions is thus confined to those whose preferences in regard to free trade can be read directly off their asset ownership: land, labor, or capital as scarce or abundant factors. It is difficult, however, in Rogowski's framework to consider how owners of complementary factors might cooperate in the production of goods and thus create a coalition that, generally, was favorably inclined toward free trade (or not). It is also difficult, in all purely political frameworks, to know how to place asset owners who are not adults and who, presumably, have no clear preferences that can be translated into political action. One advantage to employing a more purely economic meaning to coalition in addition to the political meaning is that it provides a way to address these kinds of issues.

Hidden away in the condition that there are no more products than factors of production is the presumption that the goods produced by the trading partners are homogenous: any single item is identical with all the other items.

Although this is a necessary condition of existing analyses of trade, it is obviously not an accurate portrayal of the trade in primary goods. Primary materials, or staples, were and remain important items of international exchange. Because staples have undergone only minimal initial processing of a natural product they exhibit significant variation.[3] The greater the heterogeneity of raw materials used as inputs the higher the cost of producing the standardized outputs that are industrial goods. Therefore the homogenization or standardization of raw materials—although absent from theories of trade—is an important dimension of quality for industrial purchasers of primary goods even if it is largely absent from theories of trade. Investments in reputation, whether socially through institutions or individually at the level of firms or immediate producers are one method for transforming the variation of the real world of commodities into standardized products.

## The Work of Development

Simply thinking that agricultural goods are of variable quality and that, consequently, some have important reputations is a break with the existing literature on development as well as trade. The literature on development is a continuation of the mercantilist analysis of trade and invariably argues that industrialization is the necessary path to enhanced human well-being. Explanations of industrialization and attempts to create policies to ensure that economic growth exceeds population growth have not, since World War II, have viewed industrialization and development as desirable ends in themselves rather than because they enhance the military capacity of the state. Nevertheless, many analysts of development have argued that industrialization requires a powerfully intrusive state as the power and wealth of old elites is necessarily confiscated during industrialization. The state can provide new social institutions, increased levels of capital investment, and higher levels of human capital investment than private investors will in open market economies. Contemporary analyses of economic development further claim that industrialization occurs when societies substitute the production of high-quality goods for those of low quality because the state, rather than acquiescing to decisions set by market prices, active circumvents them. For example, one analysis of East Asian development argues that industrialists there succeeded because they "are more solicitous of shop floor productivity and quality than firms that evolved as innovators, with a strategic focus on design and R&D" (Amsden 285). A related further claim is that the state in the East Asian countries has imposed on such firms the need to produce goods of high quality (Wade [1993] 157).

These arguments confuse capital-intensive goods with high-quality goods. They assume that introducing higher levels of physical or human capital create higher-quality products. Because these inputs are more expensive than production processes employing less complex machinery or less well-educated workers, it appears as if the economy has made a transition from the production of lower-quality to higher-quality goods. Quality, however, can only distinguish between goods that are effectively substitutes. A moment's reflection reveals that goods imported from East Asia have rarely been of high quality. No one would mistake a Korean Hyundai for a Rolls Royce; nor would anyone purchase a suit off the rack at Kmart, made in China, with the idea that it was the equal of one produced by Armani, let alone by a bespoke tailor in Savile Row. Industrial goods from China, South Korea, or Hong Kong rarely possess the quality or the reputation that we frequently associate with similar goods made in Japan, Germany, or even the United States. This same reflection also reveals that there are important differences in quality and reputation between similar kinds of goods.

Agricultural producers, like industrial and commercial enterprises, can and do invest in reputation and the production of goods of high quality. The existence of investments in reputation resolves a conundrum posed by Michael Shafer about why agricultural producers can have as much clout with governments as industrial producers despite their different investment profile.[4] Shafer's problem arises because he, like other writers on political economy, incorrectly links quality (reputation) and capital intensity. Although agricultural producers can, in principle, shift crops from one season to the next they have often committed their capital both to a specific crop for one season and, not infrequently, to a reputation for producing the same good of similar quality over many seasons. Reputations can be lost—by expropriation or by theft—and thus those who have reputations have another reason to influence political decisions in domestic and international politics to maintain them. To allow Pima cotton, for example, to be marketed as "Egyptian" or sparking wine from California as "Champagne" is to acquiesce in the robbery of a product's reputation.

By ignoring reputation the development literature makes it appear that agricultural countries such as Egypt had weak states and institutions that were far less robust than they appeared in practice. It is less plausible therefore to argue that development is the replacement of low-quality products by those of higher quality than to recognize it as the process of replacing inputs of lower-capital intensity (including human capital) with those of higher intensity. This process is more likely, initially, to lead to the production of low-quality goods that are, because they are produced with relatively low-quality inputs, cheap and therefore competitive on global markets.

So far I have presented reputation as it is described in the existing literature of economic analysis: as an investment made by a single economic agent who controls an entire production process and touched only lightly on its collective aspect. Thus Starbucks, McDonalds, and the Maytag company are all large firms but we treat them as if they easily aligned the interests of employers, managers, and stockholders alike in the creation and maintenance of reputation. Reputation can also arise from collective investment across institutions and firms. Sometimes it arises from the voluntary joint action of individuals ("look for the trade union label") and sometimes it arises from the activity of the state (through regulatory certification). Most commonly reputation as a collective good appears to involve both private voluntary action and the state. Trade associations and government regulatory agencies are two of the many institutions that may confer, remove, and publicize reputations. Other institutions, including commodity markets, are frequently the sites of bitter conflicts over the evaluation of quality and the reputations of goods bought and sold through their auspices.

## A New Focus for Study

It is easy enough to see why recent students of trade have confused capital intensity with quality, but in the absence of a *theory* of reputation studies of development have, like those of trade, focused on particular institutions to the neglect of others. The implications for a research agenda of considering reputation are large. Besides considering a different kind of socially held asset and a different idea of what constitutes a coalition, a focus on reputation requires that we take seriously the construction of institutions that have largely been ignored until now. That free trade required institutional structures has always been clear but for most of the twentieth century analysts focused on formal agreements between states and the monetary and fiscal institutions created by governments. These include, but are not limited to, those that made the gold standard effective before World War I and the Bretton Woods institutions that were created after World War II (Keynes [1963]; Kahler [1985]; Simmons; Eichengreen [1996]).

The development literature added a concern with another set of institutions, especially those engaged in the collective representation of asset holders. The most important of these institutions are the trade unions. Trade unions became the subject of significant description and analysis because they obviously represented those who sold labor power, which is a very large and important set of asset holders. Unions are clearly important actors in the redistribution of wealth, they often can organize political power and transform latent coalitions into overtly political ones, and their members are very likely to be immediately affected by increased or decreased levels of trade in accord with the work reviewed earlier. In addition to unions, there was also a growing interest in the political associations of other economic actors, notably businessmen, as well as in the creation of market-restraining organizations such as the World Coffee Organization and the Organization of Petroleum-Exporting Countries.

These kinds of institutions are undoubtedly important for the working of international trade and to the health of national market economies, but in places like Egypt they were never quite as important to the actual working of the economy as they have been made out to be. Instead, international markets were long connected to local firms and local firms to each other by a variety of other institutions that were frequently privately owned or of a semipublic character: specifically commodity exchanges, as well as voluntary regulatory institutions. In Egypt such institutions existed for more than a century and they appear in descriptive accounts of other countries to have been profoundly important and contentious institutions in the world economy of the late nineteenth- and early twentieth centuries. They are profoundly unstudied even as they have continued to exist and they are frequently confused with state-dominated marketing associations with which they have very little in common. Just as it is remarkable that there is no theory of reputation and trade, it is equally remarkable that we have no studies of the workings of commodity markets for the past 150 years although they have been the subject of intense political conflict and have generated immense values of financial instruments. The interventions by states in the working of these, often privately owned, institutions deserve far more scrutiny than they have received for theoretical and practical reasons. Practically these institutions were of immense importance in the actual financing and organization of production and thus they were crucial instruments to channel investments in reputation. Their practical importance made them important zones of overt and intense political conflict now largely overlooked. Theoretically they are of interest because they provide insight into the very complex ways that government and private action must coincide for economic regulation to occur. Too frequently, students of political economy have argued that the state stands apart from economic activity as a detached third-party regulator of the messy business of market warfare. The regulation of markets requires that private individuals divulge information of strategic value but state officials and political leaders are not disinterested parties seeking to acquire this information because of its necessary relation to taxation. The developmental state, wielding as it presumed to, the power to regulate and to inquire must also wield the power to tax and to destroy private enterprise. It therefore seems less likely that private parties will yield strategic information to the state with greater ease than they will yield it to other private parties. If insurance companies are subject to the risks of moral hazard and adverse selection, state officials must be even more so.

## Government Institutions and Regulatory Coalitions

Attempts are made to bridge the gap between theories of trade in which governments are the object of conflict between holders of different assets and theories of development in which the governments use their power to affect social interests. One is the "new institutionalist" framework, in which states play a key role in economic growth because they define property rights so as to encourage investment (North). This approach is not very useful for understanding complex social investments and undefined but real property rights in reputation. To the degree that these theories urge us to look at legislative and judicial functions, they point in the right direction but they remain too concerned to view government activities as autonomous acts that shape society. Regulatory agencies, whose staffs may formally or informally be made up of those whom the state seeks to regulate, are far more complex. Regulation, in this case, appears to have more in common with providing institutional solutions that conduce to the joint employment of assets for common purposes than with the assertion of the state's sovereign interest.

Stories about development, trade, and the necessity for powerful state institutions have been, at least since List, stories about the sovereign activity of the state. The sovereign power of the state is more than the monopoly over the instruments of coercion that characterize Weber's classic definition of the modern state. It is no accident that this literature is profoundly concerned with the concept of state autonomy and the ethos of regulatory officials. At the center of arguments about competitiveness and development lies a vision of regulatory agencies that constitute something called Weberian state. The "Weberian" state is a conflation of Max Weber's ideal type of the bureaucracy and the modern state. The Weberian state is thus a unitary sovereign with two faces: honest officials who wield coercive power to enforce rules and higher policy-making officials who make rules in some larger, presumably public interest.[5] The officials in the Weberian state act in accordance with general rules that allow them to make technically correct decisions. Arguments that focus on the role of state institutions to induce entrepreneurs to invest are prone to assume that information is easily obtained. Many such arguments are predicated on the assumption that states acquire information about firms in the economy through taxation. This is, as I shall show later, an exceptionally unrealistic assumption and one that impedes rather than furthers understanding economic policy-making.

It is more useful, at least when studying regulation, to adopt the stance of formal theories of regulation. Regulation may be something firms do with each other through the cooperation of third parties as much as something done to them (Bowman). The regulatory regime itself is a coalition between government officials, firms, and buyers. This coalition has a particular form: regulators arbitrate between consumers and firms by intervening directly in the market mechanism, changing the incomes of consumers, or by affecting firm decisions (Spulber). By intervening on one side or another of a transaction, government officials change the balance between buyer and seller and therefore affect the market in which they operate. Regulators, buyers, and sellers have only limited access to the private information of other members of the coalition and there will be shifts in the extent and direction of market regulation over time. This is a different approach than the more commonly accepted idea in comparative politics that regulators gain independent and reliable access to private information and can thus routinely reach the government's preferred outcomes. This very strong, but I think misleading, assumption dominates the literature on the Weberian state.

Problems with the argument favoring regulatory solutions through the creation of a Weberian state arise empirically and theoretically. Studies of regulation suggest that many (and perhaps most) regulatory problems do not have single, purely technical solutions. Cost–benefit analysis relies, for example, on assumptions that mask political conflicts and competing economic interests (Porter; Jacobs [1963]). Moreover, it is apparent that no regulation can be successful when it works at cross-purposes to the interests being regulated.[6] Successful regulation requires those who have private information to share it. The second major point of this book then is to argue that we must look at regulatory institutions as a form of coalition necessitated by asymmetric information. Regulation is not simply something the state does to a passive body but requires that divergent interests be linked together.[7] Whether the task of regulatory institutions is to monitor the quality of crops grown for export, encourage investments in associated industries, or restructure relationships between capital and labor in order to encourage physical investment their task is still political more than technical. I look at how regulatory institutions dealt with each of these challenges.

I propose therefore that we replace arguments about whether states are strong or weak by arguments about the emergence of regulatory coalitions. States will apparently become stronger as they create regulatory institutions to encourage investment in new areas. However, as Aaron Wildavsky argued in regard to budgets three decades ago, states are more likely to solve problems by creating new institutions than by utilizing general capacities of existing institutions (Wildavsky).

### The Role of Private Institutions in Regulation

Government officials need information but theirs are not the institutions that provide information nor is public regulation the only kind that matters. Yet in writing about development the only kinds of institutions that matter in eliciting information are state organizations. Recent literature has argued that governments are enabled to play a key role in the development process and in trade because they obtain information about the economy as they engage in taxation.

Private institutions play crucial roles in contemporary market economies despite their near-absence from the developmentalist literature other than as aggregators of policy interests and pressure groups. One kind of information that producers and investors require is about the future intentions of others. Surveys can provide some of this information, but people have no compelling reason to reveal their preferences to questioners. It is more common to gauge expectations about likely prices for primary goods and financial instruments through the use of sophisticated markets for future delivery. The existence of such markets provides what economists call incentive compatibility for the revelation of private information. The price system itself, however, is too crude to convey much relevant information for those engaged in economic exchange (Stiglitz [1994]). Formal associations and informal relationships are crucial for conveying information about product specifications that the price system is too crude to convey, but it is rare for governments to be privy to this information. Trade unions can also be such an institution if they provide cheaper access to information about the preference structure of the labor force than firms would gain by individual bargaining (Freeman and Medoff). This question of the economic role of noneconomic institutions is distinct from debate between the new institutionalists and their critics about the noneconomic sources of economic institutions. A third point of this book is to look more closely at the development of private institutions that help to structure markets because they provide incentives for the revelation of private information.

Dramatic change in investment strategies and especially the shift from staple exporter to becoming an industrial producer required equally dramatic changes in the regulatory institutions of the country. Specifically it was necessary to intervene in the arena of formal legislation as well as administrative decision-making to affect the structure of firms, investment strategies, and labor markets. This development-oriented strategy in much of the world mirrored the shift from classical to Keynesian and even mercantilist policies in the industrialized countries.

Cumulative investment decisions change the profile of physical and nonphysical assets. One result can be to allow firms and sectors of the economy to traverse what is called the product cycle. Widespread concern with the product cycle emerged out of a debate over competitiveness in the industrial countries and became especially prominent in the United States in the 1980s and it has affinities with the concepts of "easy" and "hard" import substitution industrialization and capital "deepening." It has long been linked to stories about development,[8] but the story of development being told can easily be elided into a moral tale in which the regulatory institutions of an autonomous state are the collective conscience of a society.[9] A description of the path by which some countries mobilize savings and dramatically increase investments in physical capital and human labor is easily rewritten in ethical terms: Countries that curb their appetites learn from those whose knowledge is superior. They can continue to discipline their unruly instincts and move from rude and simple agriculture to refined and sophisticated industrial production.

It is worth retaining skeptical distance from the development literature in order to avoid conflating government policies and individual ethics. It is, at least in part, in reaction to the implicit morality story that economists have leveled some harsh criticism against the development literature.[10] Still, as a snapshot of a path from relatively low incomes to high ones the developmentalist picture (like the modernization one before it) has much to commend it. My concern is threefold: (1) focusing on investment as the mechanism for development, (2) with investment choices, and (3) with the institutions that link producers, consumers, and officials. The developmentalist literature and especially the product cycle analysis laid a considerable burden on entering global trade as a path from the periphery. There are good grounds to be wary of the claims of this literature in regard to international trade as a reliable engine of growth (Rodrik). There are equally good grounds to recognize that because autarchy is no longer a viable policy the question that confronts governments is not whether to allow trade but how to enter global markets beneficially. It is therefore worth looking closely at exchange as a domestic and international process.

## Why Egypt?

Economic transformations will look like the commodity cycle picture, of course. There will be increased capital intensity, increased trade, and (at least in physical aggregates) increased welfare. To understand these processes that still occupy the field of vision of most of humanity is a valid undertaking but it requires an empirical look at a pedestrian process that is still important in the world.[11] Much of the world's trade is still in raw materials, agricultural products, and not-very-finished industrial goods.

Specifically I examine the questions I have raised about how regulatory coalitions are created and their impact by looking at the interplay between regulation, production, and markets in Egypt in the first half of the twentieth century. Egypt is interesting because for the first third of the twentieth century agricultural exports appeared to be a viable path to growth and because many of the institutions that guided this growth were private. For the first third of this century, Weberian officials guided the production strategies followed by many Egyptians and these strategies were predicated on investment in the reputation of Egyptian cotton. After the Great Depression agricultural exports no longer provided a path to growth and governments promoted local industry. Egyptian economists discussed possible paths to development and after 1952 the government made policies that conformed to some of the goals suggested by economists. One common point of agreement even then was the need to improve labor productivity and to press business to make greater investments in physical productivity. Egyptian history then recapitulates, well before the current concern with business, the state, and regulation, themes that continue to occupy our imagination. What this history shows is the importance of private institutions (not just entrepreneurs and state regulators) for enhancing trade, the necessity for legal changes with unintended consequences, and the necessity for continuing to attract high levels of foreign investment.

Egypt, before World War II, was a paradigm of a small, open economy dependent on trade. Until World War I, nearly 90 percent of its trade was based on cotton plant products (fiber and seed). Because Egypt was on the gold standard rather than using notes, its money supply fluctuated directly with the level of imports and exports and Egypt was an early case for discussion of mechanisms that were later believed to underlie the so-called Dutch disease (Bresciani-Turroni [1934]). If Egyptians were able to specialize in the production of high-quality cotton, they were only able to do so because they could employ public and private institutions to invest in reputation at the level of aggregate economic production. They could make these investments because they believed there was a corresponding commitment from English textile firms to buy cotton would buy reputation. We can, however, imagine a market solution to the problem of finding cotton for English mills: merchant firms specializing in the provision of high-quality cotton would buy from producers around the world. Such solutions existed because the Japanese textile industry utilized them (Lazonick, Saxonhouse). Regulatory institutions allowed firms (growers) in particular countries to reap the returns to such investments more directly but only by investing in reputation: ensuring that standard crops of a particular quality were produced.

This is, therefore, an important story for several reasons. Domestic institutions do not simply cushion the transformation of trade; they play a role in choosing the goods a country's economy will trade. The kind of commodity trade that dominated the Egyptian economy for the first half of this century may no longer be so common or so desirable. A large part of the world's trade is still in staple goods, however, and a reexamination of the theories related to such goods is therefore worthwhile. For Egypt, the debates that I recount here remain substantively important and it seems to be worthwhile to understand the likely effects on the Egyptian economy of travelling paths bypassed in an earlier era. That these were momentous questions were apparent to educated Egyptians by the turn of the twentieth century and their discussions remain of interest.

## Two Egyptian Economists Speak

The story I have told so far would work well as an analytic framework even if no one in Egypt or anywhere else ever considered the issues I have discussed. Why should we look at one country and why specifically at Egypt? I look at one country because I wish not simply to model but to explore the process of making and implementing policy and to address the large issue of how the state functioned as well as the issue of what kind of inputs are appropriate for development. Egypt was, moreover, a country whose policies were designed with the global free trade in mind.

Egyptians discussed the problem of social investments just as I have described them. Consequently we can see the emergence of policy choices in as policy makers sought to conform to a specific model similar to that I have described. Investments in reputation and quality premiums were topics discussed frankly in a variety of professional and policy-making settings; so, too, were the problems of increasing demand and rapidly increasing investment in physical and human capital.

Consider the evening of November 8, 1912 when the director of the Khedivial Agricultural Society, Abdul Hamid Abaza, delivered an address at the then newly opened Egyptian University. Abaza spoke to one seminar in a series of meetings convened by the International Federation of Master Cotton Spinners' and Manufacturers' Associations. Egyptians, alone of the world's growers, routinely took part in the Federation's meetings where they could engage in exchanges with a large fraction of the buyers of the Egyptian crop.

Abaza gave a frank exposition of the economic situation of Egyptian landowners 30 years after the English occupation of Egypt had begun. "Being myself a landowner, and a descendant of landowners," Abaza told his audience, "I wish to tell you in the name of all the farmers of our country that we give you unlimited power to make such regulations as you judge useful for the production of cotton of the variety and quality you desire, and we promise to obey these regulations, provided that you give us higher prices."[12] These comments were widely reported in Egypt. They appeared in the printed minutes of the congress and references to them were made in contemporary speeches and articles.[13] It is easy enough to read Abaza's comments as simply one more complaint about British unwillingness to pay the price landowners wanted, but to do so is obviously to miss their significance. Abaza was an important and astute member of a dominant family in the Egyptian elite and his frank assertion that the primary dispute over price was a dispute over quality should make us pause. Abaza, quite explicitly, did not consider regulation something that the state did to the landowners. Regulations to affect the quality or reputation of Egyptian cotton were to be the outcome of an agreement between growers and spinners mediated by the state. The regulatory process, to work, had to create a coalition centered on price through which growers promised to meet the needs of spinners and spinners promised to meet the price asked by growers.

However plausible in 1912 to frame policies based on the expectations of complementarity, by the end of the first third of this century such expectations could no longer be sustained. Exogenous shocks of war, depression, and technological change have been prominent features of the twentieth century and in retrospect made the expectations about complementary investments wrong. The responses of actors who specialized in order to engage in trade have infrequently been to find new areas of specialization rapidly. Rather than shift to new areas of production, they often sought to find new areas of demand. Producers of raw materials for which prices were at least adequate in June 1929 found it easy to believe in June 1930 that capitalism had a demand rather than a supply problem. Political institutions were frequently available to create increased demand for existing production at least in the short term.

Keynesian and other economic theories encouraged a concern with increasing demand in the middle-third of the twentieth century. It was even more apparent to political and economic elites in primary exporting countries that the sudden collapse of the global economy in 1929 was due to insufficient demand than to their counterparts in the developed capitalist countries. There were, consequently, broad coalitions to support moving in the direction of import substitution if local inputs could be harnessed to the task.

After World War II the global economy was created anew. The strategies that had linked the producers of primary goods as inputs to industrial processes in the developed countries no longer worked as they had before the Depression. The advantages of transforming Egypt from a supplier of raw materials to Great Britain into an industrial producer became a possibility and even (with the decline of the British economy) a necessity.

How to make such a transition exercised the imaginations and energy of Egyptian economists. Forty years after Abaza's talk to the Master Cotton Spinners' Federation, and on the verge of a military coup that was to end the liberal era in Egypt, several economists discussed the possibilities. One in particular, Said el-Naggar, published a detailed study of the Egyptian economy, *Industrialisation and Income*. Naggar was a lecturer in economics and law at Cairo University. Naggar identified the problems of labor productivity and capital scarcity as crucial bottlenecks for industrialization to occur and warned that light industries represented the most obvious source of comparative advantage for Egypt. Using the then recently published work by Paul Rosenstein-Rodan he noted, "The expansion of [industrial] employment implies the creation of new incomes that add to the stream of effective demand" as well as a rise in rural incomes that "cannot fail to strengthen the steam of effective demand for manufactured goods."[14] In a prescient vision of where world trade, but not regional trade, would go El-Naggar concluded that if local demand was insufficient

> ...The Egyptian industry will have to seek export outlets. The most natural market is that of Syria, Lebanon, Iraq, the Anglo-Egyptian Sudan, and other Arab countries...there is ample scope for expansion in this direction...the future patterns of trade inside the region will not be based on the exchange of manufactures against agricultural products, but rather on the exchange of different types of industrial products.

At least through 1930, it was plausible for landowners like Abaza to assert that economic growth could occur through a privileged relationship with Great Britain. This argument was directed not only at Egyptians but was also an aimed at the imperial power itself. Britain, the occupying power, undertook institutional innovations that encouraged investments to promote Ricardian trade. By the end of World War II, when El-Naggar wrote, this strategy for growth was no longer viable.

As early as 1930 the expectation that economic growth could occur through Ricardian trade became suspect and landowners themselves began to consider industrialization as a cure for the problem of aggregate demand. The Depression itself destroyed, over a decade, the promise that the old trade relationship could be restored both by its length and by the transformations that occurred in Great Britain. From 1930 until 1952, Egyptian economists debated theories and policy implications at the same time that the domestic political coalitions underwent significant change.

By 1952 the possibility of a new coalition emerged based on new expectations about trade and investment. In this new coalition, state officials played a much more important role than had been the case before 1930 and taxation played a more prominent role as a source of capital investment than did debt or equity investment. In this model, as in the old, Egypt had to fit into the global economy. In the Soviet Union and in the capitalist economies of Western Europe, the state played a large role in investment as well as in managing aggregate demand. Egyptians had long been familiar with the state provision of demand through its cotton support programs; during the Depression and the War they had had experience with the state as a guarantor of investment and even, on occasion, as an investor. Now, however, Egyptians saw the possibility of investing in the quality of their factor inputs and only indirectly in the goods they produced. Defenders of the new strategy appealed to the labor movement and the peasantry for popular support in the short term. In the longer term they explicitly envisaged investments in increasing the stock of human capital through education. It also sought to increase socially owned capital through electrification as a path to development.

Egypt provides important empirical material to elucidate the role of reputation in international trade. Egyptian experience is also important because it provides us with an understanding of the self-conscious way in which policy makers addressed the issues of reputation, growth, and equity. It is to our advantage not only to observe Egyptian policy-makers and their policies, but (in a new age of globalization and free trade) to enter into an imaginative dialogue with them.

# CHAPTER 3

# Growing the World's Best Cotton: Colonial Crisis or Business as Usual

The theory of reputation facilitates a closer look at the investments in prized dimensions of quality, which committed Egyptians to produce goods of above-average quality in ways that conveyed information to prospective buyers and that also allowed those buyers to punish Egyptian producers in exchange for a quality premium. If Egyptians did intentionally produce cotton of high quality with an idea toward reaping a quality premium we must dramatically overhaul our understanding of the political economy of the period by reassessing the active decisions of Egyptians and the relationship between cotton producers in Egypt and consumers outside it. We must recognize that Egyptian agency was an important aspect of the shaping of the political economy.

The quality of Egyptian cotton has been celebrated for more than a century as if it were a simple natural feature of an agricultural good. In fact, quality was measured on several dimensions and was the result of constant investment by Egyptians and the source of frequent conflict between them and consumers abroad. Much Egyptian cotton, unlike that grown in most of the United States and India, possessed an extra-long staple and this is clearly a natural feature of the plant. The production of millions of pounds of particular types of cotton was not a feature of the natural world nor was the high degree of homogeneity exhibited by the baled cotton. Although it is commonly asserted in many existing accounts that the cultivation of cotton occurred at the expense of local society and the domestic ecology and thus must have been coerced, the production of high-quality cotton was primarily a reaction to market demand.

Strategies of investment in reputation were extremely popular in smaller agricultural economies in the first half of the twentieth century. Their popularity lay in the hope of segmenting markets and thereby reaping extraordinary profits. Colombian coffee growers employed similar strategies for an even longer period of time than did Egyptian cotton growers and so did owners of Ceylonese tea plantations, Argentinean stockmen, and the peasants of West Africa who grow cocoa. Brazilian coffee growers, plantation owners in the American South (and cotton farmers in India), and Australian cattlemen all made different investment choices and none developed a reputation for quality. To invest in quality required the producers, who were often quite numerous, to know the precise dimensions desired by consumers. Because quality conveys information and provides a trigger mechanism, producers must know what qualities are desirable.

Backwardness neither promoted nor constrained the development of strategies for investment in quality. There is a widespread belief that poor countries suffer a generalized administrative failure or weak governance, but this does not appear to be an accurate description of the particular regulatory institutions necessary to ensure the production of high-quality goods. When cotton growers in the San Joaquin Valley of California, chose a strategy of investment in reputation they adopted regulatory structures very similar to those in Egypt despite a very different labor–capital ratio. These strategies required public and private investments to ensure the maintenance of quality and their actual operation is discussed in chapter 4.

The argument that Egyptians invested in reputation can be tested because it implies that an important and uncritically accepted part of the now standard account of the twentieth-century political economy of Egypt—ecological disaster—is wrong and it provides an alternative explanation for what appears to have been an ecological collapse. Although such claims are common to many descriptions of twentieth-century imperialist experiences, the account of colonial crisis in Egypt that has entered the standard histories conflates ecological and political degradation:

> After the First World War, the moral, economic, and political crisis of Anglo-French colonialism created an environment conducive to a new political order in Egypt. The nationalist movement was an effect of urban middle strata educated in modern, western-style schools—the *effendiyya*—and circles of large landowners simultaneously articulating and responding to collective anti-colonialist sentiment and action.... A central

element of the political economy of the 1892–1924 era was a multifaceted rural ecological crisis. After expanding rapidly in the 1890s, crop yields and cultivated areas reached a plateau, as agriculture attained the economic limits of the environment, deployed technology, and the social relations of production.... Consequently, agricultural yields declined by about 15 percent from 1900 to 1920 and recovered only in 1930. (Beinin [1999] 309–310)

There was certainly no general ecological crisis. Yields of crops other than cotton do not show the pattern of decline and recovery (see table 3.1). Nor was there a specific ecological crisis affecting cotton. Instead what happened was that deliberate investment choices to ensure the production of a high-quality good had effects that, when measured in a particular way, mimicked those of ecological crisis. Instead of crisis there was a discourse of crisis that initially entered Egyptian historiography as a colonial argument and was later deployed for anticolonial purposes. This discourse has had a remarkable career of its own and to understand the political economy of trade we must eliminate it.

Table 3.1    Yields of various field crops, 1913–1924

|      | Barley | Beans | "Cotton" | Lentils | Maize | Millet | Rice | Wheat |
|------|--------|-------|----------|---------|-------|--------|------|-------|
| 1913 | 5.86 | 5.53 | 3.04 | 4.70 | 6.33 | 7.46 | 5.15 | 5.25 |
| 1914 | 5.24 | 4.41 | 2.60 | 3.88 | 7.16 | 8.07 | 3.59 | 4.75 |
| 1915 | 5.6  | 4.47 | 3.06 | 3.52 | 7.41 | 8.26 | 4.34 | 4.63 |
| 1916 | 5.65 | 4.00 | 2.33 | 3.96 | 6.96 | 8.11 | 3.90 | 4.75 |
| 1917 | 5.72 | 4.53 | 2.87 | 3.62 | 7.15 | 7.33 | 4.65 | 5.03 |
| **Mean** | **5.62** | **4.58** | **2.76** | **3.90** | **7.01** | **8.08** | **4.50** | **4.87** |
| 1918 | 5.68 | 4.73 | 2.81 | 3.98 | 6.81 | 8.40 | 4.68 | 4.71 |
| 1919 | 5.33 | 4.48 | 2.71 | 3.91 | 6.72 | 8.43 | 4.25 | 4.29 |
| 1920 | 5.78 | 4.46 | 2.53 | 3.59 | 6.86 | 8.42 | 4.47 | 5.02 |
| 1921 | 5.71 | 4.46 | 2.59 | 3.99 | 6.07 | 8.07 | 3.80 | 4.78 |
| 1922 | 5.68 | 4.44 | 2.86 | 3.58 | 6.15 | 7.97 | 2.88 | 4.55 |
| **Mean** | **5.64** | **4.52** | **2.70** | **3.80** | **6.50** | **8.27** | **4.24** | **4.66** |
| 1923 | 5.64 | 4.43 | 2.92 | 3.04 | 6.78 | 8.05 | 4.26 | 4.98 |
| 1924 | 5.44 | 3.95 | 3.09 | 4.06 | 6.78 | 8.23 | 4.22 | 4.55 |

*Notes*: All yields are in ardebs per feddan. For purposes of illustrating the degree to which the series purporting to show that cotton fiber yields are in decline, "cotton" yield in this table only refers to the production of seed. Seed production, it will be noted, is quite stable across the period. "Mean" yields are averages for the preceding five years.
*Source*: Annuaire Statistique 1925.

As with other crops, improved varieties of cotton occurred at random. Improved varieties were preserved and grown over decades because prices rewarded the investments necessary to find them and grow them and because an institutional structure existed to overcome dangerous externalities (Feeny). Where institutions provide good information and encourage responsiveness, the kind of rapid changes in price differentials between long and extra-long staple that characterized the first decades of the twentieth century rapidly affected crop choices.

A story of investment in quality necessarily and deliberately abstracts away from British colonialism to focus on Egyptian agency. Although the presence of British troops on Egyptian soil and British officials in key government roles for the first third of the twentieth century is undeniable, much of what I discuss later occurred apart from the strategic power of the British. As I shall show in some detail in this chapter and chapter 4 similar regulatory schemes and decisions about the investment of public and private resources occurred elsewhere as responses to market integration. More responsive state structures in Egypt after formal independence made investments in areas other than reputation easier but the institutions and people involved were already in place by 1912 and continued to play crucial (and often the same) roles until the mid-1930s. The Egyptian elite bound themselves tightly to the English textile industry because English spinners had an unusually large demand for high-quality Egyptian fiber. Egyptians perceived British spinners as vulnerable to market power; British officials did not make their cropping decisions.

In the 1920s British basic industries including textiles underwent a long, painful restructuring but this crisis of the British economy was not reflected in Egypt (Keynes [1931]; Skidelsky 261–263). The retreat of lower-grade English textile exports and the attendant rationalization under pressure from Japanese competition caused few immediate problems for Egyptian producers or exporters. What threatened Egyptian landowners and forced a new policy was the capacity of Japanese spinners to penetrate more expensive markets with thread from cheaper non-Egyptian fiber and the introduction of synthetic fibers.

To clarify the role of market responses I proceed from the demand side (British spinners) to the supply side (Egyptian growers) for a good with a reputation for quality (Egyptian cotton). I examine the production of quality through investment in domestic regulatory institutions (government ministries, use of domestic police power, research institutes, primary and secondary commodity markets) and participation in international institutions that enhanced the exchange of crucial non-price information between actors in cotton markets (International Cotton Congresses). Finally, I place the Egyptian experience in comparative perspective by reviewing similar experiences in California and Thailand. Egyptian landowners and businessmen could, for nearly forty years, undertake extensive regulatory and other investments to maintain a reputation for Egyptian cotton higher than that of all American cotton but that of the San Joaquin Valley. I consider this evidence of powerful regulatory institutions that accomplished the most regulation can: the alignment of private incentives for public purposes.

### British Demand: Colonial Power, Labor, and Paleotechnology

There is a dramatic disjuncture between the picture of England's economic power and especially her textile mills drawn seen from abroad and seen from home. The particular dimensions of cotton quality that Egyptians produced only make sense in the context of the weaknesses of English factory organization and the structure of her commodity markets. Seen from home, the British economy and its ruling class exhibited considerable fragility even before the Great War. By the turn of the twentieth century the New Unionism already played an important role in the economy based on the expansion of Britain's economy into world trade in textiles and energy production and the extension of the franchise to most of the male population. Consequently labor commanded a larger share of the national income and profits were no longer robust (Suttle; Schultz-Gaevernitz). Socialists and other critical thinkers in the early twentieth century put these two faces of British power together to explain imperialism as the last phase of capitalism (Hobson; Lenin; Luxemburg). Although the end of imperial rule did not spell the end of capitalism, these theories point to something important: the conflicts between the European powers for hegemony in the first half of the twentieth century severely damaged world markets.

Looking at the global market for textiles allows us to see ways in which the same elites who, from the turn of the century at least through World War II, sought political independence also sought closer economic integration into global markets. In fact, they often sought political independence as a way to enhance economic integration. It is thus not surprising that their narrative has been so ambivalently written. When they are not (most commonly) ignored, they are perceived as compradors—treacherous allies of colonial rule—although the notion of such a distinct role has been largely exploded in the commercial and industrial sectors of these economies (Kasaba; Vitalis [1990]).

The extension of the market into ostensibly subsistence peasant communities in the late nineteenth century has been seen primarily as a catastrophe to which the only possible response is a strategy of resistance (Migdal; Huntington; Apter) and Egypt is no exception (Berque). Crisis and disruption arise from the demand for raw materials by the metropolis, the supply of cheap manufactures in return, and the consequent transformation of an entire culture (Mitchell; Lewis; Huntington; Migdal [1988] 93–95; Vatikiotis). There is no space in such narratives for a sophisticated strategy designed, at least in theory, to take advantage of the economic weakness of the colonial power.

Britain in this view, and it was certainly the most common view among nationalists in Egypt and elsewhere, was not only the dominant colonial power; it was the most advanced industrial economy in the world. A brief description of British power in the 1890s would note that Britain had the most cotton spindles, the most mechanical looms, the largest workforce, and the most capital invested in textile production of any country in the world. Liverpool was the center of a global market in fiber and textiles were the single most important industrial product of England and its single most important export.[1] Britain was also the world's dominant naval power and had used its warships to project force around the world (including a bombardment of Alexandria in 1882). It is thus no wonder that powerful England easily subordinated Egyptian interests to its own and exploited the Nile Valley to provide the Lancashire mills with raw cotton harvested by children.

Correct as each item is, as a whole their impression is misleading. They confound the description of Great Britain as a strategic actor with the efficiency of her industrial plant and they ignore the highly specific nature of the British investments in industrial production. Because the British cotton industry thrived as a global exporter and because imperial institutions allowed British officials to play crucial roles around the world, the shaky foundations of the British economy have rarely been integrated into studies of the colonial or semicolonial economies. Empirical studies of British firms acting abroad have nevertheless made clear the increasing reliance of firms in the capitalist core on their suppliers and partners abroad (Fieldhouse [1994]; Fieldhouse [1978]; Tignor [1990]).

As world demand for machine-woven textiles grew throughout the nineteenth and early twentieth centuries, British demand for cotton grew as well. Until 1913, British industrialists and economic analysts believed the future was one of unlimited increases in demand and were most concerned about how to expand supply rather than about excess capacity which would become their dominant concern after the war (Chapman and McFarlane; International

Cotton Federation [1912]). These fears drove manufacturers to create the British Cotton Growers Association before World War I to lobby for the extension of cotton production in the Sudan and the colonies of West Africa.

Before World War I, continental spinners and weavers, like their British counterparts, were more afraid of insufficient supply and rising prices for raw materials than of insufficient demand for finished goods. Because continental spinners and weavers faced greater difficulties in obtaining raw materials than did their British counterparts they were more inclined to participate in efforts to increase supplies and coordinate markets. A cotton shortage in 1904 and a consequent reduction in working hours by English spinners in 1904 ("short-time movement") provided the impetus for the creation of the International Cotton Federation, which was an attempt to reproduce British institutions of sectoral cooperation globally (Cotton Federation [1905], [1906]). With sufficient supplies of raw material, spinners believed they had an untapped market of at least a third of the world's 1.5 billion inhabitants (Macara, International Cotton Federation [1912]) and that the demand for cotton would increase much faster than supply could respond.

The vast expansion of cotton production was based on British comparative advantage, but decades of research have shown Victorian England's comparative advantage in international trade was neither in physical capital or human capital. Through much of the nineteenth century and into the twentieth-century British comparative advantage lay in the *organization* of unskilled and semiskilled labor in a country whose workshops often remained artisanal (Samuels; Crafts and Thomas). By the 1930s nearly three quarters of Britain's spinning capacity was at least 20 years old and it was widely understood that English industry would be hard-pressed to compete adequately with Asian industries that possessed cheaper labor and more modern capital equipment (International Institute of Agriculture [1936] 369–370). Whether the problem was caused by relative cost structures or by an insufficient willingness to innovate among British entrepreneurs has generated considerable and still unresolved conflict (Keynes; Lazonick; Saxonhouse).

If the long debate centering on British, Japanese, and American textile industries has not completely settled the issue, it has clarified how dramatically capital–labor relationships and the industrial structures of the firms in these three economies differed. Textile firms invested in looms that they expected to last for decades. The bulk of the costs in the industry were not for fixed capital but for fiber and labor. Firms consequently required high throughput to be profitable. British firms depended on plant-specific skills and cooperative capacity of their workers. Workers played an important role in the organization of production in Britain and received powerful incentives.

Unions were powerful and had been able to negotiate contracts that placed the burden of downtime on employers rather than on workers. Consequently British firms were especially vulnerable to what was called "bad spinning": the disruption of production that occurred when inferior cotton was unexpectedly mixed with that of high quality (Lazonick 503). British complaints about quality of fiber were heard first in the 1870s and they were voiced without interruption until World War II. In response, the Egyptian government intervened through the regulatory process to ensure that Egyptian cotton was of increasingly high quality (Owen [1969] 135–137). During the first two decades of the twentieth century, British manufacturers were pushed out of export markets as domestic production met demand in the United States and Japan challenged British goods elsewhere. English producers concentrated on finer products for narrower markets; their dependence on Egyptian cotton increased; England remained the largest single destination of Egyptian long-staple cotton (Todd [1927] 168).

Finer products were measured in "count" or the length of yarn required to weigh one pound. Higher counts required more expensive (longer-staple) cotton but, because British firms had not substituted ring spinning for mule spinning as quickly as did the Japanese, they also required more expensive labor. Fiber uniformity (freedom from trash and from excessive moisture that literally went into the air) was crucial if British firms were to avoid "bad spinning" and achieve high throughput. Because Japanese spinners made technical advances that allowed them to substitute lower-paid female labor for male labor and shorter staple and cheaper fiber for somewhat finer products, British spinners were pushed out of the lower end of the global markets for yarn (Lazonick; Saxonhouse; Shimizu).[2]

British spinning and weaving firms relied on unions and an extensive labor market to provide them with an organized workforce, but they also relied on the centrality of Britain in world trade. They were blessed with what economists call network externalities because they had access to highly efficient markets connecting spinners with suppliers around the world. The spot and futures cotton markets of Liverpool and later Manchester provided British spinners with sufficiently large and diverse cotton inputs in a timely enough manner to minimize their inventory costs. Neither continental producers nor the Japanese could rely on ready market access to cotton of diverse grades and consequently they invested in what were by British standards excessive inventories (Brown [1992]).

Because British spinners and weavers had lower inventory costs they were immediately affected by short-term price fluctuation. British buyers were, as a result, exceptionally sensitive to events on commodity exchanges and exceptionally fearful of concerted activity to raise prices for raw cotton. Thus, in 1904 when Daniel Sully attempted to corner the market for raw cotton and briefly drove prices to nearly double earlier levels, the ensuing panic in Manchester reinforced the belief there that supply shortage rather than demand for finished goods was the crucial danger the industry faced.

Given labor markets with large supplies of appropriately skilled employees, access to increasingly large product markets in which to sell high-quality textiles, and price stability British entrepreneurs made fixed investments in machinery. Before the Great War, Bolton entrepreneurs had invested in mule spinning machinery with an effective life of 20 years. Without complementary commitments that high-quality fiber would be available so that the expensive labor working in the factories would be employed, the machines were worth little more than scrap.

As late as 1912 spinners only needed minimal reassurance that the long-term investments would be profitable, but World War I itself marked a trend change in British growth that affected all the basic industrial producers.[3] So Egyptians in the period before World War I could be forgiven for believing that increasingly integrated global markets would drive British manufacturers to greater dependence on Egyptian cotton. During the war, the British Cotton Control Board had severely restricted the use of machinery among spinners using cheaper American cotton but not those of the "Egyptian section" and encouraged the substitution of Egyptian for American yarn among spinners despite the difficulties this caused for some firms (Henderson 20–21). Britain's return to the gold standard in 1924 and the success of the textile owners at utilizing "short-time" work supplemented by unemployment benefits to maintain the workforce and industrial capacity had been destructive for "American" producers but left the "Egyptian" manufacturers largely unaffected (Skidelsky [1988] 259–261).

Not until the 1927 meeting of the International Cotton Federation (the second held in Egypt) 1927, were the optimistic notes of earlier gatherings replaced by a strident conflict over the definition and price of quality. The British delegates sounded an increasingly urgent note and demanded high-quality cotton but refused to pay for it. "Our future in England lies in maintaining our superiority in fine cottons" said one and rebuffed Abaza's demand for higher prices by asserting that no premium was necessary for buyers to obtain a reputable product: "It is not a case of payment, it is a case of fair dealing, a matter of reputation" (International Cotton Federation [1927] 162). A paper delivered by the managing director of the Cotton Mills Trust, Seddon-Brown, was important for defining quality wholly apart from staple length when he noted that cotton "regular in staple, strong in fibre, clean, free from neps, over-ripe and under-ripe fibers" would reduce the price of yarn by 50 percent (International Cotton Federation [1927] 146–148). The conclusion drawn by William Catterall was a barely veiled threat: "All the lecturers we have heard from Egypt are building on getting higher prices for Sakel. I say you must get your Sakel prices down instead of attempting to raise them… Your cotton must improve and it must be cheaper. What we want is cheap cotton, good cotton, long in staple, fine and strong" (International Cotton Federation [1927] 164). What British spinners required, in addition to staple length, was for Egyptian peasants to provide them with raw cotton that did not, because of irregularities or foreign matter, trigger bad spinning and thereby increase their labor costs.

By 1930 spinners in Bolton found that the conventional expectations of the period before World War I no longer held. The "Egyptian" section of the trade was still in better shape than the "American one" but the claims of British manufacturers "to have elicited all costs at our end that can possibly be elicited" (International Cotton Federation [1927] 49) were simply an excuse. Fouad Abaza's retort to the spinners about the deterioration of Egyptian cotton suggests that Egyptian officials already harbored such doubts: "is it that there is nothing wrong the raw cotton and that the problem is due to some defective process of manufacture?" (International Cotton Federation [1927] 152). If British labor costs were relatively high and rising for many areas of yarn and fabric production, Egyptian labor costs were extraordinarily low although the social cost of reducing the price of Egyptian cotton was exorbitant.

### Economic Shift or Ecological Crisis?

Egyptians were acutely aware of what British spinners wanted them to produce, and they were also increasingly well informed about managing the environment to achieve quality. The scientific study of agriculture dates from the late nineteenth century and through the state the Egyptian elite rapidly acquired a powerful set of technologies for improving the quality of Egyptian cotton. Three relevant issues requiring manipulation of the physical environment confronted growers seeking to produce a highly uniform product: seed, insects, and the provision of water. The standard wisdom is that the Egyptians sacrificed the environment to produce cotton for Britain. Showing that they did not is crucial to understanding what they actually did.

Water supply is a capital-intensive undertaking and it seems self-evident that agriculture in a desert can only exist with irrigation (Hansen [1990]). Yet irrigation is preferable to rain-fed agriculture when strict control of water is needed. Large-scale investments in irrigating deserts are generally made to pay through growing high-quality goods (e.g., cotton, melons, strawberries) that would be vulnerable to climatic variation if the relied on rain. Dams built in Upper Egypt at Aswan, Assiut, Zifta, and Esna between 1889 and 1906 allowed sufficient over-year water storage to make perennial irrigation possible in much of Lower Egypt. By one estimate the value of these works was nearly 14 million Egyptian pounds (Radwan 30). A canal system of nearly 15,000 kilometers by 1912 delivered water to nearly 4.1 million feddans.[4] Perennial irrigation made possible the Egyptian reputation in cotton but it also increased the danger of degradation as percolation removed essential ingredients of soil fertility and built up surface salts.

The word ecology only entered English in 1873, but an important argument about the effects of irrigation was already underway in Egypt before World War I. In the wake of a disastrous flood in 1909 a prominent British scientist employed in Egypt discovered that cotton yields declined if the plants received too much water. His conclusion that plant survival (and consequently yield) was adversely affected by insufficient drainage and overwatering was increasingly accepted as an appropriate technical explanation for secular declines in yield mentioned by Beinin (Balls [1918]; Todd [1915] 266–269). His research was considerably more complex and relevant than the use to which it was put. Most damage to the entire crop, Balls showed, could be attributed to random variation in the height of the annual flood and it could be alleviated by drainage in the low-lying areas of the northern Delta. Balls studied more than the physical environment. His were truly ecological studies and he recognized that peasants traded off both the costs of physical effort and cash investments for income. Balls dismissed what we would now call the rational-choice model of peasant behavior and replaced it with an "evolutionary economics equilibrium" inherent in peasant learning in situations of far less than complete information. One crucial innovation that Balls—whose work is central to understanding the Egyptian investment in reputation—made was to shift the focus of his research away from measuring plant growth to measuring peasant income as a form of agency. Balls realized that yield measured the outcome of peasant decisions about domestic productivity rather than biological reproduction. In his own words, he decided to study "the number of plants per square metre, or any other unit area, as the basis of computation, instead of taking the individual plant... to obtain curves showing the time distribution of yield... it results that the greatest yield per area for the first few weeks is given by the spacing which contained most plants per area" (Balls [1915] 123). Balls's research indicates peasant practices were often (but not invariably) optimizing and this reinforced his understanding that peasant cropping decisions were related to physical effort and monetary cost (Balls [1915] 129). Changes in the physical environment could decrease yields but so would changes in the relative price of peasant inputs (labor, fertilizer, and rent) or products.

Next to water, insect infestations were the single greatest environmental threat both to aggregate yield and cotton quality. During World War I, the outline of the life cycle of the so-called cotton worm (*Prodenia litura*) had finally been identified (it like plant health) was clearly linked to "too much" irrigation water. Although the complete description of the life cycle was not available until 1916, the core of the problem was already known in 1895: the "cotton worm" was an opportunistic feeder on clover (*Birsim*) through the spring and then moved to developing bolls in nearby cotton fields in the early summer. The importance of moisture for insect survival meant that the northern Delta areas, which were also the areas suffering the most severe drainage problems, were most heavily infected with destructive results to both the size and quality of the high-quality cotton grown there. Because both insect infestations were heavier and the water table higher in the northern Delta, it is easy to see how a plausible case for environmental disaster can be made based on the system of dams that made perennial irrigation possible.

Irrigation created the possibility of uniform watering, but far more important for creating uniform crops was uniform seed. This was a daunting undertaking that had only just become possible in the early twentieth century. Creating uniform seed sets Darwinian dynamics against the logic of economic profitability. Natural selection rewards difference in the search for survival across niches in the environment; spinners in Lancashire rewarded identical fiber without regard to local environmental variation. Landlords and peasants were caught between the jaws of profit and biology.

The tools necessary to resolve the dilemma were still being forged at the turn of the twentieth century. Theoretical genetics had then only recently rediscovered Mendelian theory. In the 1890s Galton, Edgeworth, and Yule were still developing the statistical techniques required to manipulate plant genetics rapidly and effectively (Stigler [1986]).[5] Even the idea of producing uniform seed was new: it could only have emerged after it was understood that within a single population genetic variety was the norm and that the presence of selective forces would require constant human intervention working in the opposite direction to maintain uniformity (Beatty; Hodges; Turner).[6] Producing uniformity required constant vigilance against diversity in seed production, propagation, and renewal in the face of natural selection. Pure strains of seed had to be created, maintained, and distributed; physical mixing of seeds of different kinds of cotton had to be prevented; the danger of cross-pollination due to the differential survival of plants under different natural conditions had to be prevented.

Egyptian researchers and growers confronted several interrelated problems that they understood quite well. First and most important plants that produced finer (longer-staple) cotton generally had lower yields and were only profitable if the quality premium was sufficiently high (Balls; Dudgeon [1923]; Casoria [1922]). Second, annual sowing of a uniform seed tended, as Darwinian theory predicted, to decrease average yields because successive crops would be survivors of the research station environment rather than the microenvironment where they were sown. Taken together these two tendencies meant no selective pressures could be applied to increase aggregate yields through enhanced survival in varied environmental niches if the result was obtained by altering the characteristics of the plant (such as its fiber length). Third, the possibility of cross-fertilization required some regulation to ensure that third-party producers did not use nonstandard seed and thereby contaminate the pure strains being grown to reap the quality premium (Egypt [1910] 16–18).

These were problems faced by cotton producers globally. Although price differentials were one common form of incentive alignment, regulatory and administrative decisions were used to penalize noncompliance. In some parts of the world, growers created communities in which only a single variety of plant was sown so as to decrease the heterogeneity directly in the cropped plants and to decrease the possibility of variation over time. Given the novelty of the relevant techniques of genetic manipulation, research institutions—organizations specializing in the investment of human capital and the dissemination of information—were formed relatively quickly to develop and propagate strains of cotton with desirable characteristics: staple length, yield, resistance to environmental stress. The first such institute in Egypt was the Khedivial Agricultural Society founded in 1898 under the patronage of Prince (later Sultan) Hussein Kamil. It undertook agricultural experimentation and the dissemination of the results for the landowning elite directly. Because cross-fertilization was an externality (a nonmarket exchange) that reduced the reputation premium, distribution of seed to poor peasants was explicitly (in the address by Kamil at his palace in Zamalik) one of the motives for the Society's foundation (Thabit [1936]; Abaza [1941] 6–8).[7]

The Society hired agricultural scientists from Britain and undertook, in the absence of a ministerial bureaucracy, to issue reports and to hold conferences. The Society benefited from significant direct state aid, however, and is best thought of as an early "parastatal" organization. The Egyptian government contributed a significant direct subsidy, paid the salary of the secretary

(William Foaden who was seconded from the Agricultural School), and provided free use of nearly five acres in the Cairo area for an experimental farm (Thabit [1936] 52–53). The government created Department of Agriculture in 1910 at the urging of Egyptian landowners although representatives of British textile interests played some role and certainly attempted to take credit for an intervention with Lord Grey in London (FO 368/400/21850, International Cotton Federation [1913] 34; Owen [1969] 194). The Society remained an active private organization and much of the work it had begun in seed selection, dissemination, the use of fertilizer, and agricultural research was henceforth undertaken at state expense rather than at the cost of the agricultural elite. Other more specialized, scientific research organizations were created in the following years and they also carried out research and published the results; among these was the Royal Entomological Society. Although expatriates such as Ball carried out the earliest research, by the 1930s the authors of reports were almost entirely Egyptian as were the officials in both public and private capacities, a sufficiently higher rate of substitution than in other sectors of the economy that there was no need to use the power of the state to Egyptianize the personnel (Goldberg [1986]; Beinin and Lockman [1987]; Tignor [1984]; Vitalis [1995]; Papasian). The research of this and successive organizations, including the Department (later Ministry) of Agriculture provided crucial support to growers and provides historians with the crucial detail whereby to understand the political economy of cotton in the first-third of the twentieth century in Egypt.

There were two ways to simplify the biological and social regulation needed for uniformity: to create districts in which only one kind of plant could be grown or by reseeding a pure strain every year from a reliable source. Egyptians turned to the second of these alternatives. Large growers could easily obtain pure-line seed as new varieties became available. Because poor peasants generally preferred to use seed they already owned or could easily obtain from lint being processed at a local gin, there was a constant danger that the crops of the large landowners would suffer from biological (cross-fertilization and hybridization) mixture. To guard against hybridization, it was necessary to supply peasants with seed at the lowest possible cost and to limit the competition from lower-quality seed that remained as a by-product of ginning.

To accomplish these goals, seed provision was transformed from the private enterprise it had been in the nineteenth century into one dominated by the state.[8] Individual entrepreneurs, notably Ioannidis and Sakellaridis, developed the cotton varieties named after them because they hoped to profit from contractual relationships tying growers to ginning and marketing services in exchange for the provision of seed.[9] Although the government never established a monopoly over seed production, by 1930 the private development of seed varieties had ended and the commercial crop was effectively grown only from seed developed by the Ministry of Agriculture (Egypt, Ministry of Agriculture [1953] 11).

In addition to investment in the provision of seed, the state also undertook to regulate its production and propagation. A series of well-considered and apparently well-enforced laws drove fly-by-night entrepreneurs from the field. Apart from the 1916 prohibition on the import of cotton or seed, gins seeking to sell sowing seed were sharply regulated through licensing and processing requirements in 1921, 1926, and 1934. The State Domains were the site where experts from the Ministry of Agriculture and Royal Society raised pure-line seed that was propagated by the large landowners for sale to the smaller ones and took extraordinary precautions to avoid mixing seed-types during ginning. In a paper to the 1938 meeting of the Cotton Federation in Cairo Osman Abaza explained to what lengths the government went to ensure that seed to be used for propagation was uniform: "We take the gins nearly to pieces before we start to gin another variety." He suggested that privately owned gins take similar, terrifically expensive efforts (International Cotton Federation [1938] 63). After 1938 the Ministry of Agriculture specified what varieties could be grown, prohibited nonstandard varieties, and required permission of the Ministry for the propagation of new varieties. State agencies charged with testing, maintained sufficiently high failure rates to improve quality continuously and ensure that private entrepreneurs would have a moving target were they to enter the field.

Because the consumers (British spinners) were concerned about irregularities in raw cotton, an additional problem was the mixing of varieties of fiber *after* ginning. As early as 1910, British spinners proposed to English officials in Egypt that they enact legislation to prevent such mixtures. As longer-staple cottons were increasingly produced in the north, increasingly strict legislation was introduced forbidding the movement of cotton from south to north. Thus, as with irrigation, pest infestation, and the choice of inputs such as seed, state regulation ensured the reputation of the Egyptian crop but in ways that inevitably affected the distribution of gains from that reputation. Rather than seeing the regulatory apparatus as a government institution designed only to force law on unwilling and recalcitrant agents, it also served to align incentives and to provide information. Specifically, excessive regulations were, therefore, devices that *informed* foreign buyers about the production decisions of Egyptian planters just as the marketing decisions of Washington cherry packers are devices that inform buyers of their production decisions (Rosenman and Wilson 650).

Farmers, large and small, adopted new technologies with remarkable alacrity. It is instructive to compare the curve for the acceptance of a new variety of cotton, Sakellaridis, from its introduction in 1911 with the curve for the acceptance of hybrid corn in the United States (Egypt, Ministry of Finance [1921]; Ahmad and Hafiz; Griliches [1957]). Seven years elapsed from its introduction, until a ceiling of about 70 percent of the cropping area was attained. Because Sakel was highly profitable during the period around World War I, such rapid saturation may appear unremarkable, but Egyptian growers took part in an exceptionally rapid commercial "green revolution."

As a point of comparison, Egyptian farmers adopted the Sakellaridis strain more rapidly than farmers in the American Midwest adopted new hybrids in the studies of demand-driven technological innovation (Griliches [1957]). In fact, they adopted this new strain of cotton more rapidly than the highly capitalized farms of central California adopted new strains in the 1940s.[10] The relatively small area of the Nile Valley makes the rapid response comprehensible but the poverty and illiteracy of the peasantry evidently did not slow the time required for adoption. The rapid adoption of a uniform variety Sakel was not uniformly profitable for all growers but the widespread adoption and relative uniformity of the crop due to the regulatory undertakings of the state rapidly made it a recognizable type.[11]

The important distinction between the adoption of technical innovation in Egypt and in the United States lies not in the speed of adoption or the quality of regulation. Rather it lies in the area of social investment in reputation and the distribution of returns from that investment. Hybrid corn in the United States was high-yielding but did not need to be high quality: quality was observable before sale and variation in most of its dimensions did not affect its use as an input (Griliches [1957]). Seed companies therefore produced seed for many different environments and paid no concern to the uniformity of the corn itself. There were no network externalities (or other similar biological constraints) because corn is self-pollinating and because the price of corn did not depend on the specific characteristics of that grown by nearby farmers (Griliches [1957] 516). In Egypt, Egyptian the most valuable cotton had lower yields as well as significant network and other externalities that required widespread use of identical seed.

It is now time to return to the problem of ecological crisis, irrigation, and drainage. The aggregate yield declines had nothing to do with ecological crisis. They were the effect of rapid response in a highly commercialized agricultural society to demand via the adoption of technical innovation. We can test this by comparing the relationship between the proportion of the cropping area devoted to Sakellaridis and declining aggregate yields. The extension of extra-long staple cotton accounts statistically for most of the variation in aggregate yields between 1910 and 1930. Besides the quantitative evidence that this was so, I present qualitative evidence that most observers at the time knew it to be so. Drainage and irrigation were, of course, important issues for Egypt but they were not at root of an ecological crisis. There was no ecological crisis.

Figure 3.1 recapitulates the argument for yield decline by presenting the figures for the aggregate yields of Egyptian cotton from 1896 to 1930. The curve of the numbers is obvious. This is the most basic evidence, initially presented in the period around World War I (Todd [1912]; Craig) and later employed (Richards; Hansen [1991]; Beinin [1999]) to adduce an argument of crisis. For analytic purposes the aggregate "crop" for the period 1900–1930 must be divided into at least three sub-crops. Two, Mit Afifi and Ashmuni were of similar yield and staple length. The third, Sakellarides, differed significantly. As table 3.2 shows, Mit Afifi and Ashmuni yielded between 5 and 8 cantars per feddan but Sakellarides yielded on average about 3.25 cantars per feddan.[12] Deciding to grow Sakel rather than the other two crops (especially Mit Afifi in Lower Egypt) depended on the size of the expected quality premium. On average one should expect a premium of about 50 percent to induce a shift away from the higher-yielding crops to the lower-yielding one. This is, in fact, what occurred around the time of

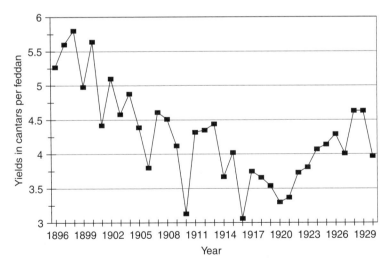

**Figure 3.1**  Aggregate yields 1896–1930.

Table 3.2  Average varietal yield

| Name | Cantar/ feddan | Ginned/ ratl/cantar | Begins | Ends |
|------|------|------|------|------|
| Ashmuni | 5–8 | 108–112 | 1860 | |
| Hamuli | | 110 | | |
| Abyad | | | 1864 | 1890 |
| Gallini | | 85–88 | 1867 | 1890 |
| Hariri | | 65–69 | | |
| Bamia | 7–8 | 100–107 | 1873 | ? |
| Mit Afifi | | 107–110 | 1885 | 1927 |
| Zafiri | | | 1893 | |
| Abbasi | 4 | 106 | 1892 | 1913 |
| Joannavich | 4 | 108 | 1890 | 1923 |
| Voltos | 6–7 | 110 | 1910 | ? |
| Nubari | 4.5 | 108 | 1909 | 1923 |
| Asili | 4.5 | 113 | | |
| Britannia | 4.3 | 110 | 1914 | |
| Sakel | 3.25 | 98–100 | 1911 | 1942 |
| Zagoura | | 110–114 | 1917 | |

World War I. Thus Sakel accounted for less than 7 percent of the area planted in cotton in 1911, but by 1921, 75 percent of the total area planted in cotton in Egypt was planted in Sakel. By 1926 it was down to about 50 percent of the area.

At all times, as shown in table 3.3 "Egyptian cotton" was a complex aggregate of subtypes, but between 1911 and 1924 it was dominated by a subtype that yielded nearly 25 percent less than the other components (Polier [1914] 323). Clearly, if 50 percent of the area of the crop was replaced by a variety yielding 25 percent less fiber, then the aggregate national yield must have decreased by at least 12.5 percent, or roughly the figure Beinin proposes for the ecological crisis effect. Visual inspection of the two curves of figure 3.2 suggests that the yield decline after 1910, the year in which Sakel was first commercially produced, is roughly the inverse of the spread of the variety. The visual impression is sustained by a quantitative analysis: the proportion of the *cropping area* in Sakel explains nearly 80 percent of the variation in aggregate yields in that decade. Confirmation that aggregate yield is explained by the switch from long- to extra-long staple is gained by looking at the reverse aspect of the switch: the role of Mit Afifi and Ashmouni (rather than Sakel). From 1905 to 1930 nearly 50 percent of the variation in aggregate

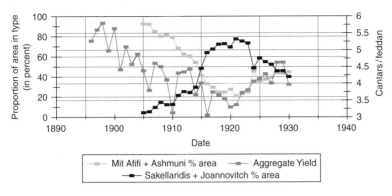

**Figure 3.2**  Aggregate yields and cotton types.

yields is explained by the proportion of cropping area of these slightly shorter staple but higher-yielding varieties in total acreage. These are very high levels of explanatory power from a single variable (acreage by type) for a biological process that is obviously extremely complex. Although early accounts had claimed that Sakellaridis provided both longer staple *and* higher yield, this was wishful thinking and it was well known to be wrong by 1920. After that date all experts in the field concluded that, on average, longer-staple cotton would always be lower yielding.

The sizes of the price differentials between varieties Egyptian cotton are shown in table 3.4 and they reflect what was needed to encourage the crop shifting that occurred. Until 1917 these figures do not mention Sakellaridis but refer to the difference between the contract grade known as Fully Good Fair for Ashmuni cotton (and thereafter for the same grade of Sakellaridis) and American Middling. The reason, of course, is that Sakellaridis had only just become an important component of the crop by that time. American Middling was medium staple, Ashmuni long staple and Sakellaridis was extra-long staple. Just as the growth in Sakellaridis area is highly correlated with declining yields, so too both price and the premium for Egyptian cotton over American are statistically correlated negatively with aggregate yield: $-0.53$ and $-0.4$ respectively. In other words, higher prices for cotton tended to be linked to lower yields. This only makes sense if growers were substituting higher-priced for higher-yielding cotton.

That growers would choose a crop that could maximize income per unit of area (rather than the yield per plant or per acre) was implicit in Balls's investigations. That rising prices affected yields through the channel of income incentive had been suggested even before the emergence of Sakel as

**Table 3.3** Subvarietal areas of the Egyptian cotton crop 1905–1930

| Year | Total area | Mit Affi | Mit Affi % | MA + Ash % | Ashmuni | Joannovitch | Sakel | % Sakel | Aggregate yield of cotton fiber |
|---|---|---|---|---|---|---|---|---|---|
| 1896 | | | | | | | | | 5.27 |
| 1897 | | | | | | | | | 5.6 |
| 1898 | | | | | | | | | 5.8 |
| 1899 | | | | | | | | | 4.98 |
| 1900 | | | | | | | | | 5.64 |
| 1901 | | | | | | | | | 4.42 |
| 1902 | | | | | | | | | 5.1 |
| 1903 | | | | | | | | | 4.58 |
| 1904 | | | | | | | | | 4.88 |
| 1905 | 1566602 | 1154923 | 74 | 92 | 293668 | 72716 | | | 4.39 |
| 1906 | 1506291 | 1163841 | 77 | 92 | 224687 | 84483 | | | 3.8 |
| 1907 | 1603224 | 1066720 | 67 | 85 | 299886 | 156867 | | | 4.61 |
| 1908 | 1620415 | 981428 | 61 | 80 | 321665 | 237194 | | | 4.51 |
| 1909 | 1597055 | 1052778 | 66 | 82 | 251548 | 199062 | | | 4.12 |
| 1910 | 1642610 | 1011343 | 62 | 79 | 292490 | 209028 | | | 3.13 |
| 1911 | 1711241 | 845665 | 49 | 69 | 329843 | 250972 | 119636 | 7 | 4.32 |
| 1912 | 1721815 | 731736 | 42 | 62 | 344265 | 239232 | 197456 | 11 | 4.35 |

| Year | | | | | | | | | |
|------|---------|--------|----|----|--------|--------|---------|----|------|
| 1913 | 1723094 | 689695 | 40 | 61 | 356485 | 173439 | 247292 | 14 | 4.44 |
| 1914 | 1755270 | 601453 | 34 | 54 | 353882 | 127532 | 394403 | 22 | 3.67 |
| 1915 | 1186004 | 259096 | 22 | 41 | 231639 | 28907 | 547923 | 46 | 4.02 |
| 1916 | 1655512 | 206048 | 12 | 33 | 343589 | 4220 | 1032140 | 62 | 3.06 |
| 1917 | 1677310 | 134683 | 8 | 30 | 361874 | 1592 | 1133180 | 68 | 3.75 |
| 1918 | 1315572 | 56976 | 4 | 25 | 273936 | 223 | 952481 | 72 | 3.66 |
| 1919 | 1573662 | 56148 | 4 | 25 | 334160 | 97 | 1146443 | 73 | 3.54 |
| 1920 | 1827876 | 74119 | 4 | 28 | 429174 | 2087 | 1270481 | 70 | 3.3 |
| 1921 | 1289805 | 12610 | 1 | 21 | 256764 | 4775 | 995479 | 77 | 3.37 |
| 1922 | 1800843 | 16063 | 1 | 23 | 402734 | 344 | 1358165 | 75 | 3.73 |
| 1923 | 1715150 | 13870 | 1 | 25 | 416540 | 4400 | 1255000 | 73 | 3.81 |
| 1924 | 1787843 | 22271 | 0 | 46 | 796362 | | 876264 | 49 | 4.07 |
| 1925 | 1924382 | 8384 | 0 | 35 | 659420 | | 1128946 | 59 | 4.14 |
| 1926 | 1785802 | 4234 | 0 | 38 | 667474 | | 981783 | 51 | 4.29 |
| 1927 | 1518199 | 4261 | 0 | 40 | 599149 | | 795740 | 52 | 4.01 |
| 1928 | 1738472 | | | 44 | 767411 | | 799523 | 46 | 4.63 |
| 1929 | 1841478 | | | 44 | 804069 | | 847950 | 46 | 4.63 |
| 1930 | 2082420 | | | 45 | 936134 | | 837344 | 40 | 3.97 |
| 1931 | | | | | | | | | |
| 1932 | | | | | | | | | |

**Table 3.4** Egyptian cotton premiums

| Year | FGF Sakellaridis | FGF Brown or Uppers | Co11/Co12 |
|---|---|---|---|
| 1901 | | 14.97 | |
| 1902 | | 22.72 | |
| 1903 | | 22.09 | |
| 1904 | | 17.63 | |
| 1905 | | 23.47 | |
| 1906 | | 24.38 | |
| 1907 | | 21.78 | |
| 1908 | | 20.28 | |
| 1909 | | 31.44 | |
| 1910 | | 24.22 | |
| 1911 | | 20.81 | |
| 1912 | | 19.63 | |
| 1913 | | 20.56 | |
| 1914 | | 19.69 | |
| 1915 | | 19.59 | |
| 1916 | | 63.3 | |
| 1917 | | 46.1 | |
| 1918 | 42 | controlled | |
| 1919 | 198 | 48.3 | 4.10 |
| 1920 | 104.25 | 65.5 | 1.59 |
| 1921 | 63.1 | 44.35 | 1.42 |
| 1922 | 39.15 | 32.4 | 1.21 |
| 1923 | 52 | 46.85 | 1.11 |
| 1924 | 75.75 | 39.4 | 1.92 |
| 1925 | 46.75 | 33.25 | 1.41 |
| 1926 | 39.1 | 28.48 | 1.37 |
| 1927 | 44 | 31.85 | 1.57 |
| 1928 | 41.3 | 28 | 1.48 |
| 1929 | 35.77 | 23.9 | 1.50 |
| 1930 | 21.85 | 15.07 | 1.45 |
| 1931 | 17.15 | 12.26 | 1.40 |
| 1932 | 19.18 | 15.37 | 1.25 |
| 1933 | 17.5 | 13.66 | 1.28 |
| 1934 | 17.07 | 14.11 | 1.21 |
| 1935 | 18.37 | 14.62 | 1.26 |
| 1936 | 24.75 | 18.57 | 1.33 |
| 1937 | 17.6 | 13.17 | 1.34 |
| 1938 | 14.99 | | |

**Table 3.4** Continued

| Year | FGF Sakellaridis | FGF Brown or Uppers | Co11/Co12 |
|------|------------------|---------------------|-----------|
| 1939 | 25.7 | | |
| 1940 | 16.25 | | |
| 1941 | 18.25 | | |

*Notes*: Prices are in "talaris"/cantar;
FGF: Fully Good Fair grade of cotton;
Brown: Regular Egyptian long staple; after 1920 Uppers replaces Brown;
Sakel: Extra-long staple introduced in 1911.

an explanation for observed yield declines before 1911:

> ...if we consider the yield (in money) per feddan, since the area has increased only 50 percent between 1897 and 1907, while the value of the crop has increased nearly 100 percent, the increase in money received per feddan amounts to nearly 40 per cent. And if as has been suggested above, the fellah has obtained this result with diminished intensity of cultivation, that is, with a less expenditure of energy, he is doubly a gainer...It is doubtful how far any efforts to persuade the fellah that the yield of cotton is diminishing will meet with success, when the evidence of his purse is to the contrary effect. (Craig)

What Craig (and all who followed him) left unexplored was whether attempts to improve the quality of the crop that was already underway by 1911 could have affected yields. For example, after 1900 Egyptians reduced pickings of the same field to ensure that less trash was being processed as cotton.[13]

As table 3.3 makes apparent there continued to be significant changes in the composition of the crop and both Mit Afifi and Joannovitch disappeared before 1930; these same forces explain the disappearance of Sakel in the 1930s. Largely due to its susceptibility to wilt disease, Sakel yields continued to decline through the 1930s but more important so did its price relative to other grades of cotton (International Cotton Federation [1938] 76).

That aggregate yields were intimately related to the composition of the crop was well known to English spinners. In July 1920 they organized a campaign to protest a rumored shift among Egyptian farmers from Sakellaridis to Pillion production because they feared Egyptians would prefer a crop with a higher raw yield and ginning outturn (FO 371/5014). The rationale behind the protest was that English machinery had been adapted to the Sakellarides variety and could not be easily changed to accept the new variety. The picture I present here was well known in the early twentieth century. By 1921 Egyptians publicly linked the extension of Sakel to the aggregate yield decline (Nahas [1952] 41) and it remained the standard explanation in expert Egyptian and international opinion for at least two decades (Ahmad 11; Black 70–71; International Institute of Agriculture 113).[14] A memorandum by Lawrence Balls in September 1920 clearly showed that the shift to Sakel (the lowest-yielding cotton) was due to its providing the highest return per unit of area. Gerald Dudgeon decomposed the aggregate yield into precisely these two components (Sakel and non-Sakel) not long after in order to explain the shift back to Ashmouni in terms of the price differential between cotton types:

> Taking the average yield per feddan for Lower Egypt, which is roughly equivalent to the Sakellaridis area, for five years and comparing it with that of Upper Egypt, which is nearly equivalent to the Ashmouni area, for a similar period, we arrive at the following averages: Lower Egypt average 3.43 [cantars/feddan] ... Upper Egypt average: 4.26. (Dudgeon 529)

Nearly a decade later Victor Mosseri[15] matter-of-factly explained (International Cotton Congress [1928] 205):

> the excess of the falling off [of aggregate yields] since 1912 is attributable, one might say almost entirely, to the combined action of two new factors, the one accidental, viz. the ravages of the pink boll-worm, the other essential, viz. cultivation of Sakel. The nett yield of this new variety is indeed *constitutionally* about 15 percent inferior to the cottons which it has supplanted. (Afifi, Assili, etc.)[16]

Mosseri was one of the two rapporteurs of the 1910 Cotton Commission that the government created to explore the reasons behind the disastrous crop failure that year and whose report is often adduced to buttress the claims about drainage. That report recommended extending the drainage system especially for the northernmost areas of the country, but the somewhat tentative findings of the commission were clearly oriented to resolving what its members were convinced was a one-time problem. The later decline in yields was, as far as Mosseri was concerned, a completely different issue.

Declining yields after 1911 were a sign of rapid response to market conditions rather than ecological crisis but drainage was an issue where landowners wanted and received state investment. How severe was drainage at any period relative to other problems? Using the data provided by Alan Richards (table 3.5), the correlation between total drain length and aggregate yield was nearly 0.77, which is very high. However these values, which presumably show the importance of drainage, apply only to the years 1922–1938, that is, after the switch away from Sakellaridis had begun (Richards 121, 145) and drainage was obviously not the cause of changes of yield in the first-third of the twentieth century. So why did drainage matter and to whom?

Of course there was a drainage problem in the northern part of the Delta where land reclamation had occurred. There had never been an absolute disregard for drain construction and certainly no lack of awareness of the need to construct drains (Casoria 145).[17] If most growers were not concerned that a crisis of drainage existed and were not prepared to exert great effort to extend the drainage system, who was? Agricultural societies and individual landowners with large investments in cotton and rice in the extreme north of the Delta were certainly affected and appear to have been consistent supporters of extending the network of drains and pumping stations (Casoria 145). Because hydraulic engineering was linked to British prestige, irrigation, and drainage were frequently foremost in the minds of British officials (Cromer [1908 ii] 463–465; Lloyd 148). There were also emergent sectoral interests within the Egyptian elite. Thus, Hussein Sirri, who was Minister of Public Works in several governments in 1937–1938, argued for the need to extend the drainage system beyond the 35–40 percent that he estimated was then currently covered. "Our aim," he said, "is to produce real drainage in the land for every plot in Egypt from Aswan to the sea" (Cotton Federation [1938] 63). Robert Vitalis has argued that entrepreneurs in the construction industry (and especially canal dredging) were crucial actors in the Egyptian political economy and Sirri was certainly an intimate of the construction magnate Ahmad Abbud (Vitalis [1995] 53). Sirri's proposal to extend drainage work far into the south where it was (insofar as reducing the water table was concerned) no issue suggests a greater concern with the profits of the construction industry than with the productivity of the peasants.

The assertion that Egypt experienced an ecological crisis does raise an important historiographical issue. Specifically, if there was no ecological crisis and if contemporary observers were aware that there was none, what drove the narrative of environmental disaster in later academic writing and why did the alleged absence of sufficient drainage become such a widely held idea? Part of the problem was a misreading of the concerns voiced by Egyptians

**Table 3.5**  Investment in Irrigation, Drainage, and Yields

| Year | Aggregate yield of cotton fiber | Net capital stock in irrigation |
|------|--------------------------------|--------------------------------|
| 1896 | 5.27 | 61.1 |
| 1897 | 5.6 | 62.6 |
| 1898 | 5.8 | 64.6 |
| 1899 | 4.98 | 66.8 |
| 1900 | 5.64 | 69.1 |
| 1901 | 4.42 | 73.2 |
| 1902 | 5.1 | 82.5 |
| 1903 | 4.58 | 90.5 |
| 1904 | 4.88 | 94.2 |
| 1905 | 4.39 | 99.3 |
| 1906 | 3.80 | 107 |
| 1907 | 4.61 | 115.8 |
| 1908 | 4.51 | 125 |
| 1909 | 4.12 | 132.5 |
| 1910 | 3.13 | 138.6 |
| 1911 | 4.32 | 142.2 |
| 1912 | 4.35 | 145.7 |
| 1913 | 4.44 | 148.9 |
| 1914 | 3.67 | 151.9 |
| 1915 | 4.02 | 153 |
| 1916 | 3.06 | 153.9 |
| 1917 | 3.75 | 155 |
| 1918 | 3.66 | 156.1 |
| 1919 | 3.54 | 156.9 |
| 1920 | 3.30 | 158.7 |
| 1921 | 3.37 | 160.2 |
| 1922 | 3.73 | 161.1 |
| 1923 | 3.81 | 162.1 |
| 1924 | 4.07 | 163.6 |
| 1925 | 4.14 | 165.4 |
| 1926 | 4.29 | 167.5 |
| 1927 | 4.01 | 171.1 |
| 1928 | 4.63 | 176.4 |
| 1929 | 4.63 | 186.4 |
| 1930 | 3.97 | 198.2 |
| 1931 | 3.78 | 211.8 |
| 1932 | 4.53 | 229.8 |
| 1933 | 4.75 | 245.1 |
| 1934 | 4.36 | 262.7 |

Table 3.5 Continued

| Year | Aggregate yield of cotton fiber | Net capital stock in irrigation |
|------|------|------|
| 1935 | 5.11 | 280.8 |
| 1936 | 5.32 | 297.1 |
| 1937 | 5.57 | 313.5 |
| 1938 | 4.67 | 329.7 |

*Sources*: Richards and Radwan.

and English spinners about cotton shortly after the turn of the century. There was, as I have shown, a persistent contention between the two sides about what was called the environmental and biological *degeneration* of Egyptian cotton. For nearly forty years, spinners complained about the deteriorating quality of Egyptian cotton and some of the arguments about environmental disaster appear to pick up on these themes.

Even in the early twentieth century, however, experts attempted to understand why yields were declining and later authors picked up their arguments. Later writers focused on one specific explanation (insufficient drainage) that was prominent around 1910 and ignored other explanations that gained currency after 1920. Divergent but plausible arguments from the early twentieth century about cotton yields had contrasting political implications. By the late twentieth century they were combined into a single, ostensibly anticolonial argument. The most surprising aspect of the anticolonial argument that colonialism provoked an ecological crisis is that it began life as an argument made by colonial officials to support their continued role in Egypt. It is now time to quickly review the hard core of the arguments for ecological crisis: they were (and remain) technical, intellectual, political, and institutional.

Explaining declining yields was an intellectual challenge. The techniques used to explain declining yields were complex and, in the early twentieth century, quite new. George Yule had only elucidated the concept of regression analysis in 1896 (Stigler 349). It was a powerful conceptual tool and English experts in Egypt began to explain it and employ it on the pages of *L'Egypte Contemporaine* within a year or two of the journal's foundation. The allure of statistical analysis has always been to uncover patterns that lie hidden within data aggregates and the use of the new technique can easily lead down a particular, but wrong, explanatory path. That these techniques were known initially only to British experts may have increased their allure (Porter 14).

Politically, the idea that Britain has been responsible for Egyptian history is alluring to both anticolonialists and apologists for colonialism; it certainly places the British nearly alone at the center directing Egyptian life. As early as 1892, long before the onset of the crisis, there were accounts that it was "the want of drainage, which completed the ruin of the Birríya, that broad belt of land, which occupies the northern and lowest portion of the Delta, adjoining the great lakes" (Milner 284). English energy and technical ability in the years after the Occupation accomplished what neither French engineers nor Egyptian politicians could in such an account. It is therefore not surprising that one of the earliest books to focus on drainage as a cause of prolonged crisis (rather than the cause of the 1910 crop debacle) was P.G. Elgood's triumphal account of Lord Kitchener's years as the British Resident. Writing in the later 1920s Elgood also blamed short-sighted Egyptian peasants for overwatering and short-sighted ministries staffed by Egyptians for responding too eagerly to the demands of peasants for water and thereby neglecting the country's future (Elgood 201–202). Elgood was sounding an old theme: British officials, unlike the Egyptian elite, were the true friends of the peasant. Despite sounding an alarm, Elgood (like most contemporary observers) placed the issue of drainage in what was then the well-understood triple context: maintaining the quality (not quantity of cotton) produced, reclaiming waste land in the northern Delta, and recognizing that it was only one among many causal agents.

Although drainage had initially been seen as one problem among many in explaining declining quality, its importance grew as later authors paid more attention to aggregate yield declines (Issawi 1947, 1954, 1963). The identification of drainage as the primary cause of aggregate yield decline, however, only emerged as a central theme in the work of Alan Richards in the 1970s. Richards was aware of the shift toward and then away from a lower-yielding crop (Richards 126), but it remains a minor part of a story told to establish the predatory and thus primarily negative economic as well as political role of British imperial rule. Richards linked a story about declining yields to a plausible characterization of why a rational government would provide irrigation but not drainage and wrote a powerful anti-imperialist narrative. Thus, an analysis that began as a tribute to imperial foresight and a concern with the profitability of investments by primarily foreign-owned companies thus came to be the basis for an attack on imperial shortsightedness, but in both cases the focus remained on the power of the colonial state as the key actor in Egyptian economic life. As taken over by Hansen (for whom the British were not inherently a negative force) and by Beinin (for whom they were), the politics of the narrative drove a widely recognized problem whose solution was always well understood into an ecological crisis that neatly supplemented other crises inherent in an imperial regime.

The explicitly anti-imperialist accounts of Egyptian history exclude Egyptians from any active role in the construction of an economic and political order that lasted more than half a century. The focus on representation makes intellectuals and imperial officials far more central to the emergence of the world in which we live than they actually were (Mitchell; Beinin [1999]), and profoundly misreads the commercial, cultural, and social connections between Egypt and England. As I have shown, the growing dependence of English manufacturers on Egyptian cotton was not due to "new machinery for the manufacture of textiles, the resulting increase in profits, and the reinvestment of profit abroad in further cotton production" (Mitchell [1988] 15). On the contrary, English manufacturers became increasingly reliant on Egyptian cotton because they did not (or could not) invest in new machinery because such investments would have been inimical to their profitability. They certainly did not themselves invest in the production of cotton and where they were able to motivate government investments to extend cotton production (as initially in the Sudan but especially in West Africa) the profits were derisory.

Drainage was only one problem in the agricultural sector that required government intervention and expenditure. From the view of the wealthy farmers many problems required government intervention: the "lethal enemy" of insect infestation, price declines, the shortage of sacking material, and the crisis of manipulation on the commodity exchanges and drainage appears to have been a problem specific only to one area (Nahas [1952] 30–33, [1954] 11–18). When Nahas discussed the problem of declining cotton crops (but not area yields) between 1915 and 1917, he singled out Sharqiya for a drainage problem but used it to criticize the newly formed Ministry of Agriculture for lack of responsiveness (Nahas [1954] 11–12). Nahas frequently employed the word crisis to discuss the situation of Egyptian growers from World War I through the 1920s and well into the 1930s. The single most common crisis to which he referred, however, was the "crisis of cotton prices." From the viewpoint of large growers the debates over price and quality were far more important than the yield because they had made significant investments in reputation that were threatened by attacks on the quality of the crops they marketed.

Because price and quality rather than yield were the most common perceptions linking ecology to cotton for the first two decades of the twentieth century, most growers were more than willing to support government funding for scientific research. Because declining quality was perceived to result from a tendency of seed to "revert the mean," scientists and engineers associated with biotechnology argued insistently for ever greater investment in providing "true line" seed (e.g., International Cotton Federation [1912] 28; Rousso [1925]; International Cotton Federation [1928]).

Having argued that there was no ecological crisis why does it matter? The argument about crisis is an argument about the failure of the state but also an argument that the primary role of the state is the provision of physical infrastructure. What I have attempted to show is that the Egyptian government successfully carried out a far more sophisticated strategy than the mere provision of physical infrastructure. This strategy aimed to maximize the reputation of Egyptian cotton by ensuring that growers could rapidly produce cotton with the quality dimensions desired by producers willing to pay a premium for such quality. Thus Egyptian growers produced, at least for a while, increasing supplies of cotton for a market that itself was increasingly turning to the production of high-quality goods. The success of this strategy was closely linked to the economic fortunes of the large landowners who benefited from it and who also frequently provided the impetus for its development (as in the case of the Khedivial Agricultural Society). It is not, of course, news that large landowners were the dominant social and political group in Egypt. The disposition of the narrative of ecological crisis also entails the recognition that the successful implementation of regulatory strategies requires not social or political support in the abstract but the alignment of incentives so that the economic gains in the regulated activity are enhanced by the regulation. Regulation by the state works, in short, as long as it involves significant levels of self-regulation. To extend this part of the argument I now turn to a second important juncture in the political economy of twentieth-century Egypt—the spot and futures markets and attempts to address more directly the price received for Egyptian cotton.

# CHAPTER 4

# Regulation for Reputation in the Egyptian Delta

Taking as a theoretical point of departure the idea that commodities in international trade are envelopes for the exchange of factors of production, an obvious question is what was the factor of production in which Egypt was well endowed? The factor of production in which Egypt was best endowed was the labor of her children and this, I shall show, was the crucial factor input for cotton production. If, as most Egyptians understood at the time, child labor was crucial for the production of high-quality cotton in Egypt, a related issue is how were Egyptians able to mobilize such a low-quality input for such a high-quality output. The answer lies in the very sophisticated public and private institutions developed in Egypt to transmit information about prices and to assure the compliance of everyone engaged in the cotton economy with the production of a high-quality good. Egypt therefore is not an example of a country with a weak or poor institutional structure but the reverse. It was a country where institutional capacity—private as well as public—facilitated the use of an abundant but seemingly unsuitable factor of production to make a high-quality good.

The most direct way to address the issue of child labor would be to calculate the relative weight of children in the workforce in Egypt compared to the world during the period 1880–1950. Unfortunately we lack adequate data to accomplish this task for the first half of the twentieth century although there is some indication that as late as 1958 the single most important factor endowment generating trade in Egypt was her abundance of illiterate labor (Leamer [1984] 203).[1] There is every reason to believe that Egypt was, in an earlier period, also well-endowed relative to the world in the labor of illiterates and children. It is also possible to show the dominant role that child labor played in the production of cotton and was understood to play at the time. This understanding of the role of factor abundance has simply dropped out of the literature along with any understanding of its importance in analyzing trade then or now.

By World War I it was already received-wisdom among experts in the field that "cotton has always been regarded as a cheap-labour crop, that is, a crop that can only be profitably cultivated where there is an ample supply of cheap labour" (Todd [1915] 107). Egypt competed with the United States, the dominant producer of cotton, by focusing on one portion of the world's market and investing heavily in reputation. Even so, Egyptian landowners had to assure a supply of cheap labor. The United States was already a high-wage country in terms of global trade and this conferred some benefit on even disadvantaged sections of the American population. Thus at the turn of the twentieth century the Black population in the Old Confederacy had begun to leave cotton production. Violent and impoverished as the American South was, especially in regard to the Black population, close observers recognized that the global situation of the United States made the situation of Blacks different from that of Egyptian peasants:

> [T]he scarcity of labour has only resulted in raising the general level of wages and enabling the negro [*sic*] to adopt a higher standard of living... The contrast between all this and the position of the Egyptian fellah, with his unlimited capacity for patient plodding work from morning till night, for almost seven days a week, and from one year's end to another, on a wage less than a quarter of that of the American Negro... is painful in the extreme. (Todd [1915] 108)

The image of the fellah is one that we immediately convert into an adult male, but children occupied, and continue to occupy, an important role in the economy of cotton production. Children were especially favored for picking cotton, eliminating insect infestations, and working in some ginning operations (International Cotton Federation [1927] 90; Richards 126; Berque 489). The role of unpaid labor in cotton production was so well understood that observers feared the end of American cotton production because of the decline in the availability of family labor in the American South although Black families were clearly still caught in the grip of the cotton economy that whites had begun to escape:

> The position is practically this, that under such conditions [prevailing in Texas, EG], cotton cannot be grown at a profit *if all the labor it requires*

*has to be paid for.* Unless the small planter has a large family to do part of the work, cotton at present prices will not pay. Such conditions may be all very well for the Negro, whose standard of living (for example, his children) has always been low; education, for example, is only now beginning to be though necessary; but they will not do at all for the small white planters... In other words, it means that cotton is, and must remain, a "black man's crop," not a white man's.... (Todd [1915] 113; italics in original)[2]

Within families the labor of children was free; outside of the family it was not free but it was certainly cheap. There are, of course, ambiguities in the category "children" and in different societies the end of childhood and dependence occurs at very different ages. However, if we define children as did the Egyptian census authorities as those aged between five and ten years, we can more easily understand the role of child labor in early twentieth-century Egypt and there appears to be wide agreement that these are years of childhood not statistically misdefined adulthood. Overall, the labor of boys accounted for nearly 35 percent of the total labor requirement for the major Egyptian crops (Anis [1950] 754–755).[3] Child labor was an important factor of production generally but it was most intensely employed in cotton, the primary export crop. For example, and in contradistinction to every other field crop except rice, more children (69) than adult males (47) were employed per acre in cotton production. Of the nearly 96 million days of labor that were needed to produce the cotton crop children provided nearly 57 million days or 60 percent of the labor input (Anis 755). The accuracy of Anis's estimates drawn from a national survey are reinforced by an account of the cost of cultivating one feddan of cotton made by Victor Mosseri in 1927. Judging that children carried out thinning, weeding, collecting insect eggs to prevent infestation, and picking, Mosseri's estimates can be used to infer that the labor of children accounted for at least half of the labor cost of production and could have accounted for as much as one half of the total cost of cultivation (International Cotton Congress [1927] 89–90).

It does not appear to be possible to estimate the total income of children nor, consequently, the cost or value of their labor in production. Nor can we be very certain about how important the income of children was for overall family incomes. On balance it appears that children earned about half the wage of adult men and about 75 percent of the wage of adult women (Anis [1950] 753).

Victor Mosseri's explanations about how difficult it was to prevent dirt and trash from being taken up when cotton was picked focused on the role of children: "Pickers are human beings: they cannot help a certain amount of dust in the cotton, and how can you prevent children from picking up cotton that has fallen on the ground here and there" (International Cotton Federation [1927] 167). Pickers were human beings, but they were, in large measure, human beings for whom education and the skills attendant on literacy were nearly impossible to obtain. Although Egyptian governments began to spend far more heavily on education in the 1920s and 1930s than had been the case under the British Occupation, illiteracy declined only very slowly. The reason that thousands of schools enrolling hundreds of thousands of students did not rapidly eliminate illiteracy had (it appears) little to do with regulatory capacity or the culture of the schools themselves. Rather it arose from the contradictory needs of the political coalitions that had emerged in a country in which child labor remained a crucial economic input. In the words of an authoritative study, "children were too tired to concentrate on lessons after a half-day in the fields, teachers working a double shift were too tired to be thoroughly competent, and the schooling offered in half-day sessions for a five-year period of erratic attendance was too meager to be effective" (Matthews and Akrawi 28). The counterpart to high levels of investment in the reputation of Egyptian cotton was inadequate investment in the education of Egyptian children.

### Institutions To the Rescue

As Joseph Nahas pointedly explained to his listeners in 1927, the production of a high-quality good for international trade required the elaboration of regulatory and market structures to combine with existing factors of production. In chapter 3 I discussed capital investments (in seed and irrigation). There were distinct but complementary aspects of investment in reputation. These were private and public institutions that, through the transmission of prices, provision of finance, or direct regulatory authority, amounted to social investment in reputation that made the investments in physical capital and the hiring of labor privately profitable. Although some of these institutions were provided by the state, others were the result of private investment and even the state institutions required significant private initiative to work effectively.

By resolving information asymmetries, investment in reputation allows complementary investments for the production of complex goods. This logic was implicit in the debates over agricultural and trade policy in Egypt between 1900 and 1940 and become explicit by World War II when the standard Egyptian analysis of the political economy of cotton was framed in terms of complementary investments in bilateral monopolies (Abbas [1946]

88–89).[4] Frequently ignored in accounts of development are the genesis and maintenance of the regulatory institutions that actually made reputation work.

The relevant regulatory institutions were not necessarily state organs charged either with enforcing abstract regulations on recalcitrant growers, ginners, merchants, or exporters or ensuring the performance of contractual relations. For reasons discussed in chapter 2 the Weberian idealization of state administrative offices is neither a very realistic nor a theoretically plausible understanding of how to regulate the production of high-quality good that requires the cooperation of a large number of different actors on many different dimensions. In place of a single actor guaranteeing quality, we find many actors and several institutional structures to monitor quality levels and to ensure rapid rewards for conformity and penalties for failure to conform: interest group associations, public regulatory authorities, and extensive commodity markets. Some Egyptian politicians attempted to employ these same institutions to manage a dramatic restructuring of the export economy in the early 1930s. What the sophisticated institutions could not overcome, however, was the historical evolution of Egypt's comparative advantage in a particular factor of production: child labor. Nor could they rapidly overcome the many consequent social disadvantages of an abundance of this factor of production. The problem for re-structuring was not that state actors lacked appropriate information about the economy or insufficient capacity to tax but that the national economy lacked crucial factor endowments.

For more than 30 years spinners, merchants, and growers debated the dimensions of fiber quality in search of an agreement so that growers could reasonably conform to the expectations of spinners and reap a quality premium. Staple length was the most obvious and most easily measured dimension and was largely genetic in origin. Three, additional, and far less easily observable dimensions also mattered for cotton's reputation: uniformity of fiber in the bale, the level of moisture, and stability of fiber tensile strength over time (Ahmad and Hafiz 41).

Uniformity of fiber within lots was necessary to ensure high capital utilization and to avoid excess labor costs. Spinners bought lots that were made up of bales produced by different growers and bales themselves could contain significantly different cottons. Genetic uniformity was only part of the solution to this problem. Uniform bales had to made up of cotton with common staple lengths, tensile strength, dye-absorptive capacity and excluding non-fibrous cotton material (stalks, seeds, roots) and they had to exclude non-cotton material (dirt, metal banding, jute coverings). At the turn of the twentieth century Egyptian bales, unlike American ones, were widely prized for their relative homogeneity. To ensure such relative uniformity growers were expected, beyond the use of common seed, to take extra care at picking and especially to ensure that cottons of one type were not mixed with those of another type. Exporting companies in Alexandria were primarily responsible for guaranteeing bale uniformity and developed their own "in-house" types of cotton for specific spinners in England with whom they developed long-term relationships. If growers attempted to produce a high-quality product by investment in seed, irrigation, and labor control they had relied on third parties to provide guarantees to consumers in Britain that the cotton was indeed of high quality. Consequently guaranteeing the quality of cotton was, at the beginning of the twentieth century, an extremely valuable asset privately held by the largely foreign-born brokers. To represent their interests in retaining control of the reputation of Egyptian cotton exporters created the Alexandria General Produce Association. Investing in such an organization provided additional guarantees to ultimate consumers of the quality of Egyptian cotton but it also sought to retain ownership of the asset in the hands of foreign-born brokers.

It is easier under the conflicts over who would guarantee the quality of the cotton and who would reap the benefits of providing that guarantee by examining a second dimension of quality: moisture content. Strictly speaking water could be considered simply as another foreign substance, but cotton like all vegetable matter contains water and only slowly dries out after picking. Some moisture was necessary for the fiber to retain flexibility, but too much moisture was a negative feature. Growers asserted that it was necessary to spray water onto cotton at the gin, but admitted that water also seeped into the bale through condensation during steam pressing. No spinners wanted completely dehydrated cotton, but European spinners who warehoused cotton for relatively long periods were concerned that the cotton not become so damp as to mold. British spinners were less concerned about mold but because they faced high labor costs, they strenuously resisted paying the price of long-staple cotton for water that evaporated due to the heat generated during spinning. The issue was not the presence or absence of water but the level of moisture.

Individual bales could be tested for water content, but it was impossible to negotiate distinct prices for each bale so the reputation of cotton brands mattered a great deal. At the very turn of the twentieth century the export houses in Alexandria were primarily responsible for guaranteeing the quality of the cotton Egypt shipped. Initially these exporters were expatriates who had extensive connections with English importers if they had not originally come to Egypt charged to purchase high-quality cotton. Growers, exporters, and spinners had to agree on what constituted an acceptable standard as well as on the institutional mechanism for enforcing the standard. Egyptian growers consequently were not averse to state regulation of the moisture content of cotton in order to reduce the proportion of the quality premium that went to third-party guarantors. In response, the exporters and especially their organization, the AGPA, made the issue contentious because they feared state regulation would strip them of the private brands they had developed, effectively expropriating their ownership of the asset of reputation.

Concern with moisture content was an issue at the second international congress (International Cotton Congress [1906] 41) and in succeeding meetings (International Cotton Congress [1912] 58, 63). Explicit collective self-regulation could have been the first step toward state regulation and the exporters strenuously imposed even this move. Thus in 1911 the by-laws of the AGPA were amended to forbid members from selling cotton with a guaranteed maximum humidity (International Cotton Congress [1927] 149). Much as exporters feared that the emergence of standards enforced by the government would make their role redundant, their unwillingness to create explicit standards laid them open to charges of unfair dealing. That exporters were engaged in fraudulent practices was sufficiently widely believed that at one meeting with them in the early 1930s a prominent official, Ahmed Abdel Wahab, accused them of all being thieves (Politi 126). Abdel Wahab was later to significantly limit their autonomy. Nevertheless fraud appears to have been less a problem than dogged resistance by the exporters to any procedure that would take the grading of cotton for export out of their hands.

Finally because spinners and end users made long-term investments in specialized machinery they were concerned about changes over time in the homogeneity—especially tensile strength—of cotton. This is the temporal equivalent of the concern for homogeneity within bales. Spinners constantly complained that the same nominal type of cotton showed evidence of deteriorating quality over time. Egyptian thread had a variety of specialized uses: although it was frequently employed in mercerized clothing, it also was prized for the warp (longitudinal) threads of many fabrics and as the foundation for then recently invented pneumatic automobile and airplane tires. There is no way to know if the concerns voiced by spinners about deterioration were accurate, but Egyptian farmers and government officials took them seriously enough to respond to complaints about the deterioration of the fiber quality over time.

Investing in the reputation of Egyptian cotton required the development of institutions that would make the relevant investments to overcome the social and economic threats to the quality of cotton just as they dealt with the biological problems as outlined in chapter 3.[5] If growers could ensure they received a minimum price for their crop, then it was necessary to create a mechanism that penalized them for failure to provide goods of appropriate quality (thereby avoiding either simple theft or moral hazard). Yet any mechanism developed also had to ensure that it encouraged committed growers to remain in production rather than driving them out (adverse selection). Social investments created institutions to accomplish these tasks that we regularly associate with a strong state: they made public policy and effectively carried it out. In Egypt (and in much of the world) they were frequently private institutions rather than state bureaucracies. The more ostentatious and expensive the regulations associated with ensuring the quality and homogeneity of cotton, of course, the more effectively they signaled the level of investment in quality (Rosenman and Wilson).

Two important private institutions linked growers, exporters, and the state: the Agriculturalists' Union and the organized commodities exchanges. The union linked them through politics and the commodities exchanges accomplished the task through markets. In 1921, the General Union of Egyptian Agriculturists was created to represent planter interests and lobby on their behalf with the government. Like the Royal Society discussed in chapter 3, the General Union was formed with royal patronage. Prince Yusuf Kamal attended the founding meeting held in Cairo on February 12, 1921 where he accepted the presidency of the group. As the Royal Society increasingly specialized in research, the General Union increasingly strove to affect government policies in many arenas on behalf of growers. Its original name, The General Union to Safeguard the Interests of Egyptian Farmers, indicated the degree to which its founders saw it as an organized interest group. From subsidies to market organization and energetic activity to promote the use of Egyptian cotton internationally the General Union always had recommendations and undertook frequent consultations with its base by issuing a stream of reports to members. Its earliest leadership was a compendium of the landowning elite and many of its leaders were closely linked to the nationalist movement through personal ties to the leaders of the Wafd party (Nahas [1952a]). Its general secretary and primary staff member was the French-trained economist, Joseph Nahas.

Given its membership, it is not surprising that the Agriculturalists' Union was a powerful group that "lobbied systematically and successfully in favor of government intervention to stabilize cotton prices" (Hansen [1991] 84). Price supports and direct payments to landowners were an important method by which the Wafd created a political base for itself in the countryside. This represented a choice by the Wafd; it was in contradistinction to policies that its political opponents followed of granting credits to rural cooperatives (Bianchi 67). The Union's influence on policy was partly structural but also due to the number of its members who frequently served in high office. Five of the nineteen Agriculture Ministers who served between 1924 and 1944 were founding members of the Union's Permanent Executive Committee (Nahas [1952b] 511–512).

That one of the few Egyptian economists then living should play an important role in an organization of landowners is indicative of the degree to which Egyptian agriculture already depended on access to the financial and political resources of the state. That Egyptian peasants were poor and illiterate does not imply that the institutions needed to make Egypt fit into the global economy were without sophistication.

### To Market, To Market

Commodity markets were a second crucial set of institutions that linked growers to processors. Commodity markets were crucial in Egypt (and elsewhere) for three reasons: they provided credit; they provided information about the current and expected prices for different kinds of cotton (price discovery); and they provided a mechanism for punishing or rewarding those who promised particular levels of quality. "Commodity markets" are not, of course, markets for commodities or at least not markets for exchange of physical goods whose names they nominally bear. They are financial markets that trade contracts denominated in commodities rather than money (unless money is the commodity being traded). Three kinds of contracts are associated with such markets: forward, spot, and futures. A forward market, as its name suggests, is a market for delivery of a good at some distant time and a spot market is a market for immediate delivery.

What distinguishes a "commodities market" is that it has a futures market or more precisely a market in contracts for forward deliveries. Contracts for future delivery allow investors to hold complementary assets. Spinners buy cotton for future delivery and thereby assure themselves of a supply of fiber and guarantee farmers that investments in fiber production will be profitable. When producers and processors sign contracts for future delivery that are honored, no commodities market exists. There is, for example, no commodities market for apples or grapes in the United States.

Where futures markets exist their mechanisms are straightforward. One party to the contract "goes short" or agrees to sell a particular amount of a good at a given price on a given date and the other party agrees to purchase that quantity of the good at the same price on the same date, known as "going long." Forward contracts can be held until they are due at which point they become spot contracts, but in a futures market they can be settled in other ways. Someone who has gone short (obligated himself to sell) can cancel his position by going long (and obligating himself to buy). Contracts at a fixed price between parties can also be settled against the difference between the market price at a particular moment and the underlying price of the contract (called "points off" or "on"). Futures markets are financial markets denominated in quantities of commodities; they have a life of their own and generate significant speculative activity. The possibility of settling contracts without having to receive or deliver the goods makes futures markets attractive to speculators and speculative activity provides the liquidity that allows purchasers and sellers of physical commodities to engage in contracts at very low cost to themselves. Speculators cannot themselves provide the goods nor process them. Therefore they usually, at some point, "cover" their initial contracts either by engaging in the opposite contractual maneuver or simply paying the relevant penalty. In Egypt, local purchasers of cotton appear to have been active in the futures markets without necessarily covering their open positions and were thus exposed to risk and ruin (Ahmad and Hafiz 21).

Although many commodities are marketed without "commodity markets," futures markets play crucial roles in the production of many internationally traded goods. Thus, Egyptian farmers (whether peasants or landowners) not only grew cotton for the mills of Lancashire; they also produced raw material for the financial markets of Manchester and Alexandria. Futures markets closely approximate the ideal type of a market where prices reflect rapid changes in supply and demand and the cost of making transactions is close to nil. Futures markets emerged historically as an institutional mechanism that increased the efficiency of markets for physical goods. Specifically futures markets provided a way to adjust inventories without having to warehouse or repeatedly move physical goods (Chandler).

There is significant disagreement about how to explain or even to model what commodities markets do because they are necessarily centers of speculation as well as of exchange and insurance. Without speculation such markets cannot attain the liquidity necessary to operate; it is common for the volume of nominal goods traded by the purchase and sale of contracts to be ten times the volume of physical goods actually exchanged in the same time period. Two major theoretical approaches to explaining why there are commodity markets (and therefore what they do) can be summarized as theories of insurance (Keynes [1936]; Hicks; Johnson; Stein) and theories of transaction cost reduction (Working; Telser; Telser and Higinbotham, Williams). The most useful approach for understanding Egypt is embodied in an aphorism by Meeker that provided the basis of Williams's approach: that short sales are debts in goods rather than money (Meeker 1). In ordinary markets goods are exchanged for money, but in futures markets goods are turned into a kind of credit. This approach sheds more light than any others on why control of the futures markets has often been crucial as the control of the country's banks (and thus interest rates). Indeed, in the absence of a fully developed central bank (and a consequent lack of political control over elements of both interest rate policy and exchange rate policy), political control of the commodity markets was even more important for Egypt than in other agricultural countries.

Political scientists have become interested in how states create rights to private property so that entrepreneurs can function in market economies. They have spent very little time examining how markets, especially highly formalized commodity markets, actually work. This is surprising because the volatility associated with speculation in these markets is politically important and because these markets, often privately owned, play central roles in organizing much of the world's trade in raw materials and financial instruments. Volatility, speculation, and the desire for political control over markets that are used by traders with no commitment to the underlying structures of production have long been consequential wherever such markets emerged— from American grain production to Brazilian coffee (Bates [1997]). Most controversial of all that occurs on futures markets is the routine selling of "uncovered" short sales in which a speculator guarantees to deliver goods that he does not own and never intends to own (or deliver).

To recapitulate: the organization of futures markets for primary commodities such as cotton and wheat by the 1860s facilitated the movement of far larger quantities of agricultural goods over much longer distances than ever before. As the volume of trade grew sufficiently large it was increasingly desirable to make contracts for the delivery of standardized goods even though the real commodities exchanged were not standardized. Standardized contracts used an existing type of good as the basis for trading in all similar goods although agricultural commodities and prices are adjusted accordingly. Because the prices of futures contracts can be so easily adjusted they also implicitly allow the creation of virtual markets for the services (transportation, cleaning, processing) required to transform nonstandard into standard goods. Futures markets therefore increase the number and sophistication of market relationships without requiring the creation of a full set of actual markets by encouraging price arbitrage to mimic these activities. Trading futures contracts makes markets more liquid just because it is possible to trade contracts without the necessity of actually delivering the underlying explicit or implicit goods. Futures trading also allows for the creation of markets in physical commodities that are quite diverse to act as if they were all identical because deliveries can also be "off" or "on" in regard to the nominal quality that defines the financial contract. If the speculator, producer, or processor were obliged to take physical possession on the one contract or even to examine the goods directly, the entire system would grind to a halt. Speculation is enabled because obligations can be canceled by a simple financial act and speculation enables producers and processors to avoid handling, storage, and interest costs.

Farmers, unlike speculators (who intend to cancel all their positions before a specified delivery date) must always dispose of their goods and processors must always purchase them. Because futures contracts ultimately come due on the spot market, the definition of the standard confers a certain market power on the traders who organize markets because they can always deliver the specified grade instead of the grade desired by processors or available from farmers. There is recurring conflict over the definition of the underlying standard good including actual samples that constitute the basis on which contracts are written. Nevertheless, contracting for future deliveries was desirable to both producers and processors because highly liquid markets allowed both sides to achieve some security on price and also to finance a necessary transaction without tying up too much of their own capital.

That the liquidity necessary for futures markets requires the existence of entrepreneurs who specialize in risk and speculation has long been a truism. "Dealings in cotton," as Herbert Knox Smith wrote in submitting a report on the organization of American markets to the House of Representatives in 1908, "must always be accompanied by risk, either to the producer, the merchant middleman, the speculator, or the spinner...It is a general principle that much of the risk should properly be borne by the speculative class" (U.S. Bureau of Corporations, 1908 v). Because of the many functions of commodity exchanges, they are, like banks, far too important to be allowed to work unregulated and the coalitions engaged in their regulation may include producers, speculators themselves, and (probably) processors. To allow them to be regulated solely in the interests of farmers (for example) is no less unsound than allowing banks to be regulated solely by the interests of borrowers.

At turn of the twentieth century, the spot and futures markets were central to the production and pricing of Egyptian cotton. The futures market (or "contracts market" as it was called in Arabic [*bursat al-ʿuqud*] and French) was a private organization whose members were drawn from the cotton-exporting agencies in Alexandria and the ranks of professional speculators. The spot market (also known as Mina el-Bassal) was where delivery actually occurred. The organization of both markets was a constant concern and growers, no less than the spinners, had an ambivalent relationship with it. The growers were frequently in conflict with the representatives of the cotton merchants over the rules governing the sale of future contracts and spot transactions and these contracts were linked because futures contracts could (but need not) be brought to the spot market for delivery. From its foundation in 1860 until the Depression, the spot market was a wholly private company (unlike the futures market that was subject to government regulation after 1909) and neither growers nor government officials served on its governing board. The emergence of an efficient market in futures was essential for the growth of the cotton industry but it often exacted a heavy price from parties that traded in it.

Egyptian growers and English spinners alike understood that they were well served by the existence of global and local futures markets. What each side bitterly resented, however, was the price of having an institutionalized futures market: the profits made by brokers and the occasional fortunes of speculators. Futures markets were originally private businesses owned by brokers who consequently made rules that benefited themselves in the short term. Their rules did not always make for more efficient trading between buyer and seller.

Futures contracts also regulated relations between growers and buyers. They were widely believed to provide an incentive to increase the quality of the crop because the full size of the premium would depend on that quality. These contracts allowed them to deliver cotton on any day during the month specified for delivery in the contract. The contract or delivery note was known as a *filière* (*filyara* in Arabic) and these were, like contracts on all commodity exchanges, what made up the market rather than deliveries. Trading in notes occurred by successive endorsements on the *filière* itself.

Until 1917 the basic contract traded on the futures market for delivery was defined as Fully Good Fair Brown (Mit Afifi) Cotton, but that year a specific contract was introduced for Sakel. The dramatic shift away from long staple to extra-long staple that appeared to cause dramatic ecological yield collapse also caused dramatic effects on the integrity of Egypt's agricultural markets (Abd al-Motaal 413). Specifically the new contract was introduced make futures trading more efficient. On the one hand there were insufficient supplies of Mit Afifi to ensure a liquid market for contracts. On the other hand, and even more dangerous, was the possibility that inferior grades of cotton could be delivered (without financial penalty) for superior ones in the spot market as long as the underlying contracts specified it for delivery. The Ministerial Decree of June 14, 1920 introducing the two types of contracts simply confirmed the shift already made in the marketplace.

Futures contracts provided cheap financing for the large landowners who could use their receipts from contracts sold before sowing to pay for the costs of production. Large growers in Egypt, as in the United States, sold their cotton "on call." Up to a contractually defined date, growers could choose when to complete the sale or "fix" the price with premiums or deductions for quality relative to the standards set by the Bourse. In exchange for an immediate cash payment that financed the crop and also gave the grower the right to choose when to complete the sale, he guaranteed delivery and agreed to mark the final payment ("points on" or "off") to an as yet unknown future Alexandria spot price. At fixing, the parties settled any difference between the cash advance and the spot price at the time of completing the sale. Exporters reportedly tried to balance their on-call sales to spinners with their on-call purchases from farmers and their success at managing the risk entailed was crucial to their success. The analytic framework provided above suggests that the most useful way to think about the exporters was as a set of bankers constantly engaged in balancing outstanding loans to farmers with demand deposits from processors. Besides the obvious financial importance of these contracts, the incentive to improve quality lay in the desire of growers to earn the maximum number of points "on." Alexandria brokers who contracted to sell cotton to spinners abroad matched those sales with contracts to buy cotton in the future.

Producers and processors constantly worried and complained about the dangers of speculation. The most extreme concern, widely voiced in the first two meetings of the International Cotton Congress, was the threat of a corner associated with insufficient supplies of the raw material. The spinners considered, and rejected, several plans to create their own stockpiles or to enter existing futures markets to depress prices. The failure of attempts to corner the market in 1904 (the Sully corner) and the expense and institutional difficulty of creating a counter-corner were replaced by continuing fears about the possible effects of speculators accentuating market volatility (Nahas [1952b]; International Cotton Congress [1905]; Hansen [1991]).

Futures contracts, so crucial to modern commodities markets, are strictly forbidden under Islamic law because of their highly speculative nature (Vogel and Hayes; Saleh). Despite constant complaints by Joseph Nahas about the inequity of on-call purchases the legitimacy of the futures markets was never challenged in reference to Islamic law or shariᶜa.[6] In this case Nahas was to some degree at odds with members of the association he directed. He seems to have envisaged the futures market largely as a source of financing and only modestly as an agency of price discovery through speculation. Anecdotal evidence suggests many growers were avid speculators. Although trading on the

Alexandria bourse in on-call options was completely legal it was often referred to as a form of gambling (International Cotton Federation [1927] and [1938]). Given the tenor of complaints it is the absence of any use of Islamic law rather than its content that is peculiar because shari^c^a was far from peculiar in its position on these issues. Short sales were illegal, after all, for periods in the nineteenth-century Germany and France (Meeker) as were options in Illinois. The reasoning behind voiding such contracts was (as would be the case in shari^c^a) that the contracts amount to a wager, and their defense (as might also be the case in shari^c^a) was that such contracts were too useful for commercial practice to be voided (Williams 176–177).

As with other institutions in Egypt, there was a distributional consequence to the working of commodities markets. Egyptian peasants who owned fewer than five feddans could not legally mortgage their land and thus were forced to contract higher-interest loans from local lenders. They also could not write contracts for forward delivery and thus could not economize on the costs of borrowing. Before the creation of the state-run *halaqas* by Lord Kitchener in 1912 such peasants sold cotton directly to small merchants who resold cotton to the large export houses (Owen [1969] 218). After 1912, the state through the local government provided much of the institutional infrastructure to bring the global market to poorer peasants in regard to the daily spot price, but not in regard to financing the crop.[7] Although traders initially opposed the *halaqas*, it turned out that they reduced search time and agency costs for traders (Ahmad and Hafiz 32).

I now shift to an examination of one of the most important government initiatives in the first half of the twentieth century embodied in the Abdel Wahab memorandum of 1930. Retrospectively, most accounts of the Egyptian political economy focus on 1930 as the year of tariff autonomy and the first steps toward protective tariffs for industrialization.

By investing in reputation and thereby attempting to segment global fiber markets, Egyptian growers hoped at least to reap a quality premium and perhaps a monopoly rent. This premium, I have argued, accrued disproportionately to larger landowners in the Delta and it was consequently those landowners who sought to limit cotton production. The size of the premium for Sakellaridis had been disappearing for much of the 1920s and new areas of long and extra-long staple cotton (especially Arizona and the Sudan) were emerging. The onset of the Great Depression dramatically decreased demand for textiles and thus demand for cotton fiber. Ahmad Abdel Wahab, an undersecretary in the Finance ministry, proposed dramatic institutional transformations guided by government policy. Because the report was presented as a technical discussion, the full political implications have been largely misunderstood. The memorandum discussed both technical aspects of demand for Egyptian cotton (Hansen [1991]) and advanced a compromise to sectoral conflict over tariff reform (Tignor [1984]) but it was also an attempt to transform the nature of social investment in reputation and the institutional framework in marketing.

Ahmad Abdel Wahab had been teaching in the Higher School of Commerce in Cairo when he was appointed Undersecretary of Finance in 1929 at the age of 39. He was president of the nonpartisan Thirty Club of young technocrats and was seen by the British embassy as intelligent, industrious, and eminently likely to be a minister (J 140/140/16; J 725/725/16). Already a bey, he became a pasha in 1930.[8] Although the policy transformations his 1930 memorandum proposed were premised on more tightly integrating Egypt into global markets, he was no friend of the exporters or the British officials in the government.

The Abdel Wahab memorandum explicitly laid out "the coordination of the efforts of the State and of the growers" as its programmatic core (Abdel Wahab [1930] i). Such coordination itself was not new; what was new was that Abdel Wahab sought to move the nature of that cooperation away from the older policy of investment in reputation to segment the market. Abdel Wahab's proposal began with the recognition that there were several Egyptian cottons. Generally speaking, these were all longer-staple varieties but they differed significantly among themselves in regard to production costs, price premiums relative to competitors, and size of the market in which they were sold.

Advocating what he called the "principle of 'mass production'" Abdel Wahab's policy was remarkably similar to the mass production competition envisaged by Alfred P. Sloan at General Motors: it was to bracket existing grades of American cotton with Egyptian cotton at competitive prices. Abdel Wahab argued for a policy designed "to produce a fifteen million cantar crop of which 9/10ths can be utilized by spinners who are now using higher grade American types, while we should be able to preserve a difference in tensile strength amounting to 20 or 30 percent—a result which would put our cotton in an absolutely impregnable position" (Abdel Wahab [1930] 14). Such a crop sold "at a price slightly higher than that of American" would have a sufficiently large demand that it would never go unsold.

The proposals in the memorandum went far to win the cooperation of the Agricultural Syndicate. This they had to do because without the grower's cooperation no agricultural policy would work on the ground. Abdel Wahab who held an office in a minority ministry led by Ismail Sidki also needed to overcome incipient partisan competition with the Wafd—the party that had historically intervened in the cotton market to maintain cotton prices generally and the Sakel premium in particular. Egyptian governments had intervened in cotton markets throughout the 1920s, but two periods of massive intervention stand out: 1926 and 1930. In spring and summer 1926, on the verge of an election, the government of Ahmad Ziwar (whose agriculture minister, Tawfiq Duss, had been a founding member of the Agriculturalists' Union) announced its willingness to preserve the premium between Egyptian and American cotton prices that was briefly on the verge of disappearing. The formation of a coalition government with the Wafd in June of that year reinforced the policy of buying cotton on the spot market as well as on the futures market and led to a government stockpile of nearly half a million cantars at a cost of more than L.E. 3 million (Abdel Wahab [1930] 51; Rizk 296). The coalition government planned an even more extensive intervention in late 1926: "purchasing all contracts offered and taking delivery of the cotton" (Abdel Wahab [1930] 51). Luckily for the government market prices rose and thus no one wanted to tender cotton at the price in the government contracts. In November 1929, weeks before a Wafd government was due to take office, a caretaker government headed by Adli Yakan announced that it would purchase spot and futures contracts. On December 23, 1929 as a new Wafd government prepared to come to office in a week, Mustafa Maher, the outgoing finance minister (and former president of the General Union), announced that the government was willing to set a fixed price for January and February contracts (Sakel and Ashmouni respectively) and a higher price for the March and April contracts (technically called a "contango"). Because distant months usually sell for less than nearer ones (the technical term is "backwardation"), the government was offering a riskless arbitrage opportunity and the Wafd extended this in February to the May and June contracts. By May, the Wafd government was buying Sakel and Ashmuni at prices than those prevailing in the spot market (FO 371 14647). It is not surprising then that nearly 3 million cantars was tendered from farmers and from arbitragers active in the futures market. These were costly operations for the government. Taken in conjunction with the role of Joseph Nahas and Hamdi Sayf al-Nasr in the leadership of the Agriculturalists' Union from its foundation until the 1930s, such policies established the Wafd as the party of agricultural price support (Nahas [1952]) in contradistinction to leaders such as Ismail Sidki.

Abdel Wahab was therefore proposing a policy that contravened both the preferences of the General Union and the analytic framework Joseph Nahas had long deployed to support those preferences. His was not a technical argument about optimal tariff policy or even about elasticity of demand (Hansen [1991]) but an attack on an important interest group. His critique of "the theory which holds that Egyptian cotton . . . has its own special market separate from that of other cottons" was aimed specifically at Nahas. Abdel Wahab may have set the government down a new policy, but he was not the first to propose such a policy.

Three years before the memorandum's publication, Victor Mosseri, speaking at the 1927 Cairo meeting of the International Cotton Federation had argued for redirecting government policy away from attempts to maintain high prices. These, he asserted, stimulated new production and also encouraged the search for substitute fibers. "Far from agreeing without further investigation to this tempting palliative which is extremely dangerous" Mosseri said, "the prudent man will seek his salvation in a sound and efficient policy, viz., the *reduction of the cost of production and not the reduction of acreage*" (italics in original; International Cotton Federation [1927] 219). Mosseri, himself a large landowner as well as an agronomist, was proposing a very different approach to Egypt's role in global trade than Nahhas's.[9] Mosseri's approach was, however, premised on continued high levels of investment in reputation. Mosseri himself championed the use of biological research and government regulation to create a system of pure seed lines. This he counter-posed not only to acreage limitations but also to the creation of districts in which only one type of cotton could be grown (International Cotton Federation [1927] 208–209). In effect, then, the proposals by Mosseri and Abdel Wahab aimed to consolidate the tendencies in Egyptian agriculture that had long been present and that Balls and Dudgeon had observed: to shift rapidly in the direction of producing whatever led to the highest return per unit of area. The relatively high levels of landed indebtedness constantly prodded producers in this direction (Owen [1969]; Tignor [1984]; Hansen [1991]) but the stream of income required to service the debt was itself the product of constant regulatory intervention and publicly funded innovation.

Abdel Wahab's proposal was far more pointed than Mosseri's remarks in its claim to repose on "natural and permanent elements...inherent in the production of cotton" so as to accord with the "well known and quite elementary proposition of Economics that it pays every country best to grow the crops for the production of which it is most highly favored" (Abdel Wahab [1930] 2, 19). It is not quite clear if Abdel Wahab was making a Ricardian argument. On balance "most highly favored" appears to mean "most favorable relative prices" but it could also imply a kind of absolute advantage. Yet the argument Nahas was entering was not simply an argument about trade theory but about the role of the state and the best way to deploy future regulatory investments in reputation. Because the argument from nature and elementary propositions of economics was clearly aimed at

Nahas, it is hard to read the report as anything other than a rebuke to claims that state investment in reputation could yield a large trade advantage or be long maintained.

Although we can see the outlines of Abdel Wahab's proposal in earlier decisions by Egyptian farmers and in Mosseri's intervention in 1927, his confidence in the memorandum's analysis derived from an article by Costantino Bresciani-Turroni then in press (Bresciani-Turroni [1930]). Egyptian policymakers were already familiar with arguments using correlation coefficients although the technique was still at the cutting edge of the econometric discipline. Bresciani-Turroni produced an article that was intellectually seminal and intensely policy-relevant. He presented quantitative evidence that the global cotton market was largely dominated by American production and that the price of Egyptian cotton was not formed independently by the size of the Egyptian crop. He thereby broke the back of the claims Nahas had long advanced. When Abdel Wahab alluded to the problem of substitution away from Egyptian cotton for tire and production and to the emergence of a Japanese industry that had shifted to using Indian cotton (instead of American) for coarse fabric, he was pursuing the path already broken by Bresciani-Turroni.[10]

Abdel Wahab took several measures to appease the Agriculturalists' Union and woo its, often Wafdist, membership. He planned to restrict Sakel acreage and to encourage its production at the level of about 1.5 million cantars in the northern Delta. This was a concession because it ensured that the landowners who specialized in extra-long staple cottons like Sakel could continue to produce without domestic competition. More important than acreage limitations, Abdel Wahab also proposed to realize a long-standing goal of the Agriculturalists' Union: to link its members directly to spinners in Europe and thereby circumvent the Alexandria General Produce Association (AGPA). To accomplish this goal, he proposed that the spot market in Mina al-Bassel be taken away from the AGPA and placed under the supervision of the government. In addition to the appointment of a government commissioner for the market he recommended that the growers, who had previously had no seats on the Bourse Commission, be given seven seats. He further moved that growers would henceforth sit on the committee to determine grades for cotton at delivery.

These were far-reaching proposals and with the passage of time, their impact has become less well understood. As early as 1915 criticisms about the monopoly power of the AGPA in creating types in a market whose existence depended not on physical merchandise but "could only arise from a conventional understanding among traders, from some regulation" were voiced (Teymur 69). Teymur, a former trader, argued that the AGPA abused its right to fix cotton types and called for establishing a formal role for growers and the state and thus limiting "an autonomous power totally sheltered from public power" (Teymur 75). As early as December 1922 Joseph Nahas had sought to subject the Alexandria spot market to state intervention on behalf of the growers (Nahas [1952] 79–89). In a letter to Makram Ubayd, who served as the Minister of Finance in the Wafd government during the first half of 1930, Nahas identified the absence of government control over the spot market and the consequence absence of government control over the standardization of cotton types as crucial steps to enhance the situation of the growers (Nahas [1951] 218–220). The AGPA, as I have shown earlier, had long rejected proposals that the state establishes standards for cotton moisture and these proposals went much further. It is not surprising therefore that staff at the British Embassy and personnel in Barclays Bank noted that there would be significant objections to creating standard types because these would undermine—if not completely destroy—the links between the largely foreign exporters and their clients abroad, the spinners. In exchange for limiting the amount of Sakel that could be grown, Abdel Wahab proposed to create a coalition between growers and the state to displace the export houses and to achieve the policy that Nahas had long sought: to place the producers in direct contact with the buyers. This was a goal that spoke both to the immediate economic concerns of the Agriculturalists' Union and to their perceptions of nationalism. The largest single group of brokers on the Exchange was Egyptian, but the largest brokerage houses were owned by foreign residents (who had often spent most of their adult lives in the country). Just as political actors deployed the concepts of national identity within the labor movement (Beinin and Lockman), the Agriculturalists' Union deployed its opposition to the role of non-Egyptians in a crucial *private* institution through the rhetoric of nationalism. In his first comments on the Abdel Wahab proposal, Nahas noted that the growers had finally succeeded in their decades-long struggle to subordinate the spot market to the government. In an obituary for Abdel Wahab in 1938, Nahas publicly declared that their joint work to limit the independence of the spot market in Mina' al-Basal was the high point of his long friendship with the late finance minister (Nahas 413).

   Although Nahas was highly critical of other portions of Abdel Wahab's memorandum and of the policies followed by Sidki, the memorandum was not developed in isolation from Nahas or the Agricultural Syndicate. The memorandum certainly proposed a break with the older policy of producing for a highly segmented market, and Nahas took issue with the proposed new policy of "mass production" (Nahas 228).[11] Nahas admitted that in ordinary circumstances Abdel Wahab's proposal might be a sound policy, but questioned whether producing more cotton would be an effective policy when cotton supplies exceeded demand and demand appeared to be dropping despite "the lowest prices imaginable." That there were no good solutions was precisely the point and Abdel Wahab had crafted a regulatory policy that gave the growers something important in exchange for their acquiescence in a new trade policy.

Viewed not as a plan to limit cotton acreage but to speed the transition (already under way) from Sakelleridis production, the government policy was immensely successful. The success of the regulatory policies Abdel Wahab proposed was incentive-compatible with the interests of the growers. In 1930 there were still almost 850,000 feddans under Sakel; in 1931 there were fewer than 480,000 feddans and by 1936 Sakel acreage had dropped to less than 170,000 feddans (Sidki 265). The slack was largely taken up by high-yielding but only moderately long staple Ashmouni (and the related Zagora) cotton and by the higher-yielding long staple varieties of Giza 3 and 7. By the end of the 1930s a new extra-long staple variety, Karnak, had been introduced and it took the same place that Sakel had between World War I and the early years of the Depression.

Support for the new government policy came from the financial sector as well as from some of the large growers and other landowners squeezed between declining producer prices and fixed mortgage payments. The general secretary of Credit Foncier Egyptien, one of the largest banks in the country, approved the new policy that he expected to restore government finances as well as private ones (Minost).

All around the world the depression of 1929 intensified the role of the state in the economy. The Egyptian state had long been deeply engaged in the development of agriculture. Two important changes occurred because of the Abdel Wahab memorandum. The first was that the particular pattern of investment in reputation was shifted away from a policy of investment in a product whose reputation created a completely segmented market to a policy of investment in a product aimed at being just slightly better than its competitors yet still able to generate relatively rents. The second was the extension of the state authority over an area of the economy—the Alexandria produce market—that had hitherto been fully private. Although this extension of state control lay primarily in the field of regulation and although it brought Egyptian practice more nearly in line with American than with European practice, it also established an important political legacy that the state had an important role to play in regulating private economic undertakings especially when they were owned by foreigners.

### California Dreaming: Regulating Mechanized Agriculture

The Egyptian investment in reputation of its cotton crop was far from unique although it was exceptionally large in terms of geography and the volume of the crop. Similar experiments in reputation investment were undertaken in the United States for crops including cotton. By the 1930s Americans had had significant experience with attempts to create single-variety territories or one-variety communities as they were also known. Invariably these required similar kinds of government regulatory intervention to those of the Egyptian government. These included the Smith-Doxey Act that provided free classification, the Cotton Improvement program that provided seed for longer-staple cotton, and agricultural experiment and extension bureaucracies.

The San Joaquin Valley provides an especially useful comparison to the Nile Delta because both areas employed irrigated lands to produce a limited number of longer-staple cotton. Before World War I, Egyptians had assumed that rising labor costs alone made the extension of cotton cultivation to California impossible (Jullien). Growers in California managed to overcome their disadvantage by far more extensive capital investments in cotton production than had been deemed possible. There were really only two important differences between Egypt and California. Egyptian cotton was produced for international trade while California produced for domestic use but under the conditions of free trade that obtained between Great Britain and Egypt until World War I, this is an irrelevant difference for my purpose.

The second was the decision to consolidate a pure-line seed strategy with that of a one-variety community. Wofford B. Camp led a political campaign to create a One-Variety Law (OVL) for the valley, which the California state legislature passed in 1925. In the United States such laws were designed to protect high-quality cotton from cross-pollination with inferior strains and varieties and to assure a uniform raw material. None of the old cotton-producing states overcame the political difficulties inherent in establishing such a large area for a one-variety crop. Hence the large number of such districts in Texas. In the United States the creation of such communities was, by overcoming the collective-action problems involved, widely heralded as an example of "progressivism." As in Egypt the successful investment in biological and ecological science to create homogenous crops led to decreasing levels of physical output. By the 1950s farmers in the San Joaquin Valley complained of declining yields and (like their Egyptian counterparts two generations earlier) understood that the problem rested in biological constraints not the engineering ones of irrigation and drainage. Despite these complaints, the California Producing Cotton Seed Distributors retained its legal monopoly over seed distribution in the valley until the U.S. Department of Justice initiated an antitrust suit in 1975 when the public monopoly was replaced by private competition to breed different varieties of Acala. The rationale for the creation of the one-variety district was the belief that it "would generate a price premium . . . for three reasons: First, farmers would be able to obtain a reputation for high-quality cotton; second, only one-variety seed would be recovered from the gin; and third, the cotton would be of relatively consistent quality, reducing sorting costs at the mill" (Constantine Alston and Smith 967–968). These are the same advantages Egyptian growers sought but whether they were real and how long they persisted is open to doubt in both California and Egypt. One clear effect of the OVL was to induce lower yields even within the relatively small area of the San Joaquin Valley (Constantine Alson and Smith 970). This outcome, which was known from early test plots, echoes the arguments about yields that I made in chapter 3 and provides additional justification to Victor Mosseri's argument against transforming Egyptian areas into single-variety locations. It also suggests that the decision not to create one-variety communities may have spared some farmers a loss of income.

Single-variety legislation and practice required far higher levels of state intervention than farming had previously required. In the San Joaquin Valley the one-variety law increased the importance of the U.S. Department of Agriculture cotton research facilities at Shafter, California: "In reviewing the early history of cotton in California, one is struck by the crucial role of government policies during an era when farming was generally free of government intervention" (Musoke and Olmstead 390).

California farmers, like Egyptians, faced high fixed costs for irrigated land. They also confronted relatively high labor costs and in response mechanized as many of the tasks associated with the growing cotton as rapidly as possible. High-yield (which California shared with Egypt) and large-scale operations (which it did not) made mechanical harvesters profitable; the major cost in mechanical picking was opportunity cost: the loss of quality or "grade loss" (Musoke and Olmstead 402). Clearly cheap labor and a concern to maintain the greatest quality premium made mechanization of Egyptian production undesirable in the first half of the century.

What is relevant is that Egyptian cotton was produced as a labor-intensive good in an economy with abundant labor whereas California cotton was produced as a capital-intensive good in an economy with abundant capital. This difference is, of course, homologous with the distinction between Egypt as an agrarian and underdeveloped society in contrast to the United States as an industrial and developed society. That similar regulatory devices were successfully deployed in both cases suggests that neither labor-intensiveness, peasant social structure, nor religious affiliation explains much about Egyptian political economy.

In fact, the *similarity* in regulatory strategies pursued by officials and growers in the Nile Delta and San Joaquin valley may blind us to the *dissimilarity* between those employed by Californians and the elites of the Old Confederacy. Egyptians and Californians pursued strategies of investment in quality, but neither mechanization nor the mere possibility of segmenting a product market explains the difference. There is an irreducible area of agency: the decision by members of the Egyptian elite to pursue the strategies of investment in reputation and to overcome by extensive production of cotton the externalities that prevented such a strategy from being successful. To get a clearer perspective it is worth looking at a case in which an elite whose income rested on agricultural exports decided not to pursue a strategy of investment in reputation. Thai experiences in the early twentieth century were in many ways similar to those in Egypt. The integration of Thailand with the global economy led to increased rice production, an increase in rice exports, a decline in domestic manufacturing, an increase in manufactures imports, a decline in real wages, and an increase in land prices (Feeny).

It is a tragic irony that Thailand arguably experienced the nonexistent ecological disaster ascribed to Egypt. The area of rice production grew faster than output and population grew faster still so that yields declined over a 40-year period. Thai rice farmers considered investing in quality: "In an effort to improve the quality of the rice grown in Thailand and better compete with the highest quality Carolina rice, seed from the Carolinas was imported in 1910 and test trials were conducted in five *monthons* in the Central plain and one *monthon* in the Northeast." Yet, no investment in reputation occurred in Thailand. After 1912, this effort collapsed despite establishment of an experimental farm for rice in 1916; "over the period 1880–1914 there seems to have been no significant technical progress in rice production in Thailand. In fact, it appears that total factor productivity declined significantly... Indeed by the end of the second decade of the twentieth century most of the modern proposals for technical change had been made in Thailand; the lack of accomplishment owed to a lack of means, ability, commitment, or resources to implement the proposals."

What distinguishes Egypt from more developed regions is not regulatory capacity or institutional development. Egyptian regulatory capacity was arguably more developed than that of the cotton regions of the American south and it would be difficult to argue that the political institutions of Egypt were inherently worse than those of the Old South, Thailand, or Korea or even the San Joaquin Valley. What distinguishes Egypt from the United States was the abundance of a crucial productive factor, unskilled labor, and a path that can only be considered economic involution.

It is not surprising that Egyptians invested in reputation or sought to segment global markets for fiber. They had certainly been told frequently that they were monopolist suppliers to one section of the British spinning industry and they could easily observe other cotton producers undertaking quite similar strategies. The behavior of British spinners from the turn of the twentieth century until the collapse of the tire boom in 1920 provided additional credence to the arguments about a cotton famine being more likely than a collapse of demand or even the creation of artificial (coal and petroleum–based) supplies of fiber. The shift by British manufacturers in the direction of higher-quality output after 1920 provided an additional reason to continue to orient Egyptian agriculture in the same direction. Large landowners used forward sales to finance the production of this high-quality good and they were, like the spinners, concerned about the dangers of manipulating commodities markets. They were not wrong to be concerned because given the relatively small size of commodity markets at the time and the power that comes from monetizing goods, there had been frequent and nearly successful attempts to manipulate the markets. Daniel Sully, like the Hunt Brothers, is a historical footnote today but for those active in such markets the risk of being caught on the downside of a major turn is frightening. Consequently landowners were as willing to come to the aid of the government in regulating commodity markets as workers would prove to be 30 years later in regulating labor markets.

# CHAPTER 5

# Economics, Development, and Egyptian Economists

Policy makers always receive and often require policy advice. In the twentieth century this advice was always political in two ways. First, policy advice necessarily engaged ideas about how to use the existing machinery of the state to enhance the fortunes of those who already held assets. It ranged from straightforward rent-seeking as owners of assets sought to increase returns above existing market levels to more complex concerns about institutions and social incentives. By the 1930s policy advice gained a second, more far-reaching, level of engagement with politics. Policy debates increasingly contained prescriptions for more intrusive state intervention in the economy and the society whether through the use of the state's police power generally or through attempts to affect entire socioeconomic categories such as workers, peasants, and owners of capital.

Ideas of planning at the level of an entire society or economy had been proposed by European socialists in the nineteenth century, had occurred during World War I in the European capitalist countries, and after 1924 had become part of a vast and unsuccessful experiment in the Soviet Union. For the West European economies, however, the Great Depression was the moment in which these ideas of massive social and economic engineering became accepted themes in economic theory and desirable norms of governmental activity. The fascist experiments in Italy and Germany were closely followed in much of the world but, like the Communists in Russia, there was some question about whether the intrusiveness of the state was purchased at too high a price in freedom. In the Liberal economies where state intervention on a far broader scale appeared, there were also discussions about it and are usually referred to by the rubric Keynes's.

The central element of Keynes's very wide-ranging work borrowed in these references is that in situations of widespread involuntary unemployment it is plausible to imagine that the primary impediment to economic growth is a shortfall in demand. Although the context of the Great Depression within which Keynes produced his most important work was the unemployment of labor, his primary economic insight was that the real gap was one of investment which, in turn, stemmed from insufficient demand for goods. Keynes's concern with labor was less economic than political. He feared that as long as involuntary unemployment was relatively large, the unemployed would generate political pressure on the government for solutions. More particularly he feared that, as in Germany and Italy, the most obvious solutions would entail the destruction of liberal society and the diminution of human freedom.

During the decade after the July 1952 coup, army officers moved Egypt from a relatively open economy in which most assets were privately held to a directed economy in which the state owned a significant portion of society's industrial assets. This transformation of the Egyptian economy, paralleled elsewhere in the Third World, is usually called import-substituting industrialization. These policies mirrored the transformation of European economies during the 1920s and 1930s where after World War I and with increased speed during the Great Depression, European governments moved economies away from open trading regimes toward mercantilism. In previous chapters I have argued for the centrality of factor abundance in understanding Egypt or other economies of the first global era of free trade. Static factor abundance cannot go far to explain economic transformations (whether called "growth" or "development") because transformations require that the proportions of factors in the economy change through investments responding, in part, to government policies. The prism of the Egyptian elite provides insight into how, over 50 years, sections of elite public opinion came to accept and even on occasions enthusiastically support such policies.

Keynesianism is a conventional term covering many different government policies that intervene in the economy to affect levels of demand for goods, services, and factors of production. Successive sections of this chapter discuss the reception of Keynesian theory and the impact of Keynesian policies on Egypt as well as whether mercantilist policies are necessarily Keynesian.

### Keynes in Theory and Politics

Robert Vitalis and Steven Heydemann argue that Allied institutional innovation during World War II is "the central mechanism behind the diffusion of Keynesian notions of economic planning into the Middle East" (Vitalis and Heydemann 103). They note that World War II marked a dramatic change in Syria and Egypt from an open economy to one in which macroeconomic planning played a much larger role. Vitalis and Heydemann acknowledge that their "reference to Keynesianism is not intended to imply that Middle East governments applied policies conforming in any strict sense to Keynes's economic theories. It refers instead to a general appreciation for the potential of interventionist approaches among the economists and planners who were posted to Allied regulatory agencies in the Middle East" (Vitalis and Heydemann 138).

Others also see the figure of Keynes in the postwar Third World. By the 1950s, according to David Waldner, many of the Middle Eastern economies were rooted in political exchange he calls "precocious Keynesianism." By Keynesian Waldner means "a set of practices and policies used to manage advanced industrial economies; the hallmark of these policies is the political and economic inclusion of an organized labor movement" (Waldner 50). By precocious he means these policies occur prior to industrialization when the state distributes economic favors "as a product of inter-elite conflict [and] embraces overwhelmingly large sectors of the population" (Waldner 51). Waldner acknowledges that his use of the term has little to do with Keynesianism "in its narrowest sense [because] Keynesianism refers to the policy implications of John Maynard Keynes' demonstration that economies can settle into stable equilibrium at less than full employment levels" (Waldner 50).

There is no single definition of Keynesianism, but there are three advantages of setting Keynesian analysis and Keynesian policy prescriptions in relation to Keynes's own work. First, we can see how Egyptian professionals came to understand the weaknesses in the neoclassical vocabulary they had used before the Depression. Second, we can see how Egyptian policy makers came to believe that there were unemployed resources in society that needed only slight changes in incentives to become productive. The claims about regulatory weakness that I challenge in this book also assume that resources are abundant and incentives are insufficient. In places like Egypt, this assertion is debatable and, I think, wrong. Third, keeping an anchor in Keynes's own thought forces us to recall his distinctive belief in retaining the central role of private ownership in an economy and a commitment to parliamentary political institutions (however imperfect) even while crafting government policies to correct market failures. Only by retaining all of these, possibly contradictory, tenets will it be possible to craft policies that enable economic growth while maintaining political liberty.

Waldner is correct that Keynes showed how modern capitalist economies can be at equilibrium with unemployed resources, but this (as Keynes argued) was a truth that had long been known. He was even cognizant that mercantilists had developed specific policies to deal with such conditions. What distinguished Keynes from other advocates of government intervention was his insistence that the tools of mercantilism be compatible with liberal institutions (Dillard 145). In Keynes's own words,

> the authoritarian state systems of to-day seem to solve the problem of unemployment at the expense of efficiency and freedom. It is certain that the world will not much longer tolerate the unemployment which... is associated, and in my opinion, inevitably associated with present-day capitalistic individualism. But it may be possible by right analysis of the problem to cure the disease whilst preserving efficiency and freedom. (Keynes [1936] 381).

Policies of demand management need not have led to authoritarian government and, in reference to Keynes's own work; the challenge to policy makers was to ensure that state intervention did not lead to the destruction of liberal institutions. Where political leaders sought to prepare for war and to mobilize private resources for its pursuit we see the emergence of governments that owe more inspiration to German or Italian fascism than to Keynes.

Truly Keynesian policies were not even possible in Egypt until the country gained a central bank in 1951. Businessmen, bankers, and economists in interwar Egypt knew how great a weakness the absence of such a bank was. In 1936 a prominent Egyptian businessman explained that a "central bank is the key stone of the financial arch, the regulator, in theory and largely in practice, of the supply of available credit, and hence of the internal price level and the foreign exchanges, a blend of watch dog, pilot and fairy-godmother" (Harari 134).[1] Egypt's bank of issue, the National Bank, had many tools but it "lack[ed] the cardinal feature of a Central Bank, *viz.* the power to make its discount rate effective and to influence the loans and deposits of the commercial banks..." (Harari 135). Egypt also lacked appropriate financial institutions to mobilize long-term capital. After the crash of 1907 no investment banks or "issuing houses" were available to fund new businesses with the exception of Bank Misr.[2] Harari's analysis is astonishingly Keynesian in its attention to financial institutions and incentive effects. Such financial institutions as had existed "failed to maintain themselves here not because the community had no need for their services, but because the net surplus of the country's annual income over its expenditures had dwindled, and those who controlled what remained were frightened into a policy of safety first. A vicious circle was thereby set up and Egypt still lies within its grip" (Harari

143). Harari's explanation for the institutional failure was close to Keynes's concept of a liquidity trap that creates an institutional failure in the entire economy despite the presence of sufficient economic resources (Krugman [1994] 33).

Egyptian politicians, businessmen, and academic professionals had had to respond to falling prices for Egyptian cotton in the 1920s, which (because production was fixed in any year) were largely understood to be the result of declining demand. The need for an adequate state policy-making became greater after 1929 as Egyptian access to markets was increasingly restricted because of technical change (the development of artificial fiber) and the unexpected collapse of world trade in the Depression.

The cause of the Great Depression remains a matter of dispute. Neoclassical arguments that markets are efficient and self-correcting, predict prices should adjust to ensure that all of society's resources are employed and thus no government intervention is needed. Besides the political cost of prolonged inaction, prices rarely adjust as quickly or deeply as the theory requires (Krugman [1994] 199–205). By 1932, Egyptians trained in neoclassical economics in France and England no longer believed that exports suffered from a temporary drop in demand or market manipulation but from a structural disequilibrium. They therefore began to think about how to transform the productive resources of the country and to utilize resources that had, until very recently, been profitably employed in international trade. They became aware, in other words, of Keynesian possibilities that Egypt possessed—at least temporarily—unemployed factors of production that could reenter the economy if the state could develop appropriate policies. The debates about tariff policies subsidies, exchange rates, and other barriers to trade are the very stuff of what has since become known as import substitution. In the Third World, this debate continued long after the Depression ended and one influential Keynesian elaboration by William Arthur Lewis claimed to see structural "hidden unemployment" in rural society.

Members of the Egyptian elite (and Europeans resident in Egypt) paid attention to experiments in Italy and Germany as well as in the United States and Great Britain. In the 1930s fascism did not yet connote genocide, and members of the Egyptian elite (and those elsewhere) looked with interest at such experiments. What has politely been called corporatism is a subset of the richly variegated politics of fascism that swept across Europe, the Mediterranean, Asia, and Latin America. Even before World War II Egyptians already had many programmatic responses to the economic difficulties of the post–World War I era. Vitalis and Heydemann correctly see institutional innovations introduced by British officials through the Middle

East Supply Center (Vitalis and Heydemann [2000] 105–106), and yet Egyptian state- and business-elites were already thinking about how to engage in demand management before World War II (Neither a Roosevelt nor Mussolini burst on the scene in Egypt in the 1930s (Waterbury 233), but at least one powerful Egyptian politician, Ahmed Abdel Wahab, closely studied American and European responses to the Depression as they unfolded, but he died before he could become prime minister.[3]

By the outbreak of World War II there had already been elite discussions about following the path of institutional change that Vitalis and Heydemann describe. The universe of discourse by professional Egyptian economists provides some access to these discussions. To the extent that these discussions were truly Keynesian, they suggested expanding the long-standing role of the state as a provider of financial rents to privately owned firms (Vitalis [1995] 12). To the extent, that these discussions were framed in the language of mercantilism and nodded to fascist styles of regulation, they were a preparation for state ownership of assets that occurred over a prolonged period after 1952.

The economists I discuss were neither wholly disinterested observers nor simple handmaidens of social interests. Like Keynes, who was both a rentier and a government advisor, Egyptian economists were highly partisan actors in the economy. They were also members of a profession and spoke to each other as well as to political leaders in the language of the profession and they all had interests in economic growth.

Discussions among Egyptian economists clarify the intellectual content of policy debates as well as reveal sectoral conflicts of interest. Robert Vitalis is correct to argue that sectoral and business group conflicts over regulatory advantage underlay many conflicts over government policy. There were also broad arguments in which Egyptian officials and influential members of the elite engaged about how to transform Egypt's position in global trade. Egyptian economists were well aware of the crucial issues of international trade. They debated whether market power existed and, if so, how it might be exercised; whether property rights were primarily rules to enhance efficiency or incentives; and whether weak Egyptian growth was a problem of insufficient investment (and in what assets) in the context of a free-trade relationship between domestic and international markets.

### Joseph Nahas and Classical Economics

Joseph Nahas received a doctoral degree in economic and legal sciences in Paris in 1897. He had graduated from the French law school in Cairo in 1896 and already had a personal friendship with Saᶜd Zaghlul, the politician who would lead the nationalist Wafd movement during World War I and become the first prime minister in an independent Egyptian state. Because Nahas's father had engaged Zaghlul as an attorney in civil litigation over real property, Nahas had a close relationship with Zaghlul (Nahas [1952a] 7) and evidently had close connections through his father with Sultan Hussein Kamil and through friends with King Fuad (Nahas [1952a] 58, 59–60). Nahas was the first Egyptian with a doctoral degree in economics and he also appears to have been the first consultant in economic affairs to a government official. Most important, he was the general secretary of the General Union of Egyptian Agriculturalists from its foundation in 1921 until well into the 1940s.[4] He had, in short, exceptionally good access to policy makers through official and unofficial connections and represented a crucial constituency, large landowners.

Nahas's publications fall into three categories: monographic studies, memoirs, and policy analyses. Except for the memoirs, Nahas's published work dealt exclusively with agriculture and agricultural policy. His earliest book, published in French in 1901 under the title *Le Fellah*, dealt with peasant society and the economy. Translated into Arabic in 1926, the book was primarily a description of the constraints and incentives for peasants as well as a review of then-recent policy decisions. Somewhat later Nahas published a study, also in French, in which he called for a change in Egypt's tax and regulatory regime to allow the reintroduction of tobacco as a cash crop. His slender volume of memoirs (1952a) provides insight into the personal dynamics of the elite that structured the development of the nationalist movement in the early twentieth century.

These collections of articles do not provide a clearly reasoned general account of Egyptian regulatory policy, trade, and the world economy, for they deal in great detail with a large number of slightly different but essentially similar topics: administrative acts, regulatory conflicts, market cycles, and secular changes in the global market for textiles. They do provide us a clear picture of how public conflict over regulatory policy occurred and the importance interest groups placed on influencing regulatory policy in the independent state formed in 1923. They also shed light on why many less-developed countries pursued policies of income maintenance and demand management after independence. Nahas's work shows that policies of demand maintenance by government intervention usually associated with Keynesian economics, had already won significant support during the Great Depression. Commodity exporters in an open global economy understood the Depression as a demand shortfall long before arguments about Keynesian demand management, economic growth, and welfare economics made the concepts cogent in other settings.

From his earliest published writings during World War I, Nahas was engaged in demanding government intervention on behalf of cotton farmers and especially large landowners (Tignor [1984] 59). He was even more closely identified with those landowners in the Delta who grew Sakellaridis or other extra-long staple cotton, and he was intimately engaged in many campaigns to invest in the reputation and production of cotton. One of his first articles in the daily *Al-Muqattam* in January 1915 called for rapid government action to eliminate insect pests—"a mortal enemy"—and he repeated this call regularly throughout the years of the war.[5] He also demanded rapid government intervention to reduce the price of simple inputs like sacking and twine as well as fertilizer or credit.

Nahas quite clearly and early differentiated between direct government provision of inputs and government regulation for reputation and he called for both. He lobbied avidly for government provision of inputs to cotton farmers, including those who were already wealthy. He also recognized the importance of government regulation to resolve collective-action problems that he understood in terms which were rooted in both Islamic and French law. In a discussion of the 1916 regulations to control insect infestations in the cotton crop, Nahas used the terminology of the civil code to argue that coercion is a valid tool to resolve what we now call collective-action problems. Thus, if a peasant allowed another's crop to be damaged he created a tort, or *darar*, that could in theory be resolved by a civil suit. The coercive power of the state was a more effective way to prevent such situations Nahas argued.

Nahas nevertheless dissented from the idea that he said was current among intellectuals ("in some newspapers") that excessive force was the *only* way to bring peasants to make the decisions that regulators desired.[6] He returned to the theme of regulation in an article later that year called "Cotton Culture and Yields" in which he entered a debate about declining yields, insect infestation, and peasant effort.[7] Nahas argued that to induce peasants to rid their fields of insects and the cotton stalks that harbored larvae, the best policy would be to announce a significant cash payment for those who took the necessary steps rather than relying on fines and denouncing peasants for being insufficiently motivated. For those whose entire future lay in the crops growing in the fields, he pointed out, what was necessary was to provide an incentive to do what was already in their interest: protect the final harvest (Nahas [1952b] 18).

In chapter 3 I alluded to Nahas's belief that Egypt had significant market power as a producer of extra-long staple cotton. Had Nahas simply represented the interests of landowners, he would not have found the Abdel

Wahab report so difficult to accept. He was, for reasons of theory and interest, a tenacious defender of the interests of that subset of Egyptian landowners (primarily in the northern Delta) who grew extra-long staple cotton. It was surprising that Nahas, who was trained in classical economic theory, should have believed it possible for Egypt to obtain market power. There was no reason to believe, a priori, that new producers could not enter the market to provide high quality long staple cotton and thereby diminish the price premium Egyptians obtained.

Nahas's argument about Egyptian market power was a pre-Keynesian argument about imperfections in English capital and labor markets. Neoclassical economics proposes that firms can shift without cost from equipment designed for one kind of input to another and to price labor without regard to down-time. If this were accurate there would have been no possible Egyptian market power. Textile manufacturers would have shifted inputs in response to short-term price signals and quality would have been irrelevant. Nahas did not let theory prevent the use of an empirical anomaly. An exceptionally revealing exchange on the question of the reputation of Egyptian cotton occurred in a meeting of the Agriculturalists' Union in 1925 presided by Mustafa Mahir, an associate of Ismail Sidqi, and Hamdi Sayf al-Nasr who was vice president (wakil awwal) of the Union and later a Wafdist Minister of Agriculture.[8] The meeting was devoted to Nahas's report of a technical mission he led to French textile manufacturers. Manufacturer's representatives with whom he talked in Tourcoing and Lille confirmed the importance they attributed to the high standardization of Egyptian cotton on several dimensions thereby reinforcing his belief that, despite neoclassical theory, Egypt enjoyed market power.

Much of Nahas's writing about cotton markets aimed at elite opinion to win support for alleviating the effect of changes in demand and the general price level on the crop. Much as he accepted the idea that Egypt was part of a world system subject to innate economic laws, he understood that the government could and should affect the market to further the interests of economic actors in a national economy.[9] Describing the formation of the Union of Egyptian Agriculturalists, Nahas noted that it was explicitly created to affect the cotton market. The second paragraph of its founding document described the existence of a "cotton crisis" that could only be alleviated by "forestalling the pressure of supply on the market in relationship to the paucity of demand until the textile industry returns to its full activity" (Nahas [1952b] 14). Initially the Union had hoped to influence the movement of price by voluntary limitations on marketing by members, but it had only weak tools with which to affect member decisions. Voluntary activity to create market power worked poorly in Egypt and the collective-action problems involved have generally precluded producer's cooperatives from accomplishing long-term control of markets. Consequently the Federation moved from voluntary collective action to demanding state purchases as a way of keeping the price of cotton high despite the significant fiscal risks to which the state was then exposed. The only plausible argument for government intervention in the markets was that it would only be for short periods and in opposition to speculative trades operated in opposition to the basic trend of global markets for fiber.

The struggle to organize public opinion and make regulatory policy was especially acute in the 1930s when the danger of defaults grew dramatically. Landowners, mortgage banks, and Treasury officials sought to compromise despite the conflicts over just who would bear the burden from falling commodity prices, unpaid loans, and the danger of a dramatic fall in real estate prices (Tignor [1984] 117). One of the ironies of the sophisticated financial infrastructure of the period is that many banks, in effect, held financial assets denominated in land (mortgages) or linked to the state's flow of income (government obligations) while large landowners held assets in money with an option to repurchase their land but with the possibility of walking away in the Depression. By 1931 bankers such as Minost were anxious to ensure that landlords did not continue to obtain price support through state purchases of cotton because such outlays diminished government credit, thereby increased the cost of borrowing, and did not necessarily provide security to mortgage banks (Minost 432–433). Minost proposed that the Agriculturalists' Union gain more control over its members rather than remain essentially an interest association of private persons.[10]

Yet, the Union remained an interest group without great cohesion although it provided its members with a constant flurry of activity. In an initial annual report the Federation noted that, in a year of falling cotton prices, it had won significant support from the government. Beyond demanding direct price support and decreasing the export tax on cotton, the Federation lobbied for everything that Minost mentioned that directly or indirectly affected the cost of production or the price of cotton and that increased the influence of the Federation itself. It also successfully pushed the government to buy cotton from large landowners in the Cotton Exchange rather than simply within the country from small producers. For this meeting the Federation sent Nahas and Ahmad Hamdi Sayf al-Nasr to the Liverpool meeting of the International Cotton Federation and deputed other members of the executive board to meet with industrial institutes in Europe to further the reputation and increase the market for Egyptian cotton. It also claimed to have succeeded in lowering shipping rates for Egyptian cotton by engaging competition between American and British lines (Nahas [1952b] 53–54).

Believing that Egypt had some market power, Nahas also believed that relatively low prices for Egyptian cotton were a temporary phenomenon caused by manipulation of the markets rather than fundamental market forces. As he put it, when he attempted to create a private cartel among growers to buy and store cotton as well as to gain direct influence over the spot market, "the cotton market, or the market for its wealth that the Egyptian nation considers to be the measure of its health, is dominated by terror and exploited by the worse exploitation of a handful of people who reach out clandestinely to affect prices as they wish" (Nahas [1954] 60). This was the domestic Egyptian counterpart to the purchasing cartels proposed by the spinners at the first meetings of the International Cotton Congress and the rhetoric was strikingly similar both in its support of neoclassical theory and its assertion that the failure of the theory was due to a small group that perverted real markets for goods. Consequently Nahas could claim that his proposed buying cartel had no desire to "define a price not in accord with the economic laws that have complete sovereignty in the marketplace" but only to counteract factors that spoiled the working of the market (Nahas [1954] 60).[11]

Nahas had a clear and plausible idea how foreign ownership of banks affected Egyptian credit markets. Such banks, he argued, loaned money to cultivators just as did Egyptian-owned banks. Because foreign banks were significantly more risk-averse than were locally owned banks and also gave their local agents less authority than did those locally owned, their activities in local financial markets were significantly different. Large cultivators sold their crops forward and these contracts were security for bank loans through which the growers got their cash. Consequently Nahas argued that when cotton prices dipped, risk-averse foreign-owned banks quickly sold the forward contracts on the open market and further depressed prices. Speculators were aware of these contractual relationships and would provoke "runs" on cotton, drive prices temporarily down, and reap profits at the expense of the cultivators (Nahas [1954] 68–69).

Statistically, there is no evidence that prices in the Alexandria market diverged much from those around the world: the correlation coefficients, taken by pairs, between prices in Alexandria, Liverpool, and New Orleans were above 0.98 (El-Sarki 48). Consequently we cannot know whether the mechanism Nahas described was at work, but it is, if dubious empirically, a plausible mechanism and provides some substance to the claim that the interests of foreign firms diverged from those of native Egyptians. Firms or individuals holding financial assets who faced important currency risks or had little information about the real economy were less likely to be Egyptian residents and had different concerns than locally domiciled investors in real assets. Nationalist discourse may have had a tiny kernel of truth from which a luxurious ideological growth arose and those who sought to increase the role of Egyptians as holders of financial assets had a story to tell.

Through the 1920s Nahas warned of a looming cotton crisis: a collapse of the price of Egyptian cotton. Nahas did not believe that the price of Egyptian cotton was materially affected by the price of American cotton and, because Bresciani-Turroni's decisive statistical study did not appear until 1929, there was no reason to. The Agriculturalists' Union therefore called repeatedly for government purchases to support the price of cotton directly and to put pressure on private demand that they believed was inelastic. The growers also sought to limit the acreage of cotton and to allow growers to keep cotton off the market after ginning (Nahas [1952b] 152, 155).

I have showed how Ahmad Abdel Wahab's 1930 report on cotton culti-vation was the opening wedge in an attempt to reformulate state regulation of the cotton economy. I suggested that, although the report relied on tech-nical arguments (such as Bresciani-Turroni [1930]) about Egyptian partici-pation in a global economy as an exporter, it implied as well the use of the power of the state to reshape the Egyptian economy. Abdel Wahab and Nahas represented distinct poles in the debate about how to employ the reg-ulatory power of the government in terms of partisan commitments, social background, institutional roles, economic theory, and understanding of the role of the state.

The Depression provoked a severe conflict over policy and in this conflict Abdel Wahab and Ismail Sidki were in decided opposition to the interests of landowners. We can see the emergent conflict in three articles published in autumn 1931 where Nahas and Sidki debated the Abdel Wahab project. In a stinging response to Nahas's demand that the government strictly limit cot-ton acreage and provide aid to landowners to switch to other crops, Sidki responded that the fall in land values accompanying the fall in cotton prices was only a problem for landowners. "One does not," in Sidki's words "eval-uate the wealth of a country or its credit by the value of the land actually offered in the marketplace but by the price of its unified or preferred debt for that is the measure of its credit" (Nahas [1954] 257). By the standard of international exchange and the creditworthiness of the state debt, Sidki argued, Egypt was doing quite well. If there was any problem, it was not that commodity prices were down but that globally money had become too expensive. As soon as the price of money came down, Sidqi expected that trade would return to normal. In reply Nahas argued that limitation of the cotton acreage was only one measure although one he had lobbied for almost from the day Sidki took office (Nahas [1954] 258).

When Nahas sought to exemplify the kind of leader he had in mind, he referred to the need to take stern methods, "on the Mussolinist path." What Nahas had in mind was less a retreat from international free trade than from an open economy with free entry to producing a high-quality good. Pursuing his attack on Sidki later in the fall, Nahas warned that the real danger for the world lay with the United States. The United States had, he explained, used the years of the Great War to win the markets of textile producers and now threatened to conquer the remaining markets of raw fiber producers. Only what Nahas called "wise national economic policy" of strengthening Egypt's role as a producer of high-quality cotton could save her from the worst of all fates: the possibility that landed property would cease to be held by Egyptians at all (Nahas [1954] 261). Nahas continued to believe that there were no substitutes for Sakel and that the Abdel Wahab policy would be self-defeating because it would expose Egypt to the danger that even England had not been able to surmount: the challenge of cheap agricultural goods from America.[12] By 1931 he momentarily embraced the exceptionalist rhetoric about soil and national community he had earlier disdained and entertained the idea that what Egypt needed was not a monarchy with limited parliamentary governance but one more closely modeled on European fascism led by a "Mussolinist."

Faced with the prolongation of the Depression, the managerial role of the state in the economy was bound to increase. Not all Egyptian political leaders saw a threat in America or thought that the energetic pursuit of change would require an Egyptian Mussolini. In October 1933, Ahmad Abdel Wahab visited the United States and shortly after his return gave a talk at the Royal Society on Political Economy on Roosevelt, the National Recovery Administration, and U.S. policies for countering the effects of the Depression (Abdel Wahab [1934]). Abdel Wahab was still undersecretary of state in the Finance Ministry when he discussed the measured taken by the U.S. government to deal with the catastrophic fall in prices. One crucial picture he drew for his audience was of the almost directly inverse relationship of prices for raw materials and world stocks between 1923 and 1933 globally and in the United States. The implication or "inevitable result was a great fall in the purchasing power of the agricultural classes, which entailed a fall in the consumption of the products of industry and a further increase in unemployment." He believed Roosevelt's decision to depreciate the currency rather than to allow a wave of bankruptcies to destroy the economy was correct (Abdel Wahab [1934] 176).[13] Both on his own and evidently from reading the work of Keynes (whom he cites), Abdel Wahab believed that the crucial regulatory policies needed to transform the American economy had to affect the banking system and the provision of credit in such a way as to raise the prices for raw materials (Abdel Wahab [1934] 178–179). Although Abdel Wahab did not draw any direct conclusions for Egypt, it is apparent that he understood very clearly the role that price supports and relatively easy credit could have, and also that the reopening of export markets, especially in America, would be crucial for the recovery of the global economy.[14]

Writing a year later, as finance minister, Abdel Wahab considered Egypt's pressing economic and financial problems. He noted the extreme poverty in which most rural Egyptians lived that included high levels of infant mortality, poor nourishment, and low levels of education, which he perceived as a moral rather than a material problem (Abdel Wahab [1935] 148). Abdel Wahab pointed to low productivity and the reliance on a single export crop as particular problems he ascribed to technological backwardness, insufficient credit, and high taxes incident on rural producers (Abdel Wahab [1935] 150–151). Abdel Wahab proposed a set of government initiatives to extend the area and intensity of cultivation which were, of course, rooted in irrigation technology, but he also proposed to increase the products available for agricultural export, to reduce taxes while raising social spending, and to use the newly won tariff independence to encourage industrialization (Abdel Wahab [1935] 157–158). One crucial ingredient for Abdel Wahab appears to have been the creation of a national bank and the assertion of Egypt's right to be free of the gold standard (Abdel Wahab [1935] 153).[15]

By 1937, Abdel Wahab went considerably beyond programs that Roosevelt or Keynes would have been comfortable with. In a paper titled "Some Aspects of the Directed Economy in Egypt During the Past Years" Abdel Wahab proposed to jettison the laissez-faire economy and move toward a state-led economy which, he noted, already existed in the sugar industry (Abdel Wahab [1937] 438). He noted that by limiting production, fixing prices, and engaging in an international agreement (by which he meant the Chadbourne accord) the Egyptian government had effectively controlled sugar production. The government understood very well how to regulate the economy to provide the rents necessary to stimulate particular kinds of investment.

In a review of Abdel Wahab's role in the political economy of this period, Robert Vitalis makes a convincing case that Abdel Wahab was part of a rent-seeking private business–official coalition acting in opposition to interests centered in the Royal administration and in the Wafd (Vitalis [1996] 90–92). Nevertheless, Abdel Wahab was also part of an emergent policy elite that opposed the Wafd and sought its own alliance with the Palace to use the machinery of the state to direct the economy into new and profitable paths for particular private interests. Thus Abdel Wahab recognized possible "intervention of the government in rental contracts between owners and lessors... as well as between debtors and creditors" as ways in which the Egyptian state had begun to diverge from a liberal laissez-faire set of policies into a far more active role in order to avoid "disastrous consequences not only for debtors but for the national economy as a whole" (Abdel Wahab [1937] 451).

Abdel Wahab envisaged a far more active role for the state toward the end of the Depression, a period in which "economic nationalism had made such advances that any move to reverse would face insurmountable difficulties." One advantage of directed economies was precisely that they allowed for the employment of millions of workers who otherwise would be jobless. Another advantage closely allied to the rent-seeking that Vitalis stresses is the emergence of a developmental strategy: "one result of a planned economy has been that the provision of public capital has led private individuals to invest in projects that were only conceived in the context of the adoption of such a system" (Abdel Wahab [1937] 452). Within a year Abdel Wahab was dead and although Nahas continued to write, a new generation arose to govern Egypt. The meditations of their policy advisers on the role of the state in the economy left far less room for an open economy than either Nahas or Abdel Wahab had assumed to be desirable.

Nahas recognized that a local textile industry could become a source of economic growth and a market for locally grown fiber, but he also recognized that such an industry would have to confront Japanese competition. When he discussed the reasons for the growth of the Japanese textile industry he diverged from the then-standard accounts. The secret of the astonishing Japanese success in the textile industry lay in the skill of the workforce and the intensity of its labor (Nahas [1954] 323).[16] He never linked the high level of skill among Japanese textile workers to the nearly total literacy in the country. To the contrary, as early as 1901 Nahas viewed education as a necessity because it increased the bargaining power of the lower classes and because it decreased the role of the state in society. He argued that the lower classes, including agricultural laborers and poor peasants, did not receive either the value of their labor or a fair share of the nation's wealth. Education would allow a civilized but illiterate peasantry to defend its own interests, "contribute to bettering its own condition," and end the need for government tutelage (Nahas [1901] 197–198).[17] When *Le Fellah* was reissued in 1927 in Arabic Nahas wrote a new introduction in which he described with some vehemence the shabby treatment of Egyptian peasants and their need for more education, higher incomes, and a more secure legal system (Nahas [1927] *lam-ᶜayyin*). Although he considered the peasant "the factor on which the country's wealth is built through unremitting toil" (Nahas [1927] *ᶜayyin*) he still was concerned mainly with whether agricultural labor received a fair return as a factor of production rather than as the primary area for investment.

Nahas's analysis of the tariff policies of the 1930s is revealing. Although the 1930 tariff reforms have been called crucial to the emergence of an industrial policy, Nahas saw them as shaped primarily to increase the state revenue (Nahas [1954] 393). Tariffs became a more important instrument to shape the economy, according to Nahas, only after Japanese competition threatened the emergent Egyptian industry. Japan was able to undersell Egyptian textiles in the home market, he argued, because of a double cost advantage: it used Indian cotton and its money had been devalued.

Nahas vigorously defended the interests of landowners, especially large landowners in the Delta, and he did so until the early 1930s in the language of neoclassical economics. His belief that Egypt could wield market power was at odds in theory with neoclassical economics, but discussions about government policy could still be conducted in orthodox language until 1929.

## Muhammad Luhayta and the "Integrated Economy"

Although now almost completely forgotten, Muhammad Fahmi Luhayta was a prominent English-trained economist in Egypt between World War I and the 1952 coup whose books included treatments of Egypt's role in the regional economy and the historical growth of the domestic economy.[18] The three-volume work I consider here, *Economic History of King Fuad: Egypt on the Path to Total Integration*, was one of the earliest systematic arguments in Arabic for the kind of sustained state intervention in the economy that we now call developmental dictatorship.[19] Along with a sustained argument for state intervention, Luhayta also makes an implicit claim for enhancing the power of the throne at the expense of local interests—foreign or domestic—that would be threatened by an explicitly nationalist industrial policy. Published in 1945–1946, the *Economic History* extended the debates about the need for powerful state intervention in the economy as a whole beyond what had occurred in the 1930s.

One subtle way in which Luhayta argues for enhanced state authority is in the dedication of the work to the former prime minister, ᶜAli Mahir. Mahir, the son of a former governor of Cairo and official in the Ministry of War, graduated from the Khedivial Law School in1905 and played a role as a young Wafdist in the 1919 revolt but later left the party. By the 1920s

Mahir, a rising star, had moved from an academic environment to a series of undersecretary-ships in the ministries of education, finance, and justice and then became the head of the Royal Secretariat. He served as prime minister for the first five months of 1936 and it was he who first appointed Ahmad Abdel Wahab as finance minister. Mahir attempted, but failed, to force the Wafd to enter a coalition government under his leadership in 1936. He formed a second government from August 1939 to June 1940 and was therefore prime minister when the United Kingdom declared war on Germany on September 3, 1939. It was Mahir, acting in advance of the British, who declared Egypt to be under a state of siege in which the prime minister was military governor (Kirk 34). Egypt did not declare war on Germany and Mahir was ousted due to British pressure as it became clear that he planned to follow a policy of diplomatic neutrality. It was also during this period that Mahir, who retained his ties to the Royal Secretariat, created the Ministry of Social Affairs. With it for the first time the Egyptian government could intervene in the distribution of welfare to society. Suspected of being an Axis sympathizer, Mahir spent a portion of World War II under house arrest.

Dedicating a three-volume work on recent Egyptian economic history to Mahir was therefore an assertion about the importance of centralized authority in which the king would play a far more dominant role than more popular nationalist officials who had debilitating commitments either to the British or to local interests.[20] More remarkable, however, were the claims Luhayta made about the crucial role of King Fuad himself. All three volumes are filled with flowery encomiums about the perspicacity of King Fuad in foreseeing and resolving difficult economic challenges to Egypt from runs against the currency (Luhayta [1945]) through the possible impact of cotton prices on political stability (Luhayta [1946a] 314) to social welfare legislation (Luhayta [1946b]). Of course King Fuad was an important political actor and the royal household was an important source of patronage and his role in Egyptian politics has never been the subject of a sufficiently serious investigation. Read now, Luhayta's work is a corrective to the post-1952 view that the Throne and the royal family were little more than British puppets. In fact, as extremely wealthy members of the landowning elite, the royal family disposed of important economic resources and the king himself had crucial constitutional powers; he therefore had significant resources at his disposal to affect policy. Even the most generous account of Fuad's reign (Thabit [1931]) does not suggest he possessed the capacities or interests attributed to him by Luhayta, but there is reason to believe that Fuad played an active role in economic management.[21]

Luhayta's three volumes focusing on King Fuad must be placed within the context of a discourse common to the 1930s about the role of genius and the search for leadership. The best-known work in Arabic in this vein is Abbas Al-ᶜAqqad's biography of Muhammad but it was a common image and in the 1930s there was a biographical tribute to the genius of Mustafa al-Nahas, the leader of the Wafd party. Egyptians were not alone in their belief in that political leaders exemplified genius. Whether a discourse or simply a popular image, the political leaders of Europe and Asia were invariably referred to in their official (and often unofficial) biographies as geniuses. The murderous official hagiography that enveloped Mussolini, Hitler, and Stalin was reproduced in milder forms elsewhere in Europe, Asia, Africa, and Latin America. A popular booklet on Germany by Thabit Thabit, for example, identified Hitler as the patriotic genius of Germany and Karim Thabit's biography of King Fuad (Thabit [1931]) made the monarch appear as an exemplar of modernity and authority. It is impossible to know if Luhayta believed that Fuad was an exceptional figure; few Egyptians and even fewer of the intellectual elite did. What seems more probable from reading the volumes is that Luhayta intended to reassure Egyptians that they had in Fuad's son, Faruq, a leader capable of forging a developmental dictatorship.

The clearest expression of Luhayta's arguments about industrialization, trade, and the role of the state are in the second and third volumes of the series. Here Luhayta lays out clearly the importance of state socialism as the mechanism that will allow a fully directed, integrated, or regulated (*al-tawjih al-kamil*) economy to replace a free-market economy in order to avoid the waste of any resources but especially human labor (Luhayta [1946b] 155).[22] Luhayta was cognizant of Marxist theory and of Soviet practice and evidently knew Egyptian communists, but his discussion of planned economies draws largely on British socialist theory.[23] He consequently envisaged private ownership of capital in an economy in which the state negotiated relationships between labor and capital (Luhayta [1946b] 157). Luhayta believed that the monopolistic structure of much Egyptian industry and the likely tendency toward monopoly in any industrialization strategy made such forms of government corporatism necessary.

Luhayta's argument that Egyptian industrialization was possible begins by asserting the necessity of using state regulatory strategies to standardize industrial processes so as to avoid the waste of capital and labor in both static and dynamic equilibriums (Luhayta [1946b] 200).[24] Of the two, Luhayta was more concerned with labor: planned industrialization would diminish structural unemployment because the state could undertake a commitment to firm-longevity incompatible with private profit and would decrease frictional unemployment because standardized equipment would make moving from one firm to another relatively easy. The consequent capital savings would increase the funds available for investment elsewhere and thus further increase employment (Luhayta [1946b] 201–202).

Industrialization itself Luhayta, like his contemporaries, viewed as a problem of industrial location and thus of specialization due to the division of labor and comparative cost advantages (Luhayta [1946] 204–206).[25] The crucial necessity for industrial production did not, in his view, lie in the availability of raw materials but in the availability of skilled and especially administrative manpower (Luhayta [1946b] 207). Administrative capacity was crucial because "location requires the appropriate decisions that allow every individual to make the maximum contribution with minimum effort to the project as a unit … if location in the past required ignoring the working and a concern with machinery, at the present it requires a concern with labor and laborers so as to increase the ability of the laborer" (Luhayta [1946b] 212). This, in turn, required aligning the incentives of the workforce with the firm (Luhayta [1946b] 212)[26] to increase productivity through increased effort, reduced turnover costs, and even eliciting suggestions for process improvement from the workforce.[27]

In Luhayta's view, labor costs for the firm and the share of labor in overall consumption played the crucial role in the success of industrialization as a dynamic process. He believed that wages were, in the long run, limited by the marginal productivity of labor; that in a free-market economy excessive wage rates whether gained by union or government intervention would cause unemployment or underemployment; and that monopoly firms were not those most likely to provide the best long-term results for workers (Luhayta [1946b] 220). Nevertheless, Luhayta's example of a successful industrial firm was not a firm engaged in a highly competitive arena but the already highly regulated sugar company that he presented as an exemplary case in which foreign capital was employed for the benefit of Egyptian and foreign interests. He praised the provision of company housing, health care, and bonuses linked to productivity for the administrative staff (Luhayta [1946b] 224–225). More regulation was needed in two areas: the general wage level and the tendency of the firm to fire older workers in favor of younger, cheaper ones. These were problems that could be addressed by labor legislation, evidently without the need for any investigation into the marginal (or any other) costs (Luhayta [1946b] 226).

Luhayta's views may now appear to be more conventional than they were. He was clearly groping with the problem that, even in Egypt, industrial wages were above the market-clearing level. In then-standard (and much contemporary) theory, there should be no open unemployment because employers will lower wages to the point at which all available workers are employed. In Egypt, this implied that wages for unskilled labor would approach the rate for agricultural labor, but adult industrial workers were paid significantly more than the market-clearing rate. Just as Nahas had no good explanation for market power but perceived that it existed, so too Luhayta recognized that workers were paid above the market-clearing wage but had no explanation as to why this happened.[28] His suggestion that what he called the "economic wage" of workers arose from competition between employers for the most skilled labor is not far from one contemporary neo-Keynesian understanding.

Luhayta, like Abdel Wahab, paid more attention to the sugar industry than have his many successors in writing political economy for whom the textile industry was invariably far more interesting. Luhayta's concern with the sugar industry was with both the direct and indirect effects of what he called the "the key to industry in Egypt" (Luhayta [1946b] 296) and the sugar industry was probably the most regulated and highly protected industry in Egypt.[29] It therefore provided a sectoral model of a managed economy. The sugar industry employed tens of thousands of workers directly, bought much of the sugar cane crop on its own account, and supplied much of the domestic market. Luhayta appears to have believed that such forms of organization could, through the effect of increased wages in industries based on agriculture, also bring about increases in rural wages that would increase rural living standards significantly (Luhayta [1946b] 65).

Luhayta argued that the evidence of successful pursuit of macroeconomic intervention lay in the debate around cotton policies in the 1930s that sought to use various regulatory instruments including direct acreage regulation, tariff control, and other policies to affect the size and productivity of cotton production (Luhayta [1946b] 108–109). Along with the organization of external trade and the creation of employer associations he also proposed strengthening the Labor Department of the Ministry of Social Affairs whose role would be to reduce unemployment, resolve conflicts between workers and owners, and intervene to enhance the living standards of the workers (Luhayta [1946b] 276–280). He did not see the trade union movement playing this role in Egypt although he recognized that these were concerns of unions in more industrialized countries.

For Luhayta, as for Egyptian politicians more generally, illiteracy was like hunger, homelessness, and illness. It was a condition to be ameliorated (Ikeda; Luhayta [1946a] 392) and education was therefore an important consumption good rather than an investment. Luhayta believed that private firms could be induced to provide such consumption goods to their employees with a proper combination of fiscal incentives and direct grants from the state because this was precisely the approach employed by the Muhammad Mahmud government to induce firms to build housing for their workers (Luhayta [1946a] 403).

Despite his awareness that wages could affect employment levels, Luhayta also believed that the government could and should set wage rates in the absence of trade unions.[30] Citing (in English) work by Herbert Silverman, an associate of the Fabian G.D.H. Cole, Luhayta proposed, "Wages rates may be decided by compulsory arbitration and enforced by the law of the State...the State itself is expected to pass laws influencing wages rates" (Luhayta [1946a] 404). Luhayta's rationale had a Keynesian flavor especially in his argument that increasing the income of workers would increase both their purchasing power and their productivity (Luhayta [1946a] 404–405).

When Luhayta turned his attention to more properly Keynesian macroeconomic factors, he (like Harari) focused on the absence of a central bank and the consequent weakness of investment at least in part due to interest-rate rigidity and the consequent problems of financing new enterprises (Luhayta [1946a] 493–494). Luhayta called for re-forming the banking system to transform what he believed was an adequate level of savings into investments (Luhayta [1946a] 495). This was far closer to a Keynesian approach and it suggests why Luhayta believed significant economic growth would be compatible with the maintenance of the parliamentary monarchy. Pursuing this more clearly Keynesian approach, Luhayta hoped that with the expansion of industry, holders of financial assets would invest in fixed assets. They would thereby increase the demand for labor and draw peasants out of agriculture (Luhayta [1946a] 565). Luhayta knew that this increased demand could raise the relative wages commanded by owners of labor and fixed capital because he had noticed precisely such an effect on the price of skilled labor and raw cotton in the 1930s (Luhayta [1946a] 566).

Luhayta understood that his proposals for industrial investments would lead to the creation of inefficient monopolies and he seems to have expected such monopolies to be the normal course of capitalist development. He predicted that the economy would require increasing levels of state influence over the domestic economy and over its foreign trade (Luhayta [1946a] 662). This, he understood, would not be economically efficient in the short or medium run, but he came down rather clearly on the side of classical mercantilism. "Industrial planning...will require creating industries not on the basis of the best exploitation of the factors of production, but out of fear of war and to defend the political existence of the state and will therefore demand the creation of basic industries.... And thus Egypt will create and preserve some basic industries even though their products could be obtained from abroad at a lower cost" (Luhayta [1946a] 663).

Luhayta's work is a mixture of normative and positive economic concerns, of description and analysis that were common in the economics literature of the mid-twentieth century. It evinces the dominant concerns of people concerned with economic policy at the time: to find ways to increase domestic incomes without at the same time increasing unemployment, providing disincentives for investment, or making Egyptian industry globally uncompetitive. Luhayta had outlined some of the dimensions of the problem and like many in the 1930s and 1940s he believed the answer would require not simply investment but state control of significant portions of investment.

## Planning for Industrialization

By the time Said El-Naggar published *Industrialisation and Income* in 1952 it had a context in the work of several generations of Egyptian academics and officials. It differed significantly from the work by Nahas and Luhayta if only because it was one of the first formal models developed by a professional economist in Egypt. Unlike Nahas's necessarily episodic concerns and Luhayta's descriptive reviews or Bresciani's concern with a single problem, El-Naggar worked within a still new professional context in which trained economists provided officials with coherent, theoretically framed and policy-relevant arguments. El-Naggar's work provides evidence that some Egyptian economists believed that industrialization was not likely to come from import-substituting industrialization but from policies designed to pursue export-led growth.

Like contemporaries, El-Naggar did not use the terms import-substitution or export-led growth but the concepts that underlie these now-common analyses were crucial to his work. El-Naggar employed the vocabulary of international location of industry and the theory of comparative advantage (El-Naggar v). There was widespread agreement in professional circles, echoed by El-Naggar, that the existing arguments in favor of protection were theoretically unsound although there was also widespread criticism that the doctrine of comparative advantage based on an assumption of perfect competition was insufficiently realistic to generate useful policy advice. Keynes's work was one variant of the renewed interest in mercantilist policies at the time. Mercantilist policy, as Heckscher pointed out, either aimed at "deflecting economic activity directly towards the particular ends demanded by political, and more especially military, power... [or] in creating a kind of reservoir of economic resources generally, from which the policy of power could draw what it required" (Heckscher 31). Heckscher noted, "[o]nce the new ideas had become established the unemployment argument found a place of honor in all future proposals and demands that aimed at measures against imports" (Heckscher 122). Writing the same year that *Mercantilism* first appeared in print (1931), Keynes appears nearly to have coined the phrase "import-substitution" when he proposed a general import tariff on all manufactured goods because "[i]n so far as it leads to the substitution of home-produced goods for goods previously imported, it will increase the employment of this country" (Irwin 195).

El-Naggar carefully worked out a proposal for industrialization based on export-oriented growth, which he proposed as a viable path for Egypt. El-Naggar employed economic theory that was then extremely novel and anticipated much of the political narrative of export-led growth. It differed from later dependency theory because it assumed that there were both domestic and international markets for Egyptian goods. Dependency theory initially had no opposition to export-led growth in principle but was based on the belief that there was insufficient demand for Latin American goods in their major market, the United States. In his original report to the United Nations, Raul Prébisch argued that the low levels of economic growth observed in Latin America were the result of relatively low levels of imports by the United States although he asserted that the reason for low levels of imports was the need to protect wages (Prébisch 16–17). Prébisch therefore noted that if the US could achieve full employment and if it could increase its imports from the rest of the world "the United States could achieve two other fundamental objectives of its economic policy: the active promotion of foreign trade and the furthering of Latin American industrialization" (Prébisch 35). Policies of import-substitution, exchange-rate restriction, and forced internal savings were not, for Prébisch, desirable policies but necessary ones to accomplish the goal of industrialization and a fuller integration of the Latin American countries into a global market.

It would be naïve to believe that the army officers who overthrew the monarchy months after the publication of El-Naggar's study would have turned to it for a blue-print on development. It is less naïve to believe that because El-Naggar was an official in the developmental institutions of the new regime we can see in his work the rationales for policies suggested by economists to the new rulers. In fact, themes he sounded were taken over in official planning documents such as the 1955 Arthur D. Little Report. We can also use El-Naggar's book in comparison with the Little Report to gain some sense of how the policies diverged from the theoretical expectations of those who suggested them. The clearest example of these departures is in the area of trade union regulation, which I address in chapter 6. Because there is considerable disagreement or confusion over how to characterize the new regime's policies, however, El-Naggar's exposition of a development strategy based on open markets and private ownership provides us with a clear benchmark by which to judge them.

El-Naggar's model is just the kind of "East Asian" model that became so popular a part of the discourse on political economy in the 1990s. El-Naggar specifically discounted the importance of allocative efficiency in favor of policies designed to increase the total amount of resources available to a developing economy (El-Naggar [1952] 6–9). Because agricultural economies had low levels of saving, he expected "foreign capital may play an important role in financing industrialization," which therefore made it necessary "to develop export industries in addition to home industries" (El-Naggar [1952] 5). Aware both that free trade ensured the optimum allocation of resources globally and that protection could only benefit a single country but not all countries (El-Naggar [1952] 23–24), how did El-Naggar expect industrialization to occur? Through the mechanism now referred to as "getting prices wrong": ensuring that the prices at which industrial products are sold do not accurately reflect the cost ratios between agricultural and industrial societies (El-Naggar [1952] 27). The crucial actor was the state. Only the state could subsidize wages (rather than employ tariff protection) to make domestic production competitive on international markets (El-Naggar [1952] 47) and only the state could undertake the investments in public goods that would make investments in industrial production profitable (El-Naggar [1952] 68). These investments (primarily in non-tradable services) would, consequently, not require tariff protection and would also increase domestic demand. More crucially, the state would be a collective entrepreneur, able to accomplish what no single investor would consider:

> [the] typical entrepreneur, especially in agricultural countries can only undertake a specific type of activity... We need an entrepreneur whose activities and resources would extend over a wide field of manufactures. Such a function can only be performed in agricultural countries by the government itself acting through some sort of a development council. This would make possible the simultaneous establish of related industries. (El-Naggar [1952] 70)

El-Naggar's proposals were within the framework of the work of Rosenstein-Rodan and others who believed that the doctrine of increasing returns made a rapid leap to industrial society not only possible but in fact the only feasible policy for governments. El-Naggar appreciated that even the task of protection "on the basis of the infant industry was argument is thus not designed to bring about an optimum allocation of given resources... The purpose is to create a *new* [italics his] factor of production, namely, industrial skill and experience" (El-Naggar [1952] 77).

Recognizing a highly specialized skill as a new factor of production, El-Naggar paid remarkably little attention to the general level of literacy as a form of social investment that could raise overall productivity. He certainly expected that industrialization would change the relative prices confronting parents and therefore that "gradual improvement in the standard of living will impair the inducement to make use of child labor" and increase the tendency to educate children (El-Naggar [1952] 94). Besides prices, he also foresaw "the growth in the power of trade unions [that] is likely to be associated with a fall in the length of working hours" and therefore further induces parents to keep children off the labor market (El-Naggar [1952] 95).

What, in El-Naggar's analysis had kept Egypt from following such a path earlier was rapid population growth, but at least as important was the ability of firms to secure rents through political activity:

> Too much emphasis was placed on the possibility of securing protection against foreign competition and too little emphasis was placed on the improvement of efficiency... the government viewed with favour the progressive monopolization of the industry and took an active part in the elimination of effective competition among local producers. In consequence the output per head in modern industry is unduly low. (El-Naggar [1952] 137)

What El-Naggar (like Luhayta before him) proposed was to use the experience of regulation in the pursuit of rents and returns to quality in pursuit of a new goal: development.

El-Naggar used relative costs to assess the most plausible investment strategies for industrialization, paralleling in this regard the work of Sir Arthur Lewis. Assuming that Egypt's relative advantage was in labor-intensive production with relatively low skill requirements, El-Naggar winnowed 144 industries into 3 categories: suitable, moderately suitable, and unsuitable. Suitable were light industries engaged in transforming agricultural products such as spinning and weaving, canning, and some electrical assembly. Especially unsuitable were industries that required large amounts of capital. Sugar refining, despite long having been considered exemplary, was within this group because the industry even after 50 years was an industry that had frequently flirted with bankruptcy and that survived only under heavy protection. Naggar also included petroleum refining and steel works under the rubric "unsuitable." One difference between El-Naggar's proposals and the development strategy actually undertaken was, of course, the decision to invest precisely in such areas that were economically unattractive but provided both prestige and were of strategic importance.

In his book, El-Naggar expected private investment to remain the central motor of the economy. The role of the state was to change the relative prices confronting entrepreneurs so as to induce more innovative and competitive behavior. Institutional changes would be necessary: since foreign capital would have to play a significant role because savings in Egypt were insufficient, the laws governing company structures, foreign exchange, and capital imports and exports would have to be changed to reassure foreign investors (El-Naggar [1952] 100). Expected increases in trade union strength coupled with increase demand from state investments in services would, along with external demand, make a path to industrialization viable and lead to the transformation of the structure of the labor market. Parents would cease to allow their children to be employed but would prefer to invest in their education. In the long run a new factor of production, increased industrial skill, would be available and it would be increasingly in demand.

The trajectory El-Naggar proposed may describe Taiwan relatively well, but it was certainly not what Egyptians actually experienced over the coming decades. One reason is that a different set of policies were set in place. Before concluding this chapter I turn to examine a study conducted by the Arthur D. Little Inc. for the Egyptian government, "Opportunities for Industrial Development in Egypt" that indicate what those policies would be.

Because the Little report is a policy recommendation, its structure differs from that of El-Naggar's theoretical study. As is usual with such documents, the Little report begins with a conclusion: a summary of proposed areas of investment many of which appear to have arisen from decisions already favored by the new government. The Little report made some of the same recommendations proposed by El-Naggar as "most suitable": spinning, weaving, and processed foods. In addition, it strongly recommended several areas that El-Naggar believed to be moderately suitable: jute sacking, automobile tires, glass containers, and paperboard containers. Yet the consultants also recommended several areas that El-Naggar had rejected: petroleum refining, vegetable oil, gypsum products, and fertilizers. In addition the consultants accepted the proposed construction of a steel mill, a sector El-Naggar had also considered unsuitable.

There is no reason to assign El-Naggar's recommendations with the imprimatur of omniscience or even economic rationality. They do, however, give us an insight into how the decisions of the new government diverged from expectations that reasonable investors and academics held before the

July coup. What they suggest is that the army officers and their advisers were attracted to the production of goods that might be of strategic importance and also that would reduce the cost of imports. The Little Report in some ways resembles El-Naggar's document with its concern to "create more goods for export, reduce imports, add value to agricultural products, increase employment opportunities, and raise the income and purchasing power of the people" (Little 1). Its concern to reduce imports, however, reveals a desire to engage in import-substitution and to conserve foreign exchange in ways subtly different from El-Naggar who understood that it was, at the most, only possible to change the structure of imports but not to reduce them.

The authors of the Little Report (like El-Naggar) and presumably their readers within the Ministry of Commerce, believed that foreign investment would be necessary for any successful policy of industrialization to occur. The Report was quite forthright about the necessary changes that would be required in the investment climate: "remittability guarantees, income tax exemption for new investments, and liberalization of foreign share holdings in Egyptian companies... Revisions should also be made in government administrative practices and in labor laws which now present obstacles and discouragements to industry" (Little 6). That the Little analysts and El-Naggar also paid significant attention to the possibility of inflation is a little strange.[31] It suggests that they may not have believed that significant reserves of unemployed resources existed. After all, one basic insight of Keynes was that inflation cannot be a problem as long as unemployed resources can still profitably be brought into production. Moreover, with the exception of the years of World Wars I and II, inflation had never been a problem for Egypt.

The Little Report placed the most favorable gloss on the new regime's actions toward the economy and projected what looked like a Keynesian plan under the Free Officers, that is, a plan in which the state created the preconditions for an investment boom from the private sector. The regime's land reform initiative was supposed to "help to create an investment climate more favorable to industry, for with the limitation on land holdings now imposed, a larger part of both accumulated and current domestic savings should be available for investment in forms other than real estate" (Little 17). Processing agricultural products provided the "best immediate opportunities for industrialization" that would lead to mechanization increasing rural productivity, which would raise wages and thence "increase the local market for industrial products which is now very limited because of the low income of the agricultural workers who make up the bulk of the population" (Little 17).

Consultants and academic analysts still enjoy these kinds of just-so stories that involve "virtuous" circles. The Little Report envisaged doubling manufacturing employment over a ten-year period and projected ambitious goals of mobilizing labor and capital. Creating 37,000 industrial jobs a year for a decade would require capital investments of L.E. 22 million per year or about half of all private savings in a country in which it was believed that because a third of all savings were held in cash or gold investors were looking for new outlets (Little 39).

The authors thought Egypt a world in which the basic Keynesian problem of a missing link between savings and investment was empirically valid. If Egyptians could only transform their hoarded wealth into investment, economic growth would occur and with it the kind of job creation El-Naggar believed was necessary. The authors of the Little Report had few problems with imagining how to fill the positions generated by investment. "While there is no over-all shortage in prospect in the total labor supply for an industrialization program, shortages of particular skills will undoubtedly be encountered," wrote the report's authors (Little 38). There was, they thought, only one important shortcoming. "One of the principal obstacles to overcome during industrialization in an underdeveloped country" the Report continued, "is the lack of trained business management and key supervisory workers such as foremen and line supervisors, technicians, shop superintendents and plant managers" (Little 38). Leaving aside doubts about whether the assets they believed were highly liquid could in fact have flowed into the banking system (Singerman 154–155); I turn to their concern with the "new" factor of production.

The authors of the Little Report made an important argument about any industrialization, import-substituting, or export-oriented when they asserted that crucial bottleneck was in managerial capacity rather than in the available skills of the workforce. This analysis drew on then-influential work by Sir Arthur Lewis: analysis of disguised unemployment. Lewis had even given a lecture in 1953 for the National Bank of Egypt and asserted that his theories applied especially well to Egypt:

> You can export almost anything if your wages are low enough. So the question becomes simply in what circumstances are wages so low that a country poorly endowed nevertheless builds up a great export trade in manufactures. The answer is obvious enough. It is the case of countries that are over-populated in relation to their agricultural resources. (Lewis [1953] 7)

Lewis was aware that countries such as Switzerland and Great Britain retained an export economy only insofar as they could "keep in the forefront of developing new skills" (Lewis [1953] 7). Egypt had what most observers recognized as a comparative advantage in a "plentiful, if not almost limitless resource . . . uneducated, untrained and unskilled labor" (Harbison and Ibrahim 135).[32] But how was a country whose population was largely illiterate and whose textile industries, for example, had never been able seriously to compete with products from Japan to undertake the kind of industrialization program proposed by the American consultants?[33] When the Little Report laid out ten characteristics of suitable industries in which Egyptians should invest, these added up to a description of a high-quality export product that used locally produced raw materials, copious amounts of labor, had an assured market, and required only modest supporting investments such as transportation. The authors seemed neither to have realized the irony of their sketch of investment opportunities nor to have realized that 40 years earlier Egyptians had already realized the possibility of investing in just such a product: long staple cotton.

Any textile industry, the authors realized would export primarily to Iraq and Saudi Arabia (Little 135) whereas any large-scale exports to Europe, besides cotton, would be fresh fruits and vegetables. For Egypt to have increased its fruit and vegetable exports to Europe, however, would have required traversing exactly the same path as had been taken to produce high-quality cotton at the beginning of the twentieth century: investments by the state or private associations to resolve "problems of grading and packing, of assembly of the crop in Egypt for export, and of coordinating the assembly of the crop in Egypt for export, and of coordinating the assembly with shipping schedules . . ." (Little 141).

## Conclusion

Writing in 1946, not long after the publication of Keynes's *General Theory*, Eli Heckscher sounded a warning about the new theory and the conditions in which it applied. The problem of unemployed resources, Heckscher argued, was a problem of the increased scale of fixed capital investment in the modern world especially in the context of global trade. He suggested that the increase in the scale of firms (that now characterizes so-called new trade theory) had caused what he called " 'intermittently free goods'—unused resources of productive factors, whether material or human, which, in themselves are scarce" (Heckscher II 357). What Keynes had analyzed, he concluded, was not a general problem of the economy but "the persistent unemployment in England between the two World Wars, a phenomenon with which Keynes seems almost to be obsessed" (Heckscher II 357–358).

Over half a century Egyptian economists and policy makers moved to embrace an expanded role for the state in the economy as an investor and employer in addition to the role of regulator and purchaser of public goods that it had long served. If Egypt was part of the Keynesian world, then increased government purchasing and investment should have created a period of sustained economic growth. In England and the United States there had certainly been productive factors, especially human, that had been "intermittently free" as Hechscher put it. What if there were not such factors in Egypt? What if, for example, despite a large and growing population, there were not actually people with the requisite skills to fill the jobs investment was supposed to create?

Until 1952, Egyptian economists (like those elsewhere), moved away from economic prescriptions that assumed self-correcting markets and proposed an enhanced role of the state in organizing the economy. If they had become more skeptical about self-correcting markets, they continued to believe most productive assets in society would be privately owned. New theoretical approaches led them to believe that the government should and could reshape the economy by affecting the choices of private investors. In so doing they also believed they could resolve the problems of poverty, illness, and illiteracy by employing productive resources that had hitherto been unemployed or underemployed. To this degree it makes sense to see the discourse of economists as having been profoundly influenced by Keynesian economics. Economic discourse was far from the only source of state policy and those policies themselves were interpreted by private investors, workers, and state officials in very different ways. It is therefore to Egyptian attempts to regulate labor markets after 1952 that I now turn my attention because the claim of the new regime was that reallocation of rural assets and reorganization of the labor market would set Egypt on a path to growth.

# CHAPTER 6

# Labor Regulation in Egypt
# After 1952

By June 1952 when a military junta seized power in Egypt, Egyptians and members of the resident foreign communities had spent a third of a century in discussions about social and economic transformation.[1] Within months of taking power the new regime issued land reform decrees that altered rural social, economic, and political relationships. Decrees affecting corporate governance and labor–management relations were issued almost as quickly but there are significant disputes about how consequential the regulations were and whether the Egyptian government had the regulatory capacity to make them work (Migdal; Chaudhry; Tignor [1995] 104–105).

What is less in dispute is that the Egyptian government did not succeed in transforming Egypt from being a country whose workforce was primarily agricultural to one whose workers were industrial. Egypt was unable to move swiftly in the direction of industrialization either through import substitution by turning cotton into textiles for home use or through an export-oriented strategy of selling them abroad. Why had a country that so successfully invested in reputation fared so poorly in using similar regulatory tools to achieve a desirable outcome requires two investigations? First, in this chapter, we look more deeply at Egyptian attempts to employ sophisticated regulatory strategies to affect the decisions of firms and workers and induce an upgrading of the quality of industrial production. This aspect of the regulatory strategy failed. In chapter 7, we look more carefully at one aspect of the dual structure of Egyptian labor markets: the market for adult labor and that for children. If labor regulation did not succeed in inducing increased capital investment by owners of firms it did, in concert with other policies, have some success in ensuring that the industrial workforce was almost wholly adult. It turns out that there is a paradox that is not entirely unexpected from a focus on quality and reputation. Strategies for development do require shifting incentives for the use of productive factors. Specifically they require moving the workforce out of the "neoclassical" model of the labor market and rewarding returns to high-quality effort and the earliest and most important aspect of that shift requires destroying the only part of the labor market that is full neoclassical: the market for the labor of children.

Egyptian experience echoes many of the arguments about the role of institutions in the so-called East Asian model of development. Egyptian policies in the 1950s are conventionally interpreted as a form of import-substituting industrialization to increase the independence of Egypt from the global economy (Waterbury 60–66; Hansen [1991] 482; Posusney 9; Vitalis 204–206). The conventional wisdom obscures the beliefs of contemporary economists that industrial development was by necessity a form of import substitution that would require changing Egypt's relationship to the global economy rather than eliminating it.[2] They certainly knew that exports would be required to earn foreign currency to pay for the capital good imports required for development and thus El-Naggar and the authors of the Arthur D. Little report agreed that Egyptians would have to enter export markets for the domestic economy to grow. In fact, what were arguably the most successful industrial undertakings in Egypt at the time, the Beida Dyers and the Misr Fine Spinning and Weaving Company, prospered because "they dominated the internal markets for textiles and realized profits from exports" (Tignor [1998] 65).

The Egyptian experience with economic regulation, industrial development, and trade is therefore an exceptionally useful point to examine claims that export-led growth is based on controlling production costs through regulating labor markets, politically limiting the power of labor movements, and the incentive effects of such regulation on decisions by investors. It is all the more important because of recent arguments that Egyptian regulation of labor markets ought to be seen in the context of exceptionalist Egyptian cultural attitudes about exploitation (Posusney).

Because unskilled labor is, for less developed countries, an abundant factor of production, Robert Vitalis is correct to suggest that we can learn much by explicitly putting labor rather than capital at the center of our analyses of how economic growth occurs (Vitalis [1995] 259). Egyptian experience shows that both the labor repression thesis and the moral economy thesis fail to give adequate consideration to the contours of labor markets, problems of unemployment, and arguments about the importance of wages, the distribution of incomes in developing economies, and the replacement of children by adults throughout the economy.

## Labor and Export-led Growth

The pervasive and influential strands of analysis known for propounding export-led growth describe it as a policy in opposition to early phases of import-substituting industrialization and the welfare policies of income re-distribution that supposedly accompanied it (O'Donnell [1973, 1978], Waterbury). Export-led growth was an argument explicitly founded on the concept of factor abundance and efficient markets: unemployed high-quality labor provides an absolute advantage to firms (Bianchi 212; Koo 174; Haggard [1987] 118; Waldner 138). Because labor is initially unemployed, employers pay low, market-clearing wages, and labor flows from the rural areas into industrial enterprises. In a neoclassical model, economic growth would exhaust the reserves of unemployed labor and create pressure to raise wages, but in an implicit model of export-led growth, wages increase because of trade unions: they wield either monopoly power or political influence. Consequently the state must restrain labor costs by repressing trade unions and avoiding "premature Keynesianism" (Waldner). Political repression of the labor movement by the state ensures "a favorable investment climate for foreign capital while enhancing business confidence for domestic capital" (Koo 174; Deyo 192–193). Evidently in the long run wages rise with productivity, and thus in a second phase of development, governments motivate entrepreneurs to switch from labor-intensive to capital-intensive production although it would not be clear why entrepreneurs would need to be induced to use less of an increasingly expensive factor of production (Haggard [1987] 119).

Such a model is nearly identical to proposals made by Luhayta and Naggar about government wage determination inducing the substitution of capital for labor and the need for export promotion. One obvious difference between East Asia in the 1970s and the Middle East in the 1950s is that the former was already abundant in literate labor while that latter had (and still has) an abundance of illiterate labor (especially children) available for employment.

The two stories of export-oriented growth that dominated policy discussions in the first half of the twentieth century were Japanese and English textile production. Since the early twentieth-century writers have sought to understand initial English dominance in the textile trade and the successful Japanese challenge (Hubbard and Baring; Royal Institute of International Affairs; The Japan Advertiser). Unlike studies of East Asia, the Middle East, or Latin America that address regulatory competence, accounts of industrialization in Japan and England focus on factor abundance (skilled labor force) and high levels of motivation among workers to cooperate with each other and with the pace of technical improvement (Royal Institute of International Affairs 32–35; Lazonick; Lazonick and Mass 12–13).[3] Egyptian economists and policy makers were familiar with English experience but knew much less about Japan. Central to success, they believed was the creation of an appropriately skilled and motivated labor force.

In England trade unions comprising about 65 percent of the workers provided the incentives necessary for labor to be employed efficiently and competitively in global markets (Royal Institute of International Affairs 37). The unions ensured that (1) piece rates adequately rewarded worker effort, (2) oversaw shop discipline, and (3) removed the threat that junior workers would replace their older ones thereby encouraging learning-by-doing for firm-specific skills. The short-time movement that led to the calling of the international cotton congresses was the direct result of the powerful role of trade union insistence that employers cut hours rather than jobs.

Japanese entrepreneurs worked within a different institutional framework. Technological innovation—cotton blending that permitted ring spinning to replace mule spinning—had allowed the substitution of cheaper (female) labor for more expensive (male) labor (Lazonick; Sandberg; Otsuka et al.). The dormitory system, in which the firms provided housing and some food, allowed employers to monitor young women in ways that have rarely been possible for young men outside prisons or military service. This looks like a classic case of exploitation where low-cost labor is substituted for high-cost labor, but a closer study of the Japanese textile industry at the beginning of the twentieth century supports a more complex, neo-Keynesian analysis (for other examples and reports of research see Akerlof [1984]; Freeman and Medoff 332–333; Doeringer and Piore; Wright). Poorly paid in comparison to English men, Japanese women received wages significantly higher than they earned in agriculture or other rural occupations (Royal Institute of International Affairs 28; Ramseyer [1996]).

The theory of efficiency wages suggests why workers receive wages above the market-clearing level (Shapiro and Stiglitz). "Efficiency wages" is a variant of the returns-to-reputation approach employed in chapter 3. Employers pay a premium above the market-clearing wage to workers who provide higher-quality labor and because higher pay also provides a trigger mechanism that can be used to threaten to fire workers whose effort is of low quality. Firms that cut wages to the point of clearing labor markets attract less committed workers. They also weaken the trigger mechanism because when markets clear, the worker who loses the job quickly finds another available.[4] Cutting wages to clear the market was, this argument suggests, a losing strategy for Japanese. Counter-intuitively, in this framework, regulation was necessary to ensure that employers paid sufficiently *high* wages to their employees rather than one that kept wages low (Ramseyer).[5]

Early variants of this theory were well known—under the rubric that cheap wages do not imply cheap labor costs—to Egyptian economists like Luhayta who had studied in Great Britain in the 1920s because they were contained in Alfred Marshall's *Elements of Economics*.[6] The idea that the reduction of wages was bad policy was already wisdom in the industrializing cotton economy of the American south (Wright 627).[7] Because Marshall recognized that labor markets often embody highly unequal bargaining power, he was favorably inclined to trade unions to ensure wages were kept sufficiently high (Reisman 229–230). Trade unions played no significant role in the analyses of Egyptian economists who appear to have believed that the state would play the necessary role in their country.[8] Knowing little about Japan they nevertheless moved in the general direction of a "Japanese" solution of higher-than-market clearing wages.

At the macroeconomic level, the theory of efficiency wages is rooted in Keynesian rather than neoclassical economics because in equilibrium the economy is presumed to have unemployed workers. For efficiency wages to be meaningful, the wage must be connected to the right of the employer to fire employees. Second, an efficiency wage implies that unskilled factory labor is paid at least two to three times the prevailing agricultural wage even if this remains an extremely low wage by international comparison.[9] Third, firms must be explicitly concerned with reducing turnover and increasing the effort expended by the workforce for as Saxonhouse argued in regard to Japan "Long-term improvement in productivity in Japanese cotton spinning occurred almost entirely because of modest changes in labor force characteristics and working conditions."[10] These were precisely the issues over which conflict occurred in Egypt.

### Regulatory Change, Political, and Economic Goals

The decrees on corporate and labor market governance changed the regulatory environment for workers and investors in important ways, but unlike the land reform later observers did not see in them any coherent set of policy concerns. The most basic purpose of the land reform was to shatter the economic power of the royal family and the landed elite connected to it (Issawi [1963] 162; Hansen [1991] 118). Selling the broken-up estates to peasants who worked on the land was supposed to generate more intensive effort from peasants who it was believed could vary their effort because they were adult men. As their efforts increased so would rural incomes and, consequently, the demand for industrial goods. Land reform also aimed to transform the investment preferences of Egypt's wealthy families from land to industry (Issawi [1963] 163; Beattie 142–143; Gordon 62). Economists claimed to have some way of assessing these choices and therefore when the Officers chose to implement land reform—against the wishes of Ali Mahir—they turned to theoretical proposals advanced by professors such as Rashid al-Barrawi. No such clear logic has heretofore been discerned in the labor law.

For specialists on Egypt the new labor law lies at the intersection of disputes about the character of the postrevolutionary state in a way not true of land reform. Did the junta seek to control the labor movement and win popular support for a state-organized labor movement (Bianchi)? Or did it make a commitment to enhance the power of investors as employers and thereby attract foreign capital (Beinin [1989]; Posusney)? There is also an argument that the new laws simply provided badly needed relief to a fraction of the population that had suffered from significant inequities (Issawi [1954]; Tignor [1982]; Tomiche). The very contradictory character of the new decrees has also been interpreted to mean that the Free Officers were initially incoherent as a policy-making group (Vitalis [1995]; Tignor [1989]).

The paradoxes of the new regime's preferences about labor are mirrored in accounts of its preferences about investors. Broadly speaking the military rulers are portrayed as pro-capitalist figures incapable of stimulating much direct capital investment (Beinin [1989]; Posusney). For Beinin and Posusney, a clear ideological choice confronted the new military rulers between socialism and capitalism. To array policies in such stark terms does not cast much light on their provenance or intended consequences. Professional Egyptian economists and policy makers at the time more commonly thought of market structures in which the regulation of monopolies, rather than the existence of private property, was the core analytic and practical problem. Labor and corporate legislation in the early years of the Nasser regime are linked because they appear to have strongly favored industrial investors. For example, it is argued, the new regime dramatically changed the legal structure easing profit repatriation, encouraging import substitution and providing tax exemptions (Dekmeijian 124; Waterbury 63).

Strictly speaking there is little reason to believe that in undertaking these measures, the new regime was radically revising the policies of the old regime toward joint-stock companies. In July 1947, the Egyptian Parliament had amended the regulations of joint-stock companies by requiring that 51 percent of their share capital be owned by Egyptians; that 75 percent of the white-collar employees and salaries be Egyptian, and that 90 percent of all workers be Egyptian (Posusney 42; Vitalis [1995]; Hansen and Nashashibi). Posusney and Beinin (Posusney 42; Beinin [1989] 78) argue that the junta on assuming power unexpectedly changed the relevant law to allow foreigners to own a majority of the shares, to make hiring foreign experts easier, and to allow repatriation of invested capital. If so, the officers completely reversed the recent course of Egyptian policy-making. A more careful narrative of the process of legal change makes clear that this is not accurate. The last civilian government had already prepared the relevant decree. It was to be issued on the day of the coup. What the military regime enacted a week later confirmed a change in policy already under way rather than imposing a dramatic shift (Ikeda 298).

All accounts of the legislation make it surprising that capitalists—foreign and domestic—did not take advantage of the incentives the new regime provided (Waterbury 63). Either the bourgeoisie was too conservative to carry out the role assigned to it by the Free Officers (Beinin and Lockman 12) or the new regime had no intention of cooperating with capitalists (Baker 62). Uncertainty despite major elements of continuity between the first four years of the new regime and the old one (Radwan 203) may have been the problem although it is also argued that capitalists were more concerned by the post–Korean War recession and intimations of where the land reform was leading (Hansen [1991] 125).

To appreciate the regulatory initiatives of the new regime we need to place them in the context of the existing discourse of economic transformation as well as the regulation of firms and markets. The new laws may have served the needs of the new political elite, but they were written by experts whose concerns had been shaped by their understanding of what constituted economic structures that they believed they could now affect. The new labor legislation, therefore like the company law and even the land reform, arose from already existing trends within the ancien regime. These policies were designed to re-shape, but not eliminate, an existing system of private property. Because they did not seize and socialize assets, they were, for Posusney and Beinin, "pro-capitalist." From the viewpoint of the ministries, however, the coup had freed sections of the existing state bureaucracy and associated experts to put into place regulatory solutions they had long sought, some of whose goals were, as I discussed in chapter 6, to transform the Egyptian economy. For a brief moment a new coalition was created in which experts such as Joseph Nahas had been replaced by younger, more cutting-edge economists, and which could be shaped to include labor for its own sake but also as a means to affect investment decisions of businessmen.

All those who elaborated strategies of state intervention believed that they could provoke a dramatic transformation in Egypt's factor endowments without eliminating the constitutional monarchy. Egypt would cease to be a country poorly endowed in physical capital as government policies drove investment rates to heights hitherto unprecedented. Less frequently discussed (although by no means ignored) was the problem of how Egypt would cease to be a country richly endowed in illiterate and poorly skilled labor and become a country with an abundance of human as well as physical capital.

Policy makers confronted three interrelated problems. First, Egypt had an abundance of unskilled labor. As long as Egypt remained an open economy, Ricardian analysis suggested that, at least in the short term, Egyptian firms should produce goods requiring unskilled labor and should increase demand for that factor. This was so widely believed to be true that even Said El-Naggar thought that in the initial stages of a "Big Push" Egyptian industry would have to concentrate on expanding production in industries in which it had a comparative advantage rather than, as some export-led theorists believe, tweaking prices and using regulatory strategies to bypass comparative advantage. Second, Egyptian politicians and policy advisers generally believed that one crucial area of investment would be human capital, although had they used that particular term they would have thought more of endowing adult workers with new skills than of increasing the supply of children with a good primary education. Unfortunately, politicians and many economists feared that in the short term the supply of educated (literate) workers would outstrip the demand for them, and thereby cause profound disaffection among the skilled workers many of whom were literate and thus intellectual leaders of the urban workforce (Goldberg [1986]; Beinin and Lockman). Third, there was the possibility that under free trade a country with a relative scarcity of physical capital would find that the returns to capital decline as it becomes more exposed to trade and thereby find that further investment in such capital decreases (Rodrik 16) limiting demand for labor.

Just as elasticity of demand for Egyptian cotton was the technical question around which much of the discussion of economic policy in the 1930s revolved, the elasticity of labor supply was the crucial debate from 1945 to 1960. In both cases, the issue was what kind of response regulatory official might expect as they intervened in a complex market economy. High elasticity implied easy movement of labor in response to wages, but it therefore also required that skills were widely dispersed so that workers could easily substitute for one another. Of course, if labor (skill) was a highly specific factor of production then workers could not shift employment very readily and elasticity would be low. In the context of mid-twentieth-century Egypt, high-quality labor (that commanded a premium) was like other goods or services with an investment in reputation a highly specific factor.

Egyptian economists believed there was widespread rural underemployment and that unskilled labor would move easily from the countryside into factories where workers would gain plant-specific skills. Once labor flowed into factories, it would be more or less immobile once employed because workers acquired nontransferable skills. The regulatory choices of the government in this regard were constitutive as well as regulatory: it could induce an economic environment more oriented toward plant-specific skills and seniority rather than one with more open labor markets.

The Egyptian government successfully extended its regulatory capacities into the new area of resolving labor–management conflict by a quasi-judicial system of arbitration and welfare legislation. European governments had been engaged in similar undertakings since the late nineteenth century and there judicial institutions played a far more important role in managing labor–management conflict than in the United States or England. Egyptian attempts to regulate labor markets necessarily resembled similar attempts in Continental Europe because the underlying legal structures were similar.

The military junta undertook steps to improve the situation of workers and provide them with the employment stability and hoped to resolve the problem of open urban unemployment. To the degree that the new laws increased security of employment they also resolved some incentive problems of skill acquisition. They provided younger workers with a reason to acquire plant-specific skills and they provided older workers with security that they could teach younger workers such skills. The impact of the law on the structure of labor markets also tilted competition between children and adults for industrial employment against children. The particular choices made by the junta improved the prospects for industrial employment by adult men and decreased industrial employment of children; they appear to have relatively little impact on the employment of women. In combination with other policy choices of the new government the new regulation increased the rate at which the overall population has become literate but they did not provide the incentives to replace manual labor with capital or to provide enough literacy to reshape the entire economy.

### The Historiographical Argument over Arbitration

Just as it was necessary to look closely at the historiography of the claim that Egypt suffered an ecological crisis to understand what happened in the first part of the twentieth century, it is necessary to look closely at the historiography of the debates on labor legislation to gain a sharper understanding of the issues at play. In 1974 Tomiche argued that the Nasser period through 1956 favored workers by strengthening the legal basis of compulsory arbitration mechanisms as well as by transforming the political climate in which they worked (Tomiche 42).[11] The contrary has also been argued, using a rudimentary statistical analysis: that there was far more labor conflict in the early Nasser period (Beinin [1989]). The new labor regulation was significantly more hostile to workers and therefore complaints brought from the factory to court were more frequently dismissed after the coup:

> [Table 6.1] indicates that, from 1952 to 1958, the percentage of cases won by workers declined steadily (except for the anomalous year of 1955 for which no explanation is apparent). Unless we assume a large number of cases brought by workers were frivolous, the high proportion of dismissed cases can be interpreted as additional evidence of an unsympathetic attitude toward workers by the courts. (Beinin [1989] 77)

The crux of the problem is what the word "frivolous" means as it applies to court cases (rather than to the underlying disputes). We do not know exactly what these disputes are, although Beinin hazards the guess that they "are the equivalent of a filed grievance in the Anglo-American style" (Beinin [1989] 77). In preparing figure 6.1 I have assumed that all court cases begin as disputes although obviously not all disputes end up as court cases.[12] I have also assumed only workers bring disputes to court.[13]

July 1952 marks a significant change in the trend of disputes. It is more clear graphically that the general trend in the number of disputes (or complaints or grievances) after the 1953 spike is downward, but the trend appears to level off after 1955. As with the claim of ecological crisis, I believe the failure is in the analysis not the numbers. One line of the graph shows the number of disputes; another line shows the proportion of disputes brought to court; yet a third line shows the proportion of disputes in which the workers were victorious. Visual inspection shows the proportion of disputes being moved into the court system increased even as the number of disputes declined. The year 1955 that Beinin finds anomalous is simply the result of its being the moment when (roughly speaking) two lines moving in opposite directions cross. Had it not been for the war in 1956 with its follow-on effects, 1955 might well have been the equilibrium toward which the two trends would have continued with about 30 percent of disputes being brought to court.[14]

**Table 6.1** Workers' complaints and trial outcomes 1953–1958

| Year | Complaints | For | Against | Settled | Dismissed | Suspended | Cases | % tried | % won | % dismissed | % lost |
|---|---|---|---|---|---|---|---|---|---|---|---|
| 1953 | 71,841 | 3,157 | 2,148 | 312 | 2,187 | 370 | 8,174 | 11.4 | 4.8 | 26.8 | 26.3 |
| 1954 | 56,874 | 4,370 | 5,175 | 584 | 3,774 | 737 | 14,640 | 25.7 | 8.7 | 25.8 | 35.3 |
| 1955 | 46,415 | 6,470 | 4,254 | 497 | 5,295 | 504 | 17,020 | 36.7 | 15.0 | 31.1 | 25.0 |
| 1956 | 32,057 | 3,703 | 4,839 | 374 | 5,186 | 473 | 14,575 | 45.5 | 12.7 | 35.6 | 33.2 |
| 1957 | 35,836 | 2,742 | 3,906 | 181 | 6,301 | 460 | 13,590 | 37.9 | 8.2 | 46.4 | 28.7 |
| 1958 | 37,166 | 2,860 | 4,456 | 141 | 5,235 | 438 | 13,130 | 35.3 | 8.1 | 39.9 | 33.9 |
| Average | 46,698 | | | | | | 13,522 | 32.1 | 9.6 | 34.2 | 30.4 |

*Notes:* The column "complaints" gives the total number of grievances listed in Beinin; the column "cases" lists the total number of actions brought to courts by workers in Beinin. These are two different series. The columns "for," "against," "settled," "dismissed," "suspended" all refer to the series of "cases." The column "% tried" is the proportion cases/complaints; the column "% won" is the proportion of "for"/"complaints." The other proportions refer only to outcomes and cases.

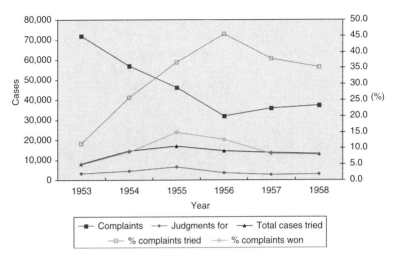

**Figure 6.1**  Workers' complaints and trials, 1953–1958.

If Tomiche was right, the crucial issue is whether the workers had easier access to the courts rather than whether they won more cases there. As it turns out, the courts generally found an almost constant proportion of original disputes in favor of workers. The courts decided, on average, that in about 10 percent of disputes the workers clearly ought to prevail.[15] Visual observation also suggests something else. The trend line of disputes won appears quite similar to the trend line of the proportion of disputes brought to court; it is simply displaced one year to the left. A regression analysis shown in table 6.2 of disputes brought to court against disputes won the previous year confirms the similarity.[16]

Tomiche was right. The new regime was more pro-labor than the previous regime, but it was more pro-labor in a very specific way. The crucial point is not whether there were more conflicts between workers and employers but whether workers were bringing more of their conflicts with employers to court. They did so because the regime had made it much cheaper to bring cases to court and it had allowed many more workers to use the courts, although at the price of curtailing the right to strike.

Workers were acting frivolously in the simple sense that they took disputes to court they had not been likely to win there in earlier years but not necessarily in a deeply normative sense. They could do this because of mechanisms contained in the new labor legislation. Before turning to the legislation I reiterate that the courts were not generally strongly pro-worker, but

**Table 6.2** Previous victories and current filings

| | |
|---|---|
| 0.048 | 0.198 |
| 0.087 | 0.367 |
| 0.15 | 0.454 |
| 0.127 | 0.379 |
| 0.081 | 0.353 |

The proportion of cases won the previous year
is the independent variable and the proportion of
complaints brought to court is the dependent variable

| Regression Output | |
|---|---|
| Constant | 0.1422434 |
| Std Err of Y Est | 0.0460188 |
| R Squared | 0.8187845 |
| No. of Observations | 5 |
| Degrees of Freedom | 3 |
| X Coefficient(s) | 2.1090932 |
| Std Err of Coef. | 0.5728594 |

they also do not appear to have become any more pro-capitalist in the years represented earlier. This may not constitute objectivity or neutrality but neither does it constitute an increased anti-worker bias.[17]

## The Labor Legislation

What was the new dispensation and why did it encourage more resort to the courts even as it discouraged strikes? On December 8, 1952 President Muhammad Najib promulgated ordinances 317, 318, and 319 dealing with individual labor contracts, the regulation of labor conflicts, and the status of labor unions respectively.[18] These laws modified the individual contract law and provided workers with a set of legal remedies for conflicts with owners so as to diminish the role of an independent trade union movement and ultimately replace it.

Ordinance 317 was written by a committee headed by a member of the Revolutionary Command Committee, ᶜAbd al-Munᶜim Amin, who was notorious with the left for chairing a summary trial in Kafr al-Dawwar at which two textile workers were condemned to death for reasons of political expediency.[19] The committee also included the director and a second official from the Labor Bureau, two prominent trade union leaders and the secretary general of the Egyptian Federation of Industry. The law had somewhat contradictory features: it made labor more expensive, which should have encouraged capital investment. Because it did so by making dismissals harder it weakened any efficiency wage effect at the same time. In other words it introduced an element of moral hazard into the factory.

The new law provided immediate and tangible benefits for the small fraction of workers in firms with more than 50 employees. Covered workers gained two weeks vacation with full pay after a year's service (Art. 20); paid holidays (Art. 24), and paid sick leave. The law forced owners to keep more and better records (Arts. 31 and 32) and also forced them to provide something like due process for infractions (Arts. 29, 30, and 31). The time, place, and manner of disciplining workers through fines or layoff were circumscribed and fines had to be used in a manner prescribed by the Ministry of Social Affairs.

Critical paragraphs of the law addressed how workers could be separated.[20] The law assumed that workers labored under an individual contract without a specific expiration clause. Article 40 explicitly forbade the employer to abrogate this implicit contract (*faskh al-ʿaqd*) without forewarning the worker and making a severance payment unless the worker was still on probation or had committed a crime such as perjury, assault, or malicious mischief, caused a serious loss, or was likely to cause one because of severe incompetence, unexplained absence of more than two weeks, drunkenness, or drug abuse on the job.[21] Strictly speaking this list defined a category of offenses meriting disciplinary separation (*fasl taʾdibi*) as opposed to contract abrogation. Legally, three different issues were involved in this paragraph: disciplinary separation, probationary separation, and contract abrogation (Hasan 56–59). In theory the new law strongly limited the right of employers to terminate workers after the probationary period for showing (from the employer's viewpoint) insufficient attention to work.

Workers who were fired without due cause were entitled an indemnity of the foregone earnings in addition to the normal severance payment. Workers in firms with more than 50 employees could seek resolution of severance pay and indemnities before a tripartite panel consisting of a labor, management, and ministry representatives (Art. 40). These key sections of the law, coupled with the increase in the probationary period, were consonant with the idea that to be successful Egyptian industry needed workers with significant experience and plant-specific skills.

Workers who had been separated for reasons not mentioned in the law retained the right to seek further damages in the courts (Art. 39). This section of the law was and remains the subject of considerable controversy. Amin ʿIzz al-Din, a prominent labor historian and official in the labor ministry who attended several private discussions about labor legislation in his official capacity, has argued that this paragraph gave employers, for the first time, the right to fire employees without excuse (Posusney 48). Allowing workers recourse to the courts was, he suggests, understood to have been derisory.[22] On April 9, 1953 Law 165 amended Ordinance 317 to eliminate that possibility. The original law had been written in neutral language that, like modern Dutch law, provided both worker and owner with redress for breaking the employment contract without a legal excuse. The amended Article 39 provided the reinstatement of workers fired for union activism and accelerated administrative and judicial redress for workers who felt they had been unjustly separated. The amended law increased pressure on owners by mandating a 50 L.E. fine for employers who did not reinstate workers when ordered to do so by the court.[23] Therefore the law criminalized behavior that had previously only been subject to civil procedures.

Ordinance 318 accompanied Ordinance 317 and provided the machinery for dispute resolution in two separate but parallel bodies to resolve disputes: a conciliation committee and an arbitration committee. The former was headed by a judge of the court of first instance; the latter by a judge of an appellate court. Both had labor, management, and ministry representatives.[24] The conciliation committee was empowered to resolve conflicts by getting the two parties to agree; the arbitration committee could exercise judicial power through a majority vote that presumably was decided by the ministry appointee (Art. 16). The law created an accelerated process that in principle should have lasted little more than six months (various articles provide time limits) and in which attorneys could not appear (Art. 18). Strikes and lockouts were forbidden under penalty of imprisonment. Criminalization of noncompliance intensified and was differentiated. Owners could be fined up to 1,000 L.E. for noncompliance with decisions and workers up to 1,000 piasters (10 L.E. [Art. 17]).

Ordinance 318 had two unusual features. First, the conciliation commission served without fees or costs for the first month of its examination of a conflict (Art. 15). Second, if the workers won their case, owners had to pay their travel and maintenance costs but workers had no similar obligation to employers (Art. 20). Consequently the costs for workers of bringing disputes to court plummeted while the costs to owners increased. In the context of Egyptian law, these laws clearly shifted bargaining power to the side of workers even if they did not provide significantly greater power to trade unions or socialize industrial assets.

The great contention over the right of factory owners to fire or lay off workers in Egypt in the 1940s and 1950s framed these laws. The basic law governing the employment relationship in Egypt defined it as an individual contract of indefinite duration and thus labor law was a species of contract law. Consequently neither party could unilaterally void a contract as long as the other party stood willing to carry out his obligations and thus employees who were ready to work could not be fired. In practice these contractual requirements remained largely theoretical before 1952 but there was considerable pressure to make them real.

The first regulation of labor contracts, Law 41/1944, introduced the concept of arbitrary firing into the Egyptian legal system (Hasan 45). Egyptian legal practice distinguishes between breaking a contract for a disputed reason and firing someone for reasons unrelated to his performance at work (Hasan 49–50). There is thus a distinction in Egyptian law between the unilateral revocation of the labor contract and dismissal without cause. The 1944 Law introduced the tripartite conciliation commission to adjudicate individual and collective conflicts and thereby eliminate some of the legal ambiguity and to resolve labor conflict.

Nevertheless until 1952 the general law governing labor was the Civil Code, which defined the individual contract in ways similar to the American tenure-at-will contract.[25] The relevant sections of the 1948 Civil Code mandated that breaking the individual contract required only the provision of due warning, which was to be specified in labor legislation. Breaking the contract without due notice was a specific example of the more general problem of arbitrary termination of a contract. In such situations the injured party had the right to receive compensation,[26] but the right arose as a tort (*darar* in Arabic) and a succeeding paragraph introduced the owner's intent into the decision about whether the breaking of the contract was arbitrary.[27]

Before 1952 these provisions about contract law meant little. Workers left jobs without notice and were certainly fired without any recourse before 1952 and suits appear to have been rare. This is why we can easily assimilate the individual labor contract to what is known in the United States as the "contract at will" (Posner; Epstein; Freed and Polsby) where employers can fire workers for any reason or for no reason and employees can quit for any reason or no reason at all.

In Egypt, as in most Western European countries, the underlying relationship between employer and worker was not one of "contract at will." To the contrary, the terms of employment for many union workers in Europe and Egypt derive from labor legislation to a far greater degree than is true of the United States where collective bargaining has been more important. In these countries, "the individual labor contract remains the formal foundation of the employment relationship. This contract usually does not exist as a physical document, but it has a very real existence as a legal concept and embodies any understandings between the individual employer and employee together will all provisions of law and collective agreement that are applicable to the particular position" (McPherson and Meyers 5). In Europe, unlike the United States, resort to the courts is common and more than a century of institutional development has led to a specialized court system to address such issues that the United States lacks (McPherson and Meyers 2; Davis [1929]; Cole [1941]). Consequently the state can profoundly change the relative bargaining position of labor and management by administratively amending the relevant regulations.

Besides contract law and rudimentary labor law, labor–management relations were also affected by body of law regulating firms in the public interest. These laws are usually ignored in discussions of labor relations although their existence forms the core of the notion that war planning brought "Keynesian" macroeconomic demand management to Egypt. The earliest regulation limiting the separation of workers was Military Order 75/1940 that limited the right of employees to leave their jobs and of employers to terminate their employment. The decree, issued in the wake of the declaration of martial law at the outbreak of World War II, explicitly proclaimed that it was not labor legislation.[28] It affected employment directly because it provided criminal and civil penalties for any employee leaving regulated enterprises and even more severe penalties for inciting someone else to leave. It also forbade businesses to cease operating without a license from the Defense Ministry although it did note the condition of zero profitability as allowing (but not requiring) such a license to be issued. It forbade firing more than 10 employees at a time and required all disputes in such firms to submit to arbitration (Ministry of Social Affairs 78–79). A ministerial decision of November 25, 1940 listed the sectors considered regulated public utilities: public transport (including the railroads and trams), concerns that dealt with pharmaceuticals or chemicals, firms that prepared, transported, or exported cotton, firms in the fuel sector (including gas and electricity production or transmission), firms producing textiles for clothing, concerns engaged in food production or preparation, building materials, and a few other areas of the domestic economy (including the waterworks).

The extensive efforts of many Egyptian governments in regulating labor–management relations suggests that the postrevolutionary laws limiting the right of employers to fire were not the reflection of the non-capitalist ethos of the workers (Beinin [1989] 74, fn. 8). They developed out of existing Egyptian regulatory practices that aimed to affect both labor and owners. In addition to providing a judicial forum for workers (as well as increased responsibility for the Labor Department) that is presented as a liability in recent accounts (Posusney) did not appear to be so before 1952. Between 1945 and 1952, Egyptians assessed willingness of parliamentary governments to enact such legislation as one way to assess their progressive nature. "The injustice of a capitalist government has reached such an extent," wrote the left Wafdist editor Muhammad Mandur in 1946 "that a government such as the Sidqi government is not ashamed to obstruct labor legislation such as the conciliation and arbitration bill..."[29] Employers had, a decade earlier, made strenuous efforts not only to avoid recognition of unions but to ensure that labor received the most limited recognition on government bodies.[30]

Workers had wanted to limit the right of employers to fire them. In 1942, Salim Sulaiman, writing in the newspaper *Shubra* that generally expressed the ideas of the left-leaning Shubra al-Khaima textile workers' union, complained about factory owners who closed plants that were insufficiently profitable. "What crime is it of the workers," he wrote, "if the owners of a company decided that the profit on five pounds was to be 40 piasters and lately have decided to close factories as long as a pound does not bring in 10 piasters... thereby idling the plant and impoverishing the workers."[31] When an Egyptian labor court followed similar reasoning after the coup in awarding a victory to workers in a conflict it was both implementing long-held legal norms and the example of the English political economy. For example, in a dispute at the Anton Shusha textile firm in Zaytun, the conciliation commission decided to award the workers what amounted to the "bad spinning" penalties that English workers enjoyed 50 years earlier. In the commission's language: when workers' wages declined due to "the poor condition of the machinery or their being antiquated then the problem is external to the willingness of the workers [to work] and it is only fair to compensate the worker by raising his wage."[32] The court weighed the intent of the owners and determined they had shown "tyrannical behavior." The words of the explanatory materials echo the 1948 Civil Code:

> If the interest that impels the possessor of a right to employ it is so small that it is not commensurate with the hardship suffered by another because of it being sought then the insignificance of the interest can be taken to imply that doing harm is the real intention of the possessor in the employment of his right.[33]

These definitions introduced by both regulation and court decisions were consequential because they denied investors the ability to reap economies of scale that resulted in reduced employment. More capital or more efficient structuring of the labor process by management can only increase the return to investors by a fractional amount while the loss of employment incurred by an individual worker is, at least in the short term, catastrophic for him or her. They also often result in higher wages for those workers who survive the restructuring with their jobs intact.

Owners who suffered severe material losses or had zero profitability could fire workers, but such firms had to show real losses rather than the opportunity costs of larger profits foregone even though there could no longer be any argument that the exigencies of war required inefficient firms maintain production.[34] At the dawn of the Nasser period, the appellate courts further limited the rights of owners to let workers go when a firm was reorganized. The owner was expected to retrain the worker as long as he was faithfully performing his job because "the right of the owner in organization and administration is limited insofar as he cannot touch the basic rights guaranteed to the work by labor legislation."[35] The only remaining period during which employers could fire workers at will was during the probationary period, which the new law defined as a maximum of a year. These transformations in labor regulation were designed to encourage firms to choose workers whose labor would be of high quality and to substitute machinery for increasingly expensive labor.

### How Did Investors Respond?

If the aim of the new legislation was to induce firms to invest more in fixed capital, it did not succeed. Employers objected vehemently to the new labor legislation and especially to the amendment of Paragraph 39 insofar as it forced them to re-instate union activists:

> Until the passage of this provision, Egyptian employers enjoyed almost complete freedom to dismiss workers for any reason, and they viewed with alarm any procedure which provided for interference by government officials and for judicial review of their prerogatives in this area. Many employers at first thought the intent of this provision was to deny them the right to fire workers even for just cause or to deny them the right to release workers whose services were no longer needed. They pointed to some early court cases as evidence of such intent. This fear was strengthened by the early practice of the lower courts in granting practically all requests for stay of dismissal . . . This fear has diminished as a result of later court decisions . . . .[36]

The new law introduced a profound change for employers because it was the first time any regulation of dismissals occurred. It therefore made the state a significantly more intrusive actor within the firm and allowed it to use the workers complaints to discipline owners. In addition, as the Little Report noted, employers in 1952 were also still constrained by the martial law regulation of 1940 and were therefore "not permitted to stop or reduce their activity without permission of the Minister of Supply. Therefore a layoff, shortening the hours of work, or going out of business is illegal without government approval" (Little 159). The consultants believed that the post-1952 legislation provided a legal basis for workers to contest the layoffs (up to 10 percent of the workforce) that had been permitted under the old regulation (Little 159). When individual employers, such as Robert Gasche, protested that "the single factor most responsible for increasing the costs of production was the existing labor regime and, in particular, the obstacles that the government had erected to reducing employment levels" these were the features he had in mind (cited in Vitalis [1996] 206).[37] Both the legislative and judicial language explicitly made maintaining employment a higher priority than maximizing the return on capital and thus provides reason to believe that Gasche was accurately reporting his beliefs rather than a strategic version created to affect government decisions. This suggests investors reacted to the new regime with caution.

Entrepreneurs could be cautious even if, unlike workers, they were not hustled before drumhead courts and executed. It can hardly have been reassuring for capitalists to have seen dozens of men like themselves tried for political crimes committed in the old regime and given death sentences (later commuted), deprived of political rights, or subjected to the confiscation of their property.[38]

Beyond, complaints, rumors abounded that capital flight was underway. Discussions of the need to regulate private holding of foreign currency assumed that capital was leaving the country either through the banknote exports, gold exports, or the issuance of false bills of lading (Saqqaf [1954] 158–163). Egyptians in the textile business had become familiar with these techniques thanks to Italian entrepreneurs who exported capital to Egypt from Fascist Italy by using them during the 1930s (Eman 35). One widely circulated story at the time was that companies were increasing dividends significantly enough to diminish the book value of companies and these stories centered on two of the largest industrial conglomerates, the Misr and the ᶜAbbud groups, were engaged in just such maneuvers by 1956 (Owen [1989] 371).

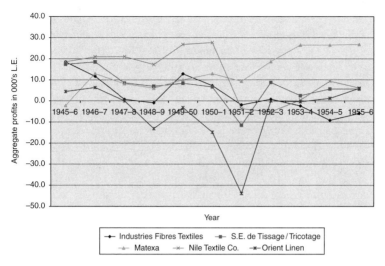

**Figure 6.2** Profits of Egyptian textile firms.
*Source*: Tignor [1989].

We can hazard a better guess at investor responses than listening to their complaints and retelling their rumors simply by asking whether they required higher rates of return afterward to justify what they perceived as riskier investments. The junta came to power just as the economy was slowing and the profits of private firms, especially in the textile industry, had slumped. As shown in figure 6.2, 1952 marks the bottom of the postwar slump and profits and employment could be expected to continue to decline for another year or so.[39]

What would have been clear to most capitalists, however, was that plans for the kind of capital spending Naggar had proposed and that the new government foresaw in building a High Dam at Aswan, electrifying Egyptian villages, providing better health care and education to all Egyptians, and creating the national resources to maintain a war footing with Israel would be far too expensive to be paid for out of then-current tax revenues.[40] Contemporary economic theory tells political rulers that borrowing is as good as taxing but the received version of recent history in mid-twentieth-century Egypt had a different moral: the imposition of foreign rule for unpaid debts. If neither borrowing nor current revenues sufficed, then only high levels of taxation remained to finance the various schemes.

We can use the stock market as a gauge of investor confidence in the new government. Long-term sovereign debt is the least risky investment available and it frequently provides a benchmark to assess how risky other assets are. I have therefore used the interest rate on the 30-year bond issued in 1943 as a proxy for a risk-free Egyptian investment and compared it with financial instruments that include the risk of owning fixed assets in the Egyptian economy (stocks). There are many problems with the data, which are suggestive not conclusive.[41] I have been able to find relevant information to calculate portfolio yields for three companies between 1943 and 1952: the Cairo Water company, the Alexandria Cotton Pressing Company, and the Kafr Zayyat Oil Company. Because ownership of specific assets is riskier than ownership of the state debt, we expect that the dividend yield on stocks will be higher than on government bonds and leave aside the issue of total return including capital gains.[42]

In figure 6.3, I compare information for the period during World War II (when German forces operated in the Western desert and high returns should have been required to induce investors to hold shares or public debt) with the dividend premium in September 1952 in three important firms in three crucial

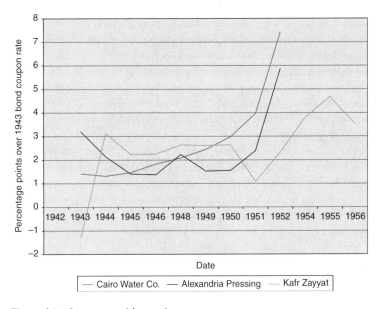

**Figure 6.3** Investment risk premium.
*Source*: Egyptian Stock Exchange Yearbooks, 1947–1958.

sectors of the economy relative to the risk-free yield.[43] In 1952 portfolio investors demanded a premium over government bonds twice as large as they had in the preceding decade, more than during the slump after the Korean War and more even than they had during the depths of World War II. The premium rose because shares were selling for a fraction of their former values not because dividends were higher. If portfolio investors were not interested in holding shares of industrial firms, at least one of which (the water company) did business under state regulation, it is hard to imagine that investors would be interested in making fixed investments in the economy without very special inducements from the state.

On the available evidence the labor legislation of the new government had a negative impact on investment for three reasons: it weakened the perceived link between wages and firing as a mechanism to increase worker effort, it signaled an increased willingness of the government to intrude into the internal workings of firms, and (at the same time) it signaled that the political environment for large firms operating under state protection was on less solid ground than in the past.

The new labor legislation succeeded as regulation to the degree that it was promptly enacted and comprehensive. It also succeeded to a degree at least commensurate with the legislation of the old regime about cotton. It accomplished the aim of creating a new coalition linking together state actors, organizational leaders (the trade union hierarchy), and the spontaneous activity of individuals in society (workers who filed grievances). To the degree that its aim was to channel the protest of workers it certainly was a success. It affected investment decisions, but not in the way its framers planned. The labor legislation shows a high degree of government competence in drafting new regulation and putting them into practice with new social partners even if not in using the legislation to induce a shift in the strategies of those who were the objects of the new legislation but not partners in its drafting.

# CHAPTER 7

# Efficiency Wages, Moral Economies, and Involution

L ike land reform, the new labor legislation conferred immediate political benefits on the new regime by providing it with potential social support (Beinin and Lockman; Bianchi; Posusney). The economic discourse that surrounded the legislation suggested, as well, that the particular choice of instruments to attain these goals would induce higher levels of capital investment. That the labor legislation did not attain this goal is obvious, but it had other goals beyond the search to win political allies through the provision of rents or the attempt to affect investment decisions. The new legislation strengthened the role of adult men in labor markets and had some important effects on the markets for adult and child labor. Although it did not transform the structure of Egypt's factor endowments, raising adult wages and limiting competition from children was also an important goal of the new government and we can see these policies at play in the labor legislation.

To look more carefully at these issues allows us to look beyond the issues of wages and labor cost to a more fundamental issue: the links between efficiency, development, and child labor. Industrialization may require not only that labor be paid more than a market-clearing wage but the creation of markets within which such wages can be paid may require the elimination of the most efficient of all labor markets: that for the labor of children.

Even the most vocal defender of the Egyptian labor movement observes, "(m)ost blue-collar industrial and service employees ... did exert effort, and apparently believed that they were productive even if their efficiency was below international standards" (Posusney 17). In other words, Egyptian labor productivity is below some international norm, and the workers make choices about effort. This is part of the larger argument in comparative politics about labor cost and productivity. Labor historians argue that low productivity is best understood as a form of resistance to market mechanisms and indicates the presence of a moral economy paradigm among workers that may be specific to Egypt or at least the Third World.

Were Egyptian workers really exceptional either in their distaste for market relations or in fending off declining wages? Rigorously implemented neoclassical economic policies should indeed have led to declining wages to clear labor markets so that no unemployment remained. Yet is it surprising that Egyptian industrial workers, like industrial workers around the world, successfully resisted the decline of nominal (money) wages?[1] Egyptian workers were not exceptional and it is not surprising that even in Egypt money wages tended to remain stable even during periods of economic downturn because money wages rarely decrease to the point of clearing markets.

The point of departure for Keynes from neoclassical economics was that in the most developed capitalist economies wages were not sufficiently downwardly elastic to clear markets. Why should wages have been more elastic where labor markets were presumably less efficient and the supply of skilled labor lower? In this limited sense—that urban and industrial money wages were not flexible enough to clear the market in advance—there is no puzzle to be explained in Egypt if markets did not clear. It would be far more surprising if nominal wages were so flexible.

Of more enduring interest is that the evidence adduced to support the moral economy argument suggests that workers can vary their effort and that, in turn, suggests that Egyptian workers—like those in Europe and the United States—may well live in a "Keynesian" world described by theories of efficiency wages.[2] Exploring the idea of efficiency wages and moral economy throws some light on the situation of adult male workers and it also unexpectedly suggests that markets for the labor of children and adults differ systematically.[3] Adults, it appears, live in a moral economy and children in a neoclassical one.

The particular model of moral economy and efficiency wages that I find useful models "labor contracts as partial gift exchange." In this model, workers exert more than minimum effort, employers pay more than minimum pay, and affective ties among workers prevent the employer from treating workers individually (Akerlof [1982] 544). This is a plausible underpinning as well as a powerful model for efficiency wages, dual labor markets, and equity theory (Akerlof [1984]; Akerlof and Yellen). The experience of industrial wages in the American South casts light on the Egyptian experience just as did Southern experience with field production. Although industrial wages in the American South were 30–50 percent lower than in the North, industrial development in the South did not proceed with the rapidity that neoclassical theories suggest. Nor did Southern wages drop to levels that cleared labor markets there. On the contrary, in the "underdeveloped" American South in the 1920s, we observe

> the persistence of wage rates in the face of excess labor, well before the emergence of the institutions commonly held responsible for this state of affairs. The South in the 1920s had virtually no unions, no welfare system, no minimum wage laws, and no extensive public sector employment. Yet when real wages peaked during the postwar boom of 1918–1920, it proved extremely difficult for employers to bring them down thereafter. (Wright 626)

Employers had difficulty reducing wages because "workers who had grown up in the mills and committed themselves to mill work as adults had also developed some fairly firm notions of equity and fair dealing … cuts in the money wages could be counted on to generate a cohesive response because they were taken as acts of class warfare, violations of the 'moral economy of labor relations'" (Wright 627).

We do not have a clear description of the mechanisms through which workers resisted cuts in money wages. It is possible that workers were all sufficiently angry to respond identically so that no strategic calculations interrupted spontaneous anticapitalist collective action (Posusney). The efficacy—let alone the existence—of such a mechanism over decades seems unlikely. In place of uniform anger, Wright proposes that the American workforce was able to resist cuts in nominal wages because it was made up primarily of adult men rather than younger women or children of both sexes.

The social networks of men, their connections through endogamous marriage, informal violence, and the better-understood (at least formally) relationships of frequent interaction that make up community, are more likely to be relevant here than formal institutions. Men may be more likely to cooperate with each other directly than in support of their children, their wives, or their sisters than can their children, wives, or sisters. Mechanisms of cooperation through familial and local structure made it possible both for men to resist cuts in their nominal wages and to monitor their own provision of effort to maintain the moral economy bargain.

Before going any further we might ask if there is any evidence that Egyptian men, before or after 1952, were being paid efficiency wages

**Table 7.1**  Agricultural and industrial wages

| Year | | Men | Women | Boys | |
|------|---|-----|-------|------|---|
| 1937–1940 | | | | | |
| | Agricultural wage | 3 | 2 | 1.5 | |
| | Food industry | 9.85 | 5.45 | 2.79 | |
| | Construction | 8.25 | 3.75 | 1.54 | |
| | Textile | 6.63 | 5.24 | 1.44 | |
| | Contracting | 12.37 | 12.57 | 2.61 | |
| | Other industry | 10.37 | 7.19 | 2.19 | |
| | Average | | | | 7.76 |
| 1943 | | | | | |
| | Agricultural wage | 6.3 | 3.9 | 3 | |
| | Average | | | | 12.86 |
| 1945 | | | | | |
| | Agricultural wage | 9.3 | 5.7 | 4.6 | |
| | Average | | | | 16.43 |

*Notes*: Wages are piasters per day.
*Source*: Mahmoud Anis 753, 803, 805 with underlying citations to surveys by government agencies.

(see table 7.1). Efficiency wages are necessarily those above the level that would clear the market and thus eliminate any involuntary unemployment. The existence of efficiency wages, like any quality premium, both draws workers into the factory and provides employers, as long as they can easily fire, with a trigger mechanism to maintain high levels of productivity. Efficiency wages, Keynesian economics, and moral economy arguments all require that workers be paid more than the market clearing wage.

Egyptian economists in the middle of the twentieth century knew about efficiency wages, in contradistinction to the arguments about East Asia discussed in earlier chapters, that wages in Egypt were too low. In addition to general arguments following the work of Alfred Marshall, specific studies of Egyptian industry followed the same vein. Writing in 1948, Gamal Eldin Said argued that besides illiteracy and low levels of general knowledge, Egyptian industry was especially hampered by high levels of turnover and hourly pay schemes that generated perverse incentives (Said 499–503). William Carson's study of Mehallah al-Kubra in 1952 also suggested aligning pay so that it would provide incentives compatible with increased production, allowing an independent union to engage in collective bargaining, and ensuring dramatically greater job security so as to reduce turnover (Carson 121–122).

Writing in 1948, Ali El-Gritly more specifically asserted that Egyptian wages were too low in relation to the "irreducible minimum required for maintaining efficiency" and that the range of wages between industrial and agricultural labor was extremely narrow (Gritly 529). Gritly, who was chosen to be a member of the National Production Council after the 1952 coup, argued that wages reflected both low real marginal productivity (531) and the monopoly power of employers that kept the price of labor below marginal productivity (535). This argument may reflect its Marshallian origins as much as Egyptian empirical reality since we have no idea what the marginal productivity of firms in Egypt was at the time (Marshall 569, 703). Nevertheless Gritly clearly was preoccupied by a situation similar to that described by Ramseyer about Japan: individual firms made decisions that led them to pay wages too low to evoke the quality of efforts necessary for industrialization. He correctly identified low productivity in the Egyptian textile industry with a fundamental problem of insufficient effort by workers: "where less looms per worker are used than in comparison with Japan, Lancaster or the U.S.A." (534). Gritly therefore proposed state regulation of wages to increase the share of labor in national income at the expense of capital. He expected such a shift to force employers to use labor more efficiently and he also believed it would increase domestic demand (especially for industrial products). Because the bulk of the effect would occur in industries already subject to public or private monopoly, Gritly believed inflationary pressure on prices to decrease if profit margins were reduced (535).

Gritly's impressionistic observations highlight the importance of the issue to contemporary policy-makers. Although the data is not very good there is some useful evidence indicating that industrial employers already paid unskilled adults wages above the market-clearing level, although perhaps not altogether high enough to evoke the performance they desired. Table 7.1 provides some support for the idea of efficiency wages with an unexpected nuance. The uppermost row of the table gives the average daily wage in piasters for unskilled agricultural labor and successive rows give average wage rates for selected industries. The aggregation is extremely crude in comparison to the kind of data available for the United States or Japan at the same time. Nevertheless, the data in column 2 suggests that within the textile industry men received at least twice the daily agricultural wage and that even in construction where the skills would be quite similar to those in agriculture wages were significantly higher than in agriculture. Because the data provides separate estimates of wages for women and children, we can pursue the argument a bit more deeply. Women received, on average, lower wages in agriculture than men. Because women's contracting wages are so high, the dispersion of women's wages is even greater than men's, but generally women appear to have received wages closer to their market-clearing rate than did men. Children's wages (column 4) show the least dispersion; children never appear to have received more than double what they were paid in agriculture and in important cases (including textiles and construction) children received essentially the same wage.

The table suggests that, even before World War II, Egyptian employers paid efficiency wages to adult men. Therefore the basis for a "moral economy" existed among adult men in industry. Women were not generally paid efficiency wages and barely participated in that moral economy. Children, distinctively, lived in the neoclassical economy: their wages in industry were nearly identical to their wages in agriculture. These findings concur with all of the theories of efficiency wages, dual labor markets, and moral economies. Children are the most completely unskilled of all labor, the supply of child labor was wholly elastic, and children are the least likely of all workers to be capable of varying their effort.[4] Thus although Egyptian employers paid efficiency wages to a fraction of their workforce they also had a significant workforce to which they paid market-clearing rates.

Child labor impeded the possibilities discussed by Naggar, Gritly, and Luhayta that Egypt could undergo a "big push" toward industrialization where higher wages would evoke more intense labor, create new markets for domestic products, and consequently induce private capital investment or at least absorb public investment. This rosy scenario did not characterize the Egyptian economy in the early 1950s because the labor force was still largely illiterate and exhibited low productivity. Recognizing that children competed with adults in some sectors of the economy also helps us understand the Egyptian labor legislation after 1952 more clearly.

Legislation changed the ways in which children competed with adults in the labor market by regulating the probationary period. Law 317 defined a probationary period during which workers over 17 years of age could be separated at the discretion of the employer as comprising two six-month intervals. Workers under 17 years of age were liable to serve a probationary period of up to two years. If indeed this marked an increase in the probationary period from three months then it did amount to a "significant setback to workers" (Posusney 48). Yet the explanatory materials for Law 317 describe the relevant paragraph as simply organizing the probationary period so that employers could not abuse it.

Because Posusney describes the probationary period as one in which workers were not entitled to full pay, I believe she has (quite possibly in accord with Egyptian practice during the time she did field work) conflated the probationary period (*fatrat al-ikhtibar*) with the training period (*muddat al-tamrin*). Ministerial Decree 451 of December 3, 1943 defined a training period for adult manual laborers of three months (and six months for intellectual workers) during which they were not entitled to the pay of regular workers.[5] The same decree allowed employers to extend the training period to two years for workers under 17 years of age.

Before 1952, the training period was a device to ensure that changes in contract law did not interfere with children routinely receiving lower pay than adults for similar work.[6] Not coincidentally the earliest legal reference to training occurs in the child labor legislation of 1933. Expressly prohibiting children from working in a variety of industries, it also recognized that "accepting adolescents into a factory or workshop for the purpose of training or technical education is not considered employment within the meaning of this provision" (Ministry of Social Affairs 5).

If, in practice, Law 317 did what Posusney believes—extended a trial period at less than full wages—it marked the first time in Egyptian history that children, when hired, did not receive wages that were legally lower than those of adults and thus eroded their economic advantage. When the 1959 labor law reduced the probationary period to three months and no longer distinguished between adults and adolescents, the hitherto legally enshrined "advantage" of children as recipients of lower wages in industry disappeared completely. In terms of labor markets and culture in the early Nasser years adult men managed, with the aid of the state, to drive away children from the formal sectors of the economy.

In chapter 3 I discussed the ways in which the demand for the labor of children and the acquisition of literacy are inversely related. I also pointed out that industrialization often increases the demand for child labor even if economic development seems to require an increase in literacy in society taken as a whole. In Egypt these two trends interacted during the first half of the twentieth century so that children worked in the fields but they also worked in factories and literacy increased at a glacial rate.

### A Case Study

It may seem far-fetched to suggest that the theme of regulation and quality affected industrialization either directly or though the efficiency wages. It is possible to follow out precisely these themes to understand how, despite significant and effective government regulation, involution occurred in one industry that attracted Egyptian capital. Egyptian economists and others engaged in policy making had empirical reasons to believe that without increasing wages, industrialization would be doomed. Most research on Egyptian industrialization focuses on spinning and weaving but they were neither the only nor even the most successful areas for industrial investment. Cotton ginning and pressing were among the earliest areas in which Egyptians invested in industry and they employed tens of thousands of workers. Although ginning was the necessary service through which the raw seed cotton was transformed into a commodity for global trade, uniform fiber, it is easy to overlook its importance.

Cotton ginning is an activity of theoretical and practical interest because seed or raw cotton is what economists call a joint product. The peculiarity of joint products is that the production process creates a "waste" stream of valuable and saleable goods. Consequently depending on the relative prices of the markets for the intended "original" good and the "waste by-product" it may be that for one or the other product there is literally no cost of production. With the cost of production equal to zero, a very difficult collective-action problem ensues in which producers can drive each other out of business. One classic example is the production of meat and hides (for leather), but separating oil-bearing seeds from cotton is clearly another one.

Egyptian investors rapidly dominated large sections of the highly competitive ginning industry, but ginning experienced a severe form of involution rather than development. Despite the efforts of private individuals and frequent attempts by the state to intervene, the sector proved highly resistant to rent-seeking, remained of low profitability, and did not attract new equipment. To the contrary, over time gin owners substituted cheap labor for expensive capital and, as in the case of many field tasks, discovered that the cheapest labor was that of children.

Policies to spur investment in industry in Egypt in the 1920s and 1930s were often directly concerned with the ginning and oilseed industries both because of local Egyptian investment and because they appeared to be immediate "forward linkages" from agricultural production to industry. These policies had to balance the demands of investment in reputation that required strict biological controls over seed and the perception that such controls were constantly enforced with the appropriate scale of investment for ginning and seed crushing consistent with profitability. Both investors and the state sought, within the confines of the basic agricultural policies of reputation investment, to meet growing consumer demand for edible oil and oil-based products.

In an apparent anomaly politicians associated with landowning interests supported the creation of cartels that enhanced capital investment and politicians associated with the Egyptian Federation of Industry evidently opposed such policies. Egyptians were aware of the collective-action problems involved but finding solutions to them was more difficult than investing in reputation for the crop as a whole because of the intense competition in the ginning industry and because ginners and planters had fewer reasons to cooperate than did planters and spinners. Unfortunately as it became hard to ensure profits to higher levels of capital investment, the particular path of "forward linkage" industrialization in Egypt reinforced the demand for child labor.

The problems that faced the ginning and oil pressing industries were widely known and, like the reputation of the fiber crop, openly discussed. These discussions, too, have largely disappeared from the academic reviews of policy making or the Egyptian economy before 1952. The nationalist party in Egypt, the Wafd, was the dominant political party in Egypt between 1919 and 1954, but the existing literature ignores its domestic policy and occasionally questions whether it had an internal domestic policy.[7] The Wafd was the party committed to government price supports for cotton, and it was also the party most committed to a strategy of encouraging rural industry. In most accounts of Egyptian political and social history the Wafd is portrayed as the relatively transparent representative of social forces and appears to have no institutional life of its own. Its huge popularity is alleged to have been based on an inexhaustible reservoir of nationalist sentiment and very little on its program. As the most complete study of the Wafd puts it, even as late as 1935, "there was no sharp demarcation between the Wafd as a nationalist movement and the Wafd as a political party."[8] This is, I think, not correct. Just as Wafdists played a significant role in developing policies of investment in reputation, price supports, and government purchases of cotton, they also played an important role in creating a ginning cartel to encourage capital investment in the industry.

The cottonseed pressing industry originated in 1889 when the Egyptian Oil and Soap Company was formed. Initially Egyptians found it far more difficult to penetrate markets for edible oil than for high-quality fiber and thus in the late nineteenth century seed was more commonly exported than pressed oil.[9] A customs arrangement was reached with the Ottoman government and Egyptian oil exports gained market share abroad. The collapse of the Ottoman Empire in World War I reversed the situation and Egyptian oilseed producers feared competition from Turkey in the Egyptian edible oil market in the postwar period because Turkish producers had access to cheaper (and noncompetitive) seed. Egyptians also found themselves bidding up the price for seed in a competitive international market.[10] Oil and soap producers were acutely conscious of the price advantage they gained by having copious supplies of inexpensive raw materials available locally and of the possibility for expansion in a growing local and regional economy.

Oilseed industrialists desired to end restrictions on the import of seed but were unable to do so. Ginning and oilseed production accounted for a significant proportion of the Egyptian industrial plant at the time and one of the largest firms engaged in making oil appears to have been steadily profitable through at least the two decades before World War II.[11] Oil (and associated soap) production employed several thousand workers and they made relatively high wages in Egypt although they were not numerous, for only 1,100 people worked in oil extraction firms (Luhayta [1946b]).

In 1935, at a mass meeting organized by the Wafd in Cairo, Ibrahim ʿAbd al-Hadi argued explicitly in favor of government policies to aid the edible oil-related industries:

It is exported in large quantities, especially to Europe, and we wish that Egyptian capital participated in this industry, a participation that would conduce to its Egyptianization.

Egypt was uniquely situated in the international market for raw cottonseed; although a small producer of fiber, Egypt was the dominant supplier of seed in global export markets.[12] Despite producing large quantities of cotton seed, Egypt was not an important exporter of the associated oil in a rapidly changing global market. Egypt exported well over 11,000 tons of oil for most of the 1930s but the major oil exporters by 1936 were the United Kingdom (obviously re-exporting oil from imported seed), Brazil, and China.[13]

Why did it prove so difficult for Egyptians to move from producing a raw material for export to producing a more finished product? A paradox of Egyptian political economy was that although there had long been excess ginning and crushing capacity inside Egypt there was also insufficient capacity for Egypt to become an important exporter. Excess capacity ginning existed because entry into the industry was easy, and because there was a tight world market for cottonseed and derived products, entry was attractive to would-be Egyptian industrialists. To enter global markets would have required a very significant increase in capacity.[14] Crushers, however, could not rely on sufficiently large throughputs of seed to be internationally competitive. The 1916 prohibition on importing raw cotton into Egypt made it impossible to augment domestic seed production by purchases from abroad. Some other large cotton producers enacted similar legislation and these laws were clearly attempts to regulate relations between growers, ginners, and oil crushers.[15] As soon as the law was passed local business interests, both in textiles and oil production, protested it.[16]

Egyptian industrialists were initially in a less favorable position with regard to global markets than were cotton growers. There was an intense conflict over prices and seed between ginners and crushers. Because an efficient international market for seed export existed, ginners were not obliged to sell directly to the crushers although the crushers were obliged to buy from the local ginners.[17] There were complaints that the ginners sold to exporters in Alexandria rather than to crushers in Kafr al-Zayyat and that the price of domestic seed was further increased by the existing tariff structure of the Egyptian State Railways.[18]

There were prolonged periods of expansion and contraction, and the number of gins tended steadily to increase. At the turn of the century there were 105 establishments with 3,521 gins, about a third of which were owned by local Egyptian or Syrian residents.[19] The industry employed then some 25,000.[20] In 1938 there were 119 ginning establishment with 6,406 gins of which 105 factories (5,852 gins) were active. Some five million Egyptian pounds was invested in the industry in both large, modern plants and small, worn-out dilapidated ones. The largest ginning firm was owned by a Bank Misr company.[21]

Contrary to the conventional view that capital-intensive production drives small firms out of business, however, it was the small worn-out gins that provided "unfair" competition to the large modern plants. With low overhead they could (especially when the cotton price was depressed) cut costs far below those needed to make the large gins minimally profitable. The gin owners were incapable on their own of creating a cartel to raise the price for ginning. Without help from the state it was far too expensive to create the administrative machinery required to police hundreds of factories spread across Egypt in regard to the prices they charged.

Here and elsewhere in the production of cotton it is apparent that low wages and low productivity inhibit industrialization. There is good reason to believe that the failure to mechanize the cotton harvest in Soviet Central Asia—along lines that had already occurred in California—was due to labor productivity that was, even in 1953, lower than in Egypt (Pomfret 184). The idea, so prominent in the development literature, that mechanization is a form of improved efficiency or that the state can readily tweak incentives to make it so is not only clearly a myth but is known to be so from the long history of Soviet experience in Central Asia where machinery was supplied as a free good but where its use also imposed a quality penalty on growers (Pomfret).[22]

By 1935, firms engaged in the oil processing industry as well as in the ginning industry found themselves caught in the toils of the dilemma of joint production. For example, to meet their contractual obligations to provide cottonseed cake to consumers the companies were obliged to produce more edible oil than the home market could support and then to cut prices to move the oil off the shelves.[23] Rural industrialists began to long for the creation of a cartel:

> Cet état de choses donna lieu a une concurrence déstastreuse entre les presses qui aboutit pour le bien commun à une entente entre les différentes huileries sûr une saine politique de production et de vente.[24]

With joint products, regulation is not required to gain information but to preserve the provision of a valuable good or service. Just as they had done with the creation of a futures market for fiber, private parties had arranged contractual relations to resolve some of the problems of the value of the seed that dropped to the bottom of the gin.[25] The entry of the government into regulation of fiber quality had had an unexpected consequence for the ginning and pressing industries. Whereas at the turn of the twentieth century the provision of seed was often tied to contractual obligations for ginning, when private companies moved out of the provision of seed, price competition for seed as an input intensified and gins had to pay the going rate.

What did the Wafd do in 1936 to resolve this tremendously difficult problem with a variety of interests tugging in different directions? It appears they resolved the issue by allowing ginners and oil producers to share profits at the expense of the growers. This is a surprising outcome given the conventional image of the Wafd as the straightforward instrument of the large landowners. It suggests some higher degree of cooperation between the Wafd and the Egyptian Federation of Industries than is usually taken to be the case. It may also be testimony to the relative unimportance of the legislature in making laws rather than blocking them given the majority of large landowners on the relevant committees.[26]

The EFI created a Chamber of Ginning Establishments and in 1936 began negotiations with the government according to Ali Al-Gritly.[27] Such negotiations could have begun under the Ministry of ᶜAli Mahir (January 30 – May 9, 1936) but is more likely that it began under the Wafd ministry of Al-Nahas, which began May 9 given that Nahas's Minister of Trade and Industry, ᶜAbd al-Salam Jumᶜah, had shown special concern for the industry at the 1935 Congress. Certainly it was the Wafd government that showed the "moral support" (in Gritly's words) necessary to establish a cartel agreement because an agreement for Upper Egypt was signed on May 14, 1937 while the Wafd was still in office.[28] The cartel arrangement was designed to ensure that no individual ginner would chisel on the arrangement designed to increase the price of ginning and to retain relative shares of the market for existing businesses. The agreement in 1937 and a second one covering Lower Egypt signed in 1938 fixed a floor for the price of ginning, assigned quotas based on installed capacity (thus benefiting larger establishments), and taxed members to compensate "firms operating in districts where non-members charge rates below those fixed by the cartel, or where other members fail to honour their pledge."[29] Compensation was also to paid to "any member who fails to attain the quota assigned to him because cotton-growers and dealers in his area find it more advantageous to send their cotton to be ginned in non-member ginneries situated elsewhere."[30]

The expansion of the ginning industry had an important social consequence: it increased the demand for child labor. Poorly capitalized firms competed efficiently with those that had far more modern equipment by using the cheapest possible labor: children. When Macara visited Egypt in 1911, he was impressed by the "antiquated methods in use" relative to American practice and by the unwillingness to invest in more modern technology (such as suction pipes) by the European firms. Gin owners, he was told, substituted cheap labor for expensive capital. Macara did not expect child labor to continue for long especially given "that wages in Egypt have considerably advanced and will still further be raised, especially when schooling becomes more general, and the vast amount of child labour ceases" (International Cotton Federation [1912] 159).

What confounded Macara's expectations was the concern of growers and shippers with the quality or reputation of Egyptian cotton. Consequently ginners also had to be concerned with the grade of cotton they produced. "Ginning," as one handbook expressed it "greatly influences the trade by its relationship to the grade of cotton insofar as the cleanliness and uniformity of the cotton after ginning" (Ahmad and Hafiz 48). Feeding the gins required that the operators, squatting on their heels, "as their sole task pick foreign matter out that was found in the raw cotton" (Sidqi 273). This kind of work, like much at the gins, in the words of one observer considered work in the gins was totally unskilled ("n'exige aucune connaissance speciale … le fellah le moins instruit et le moins habile peut donc entrer comme ouvrier dans une usine d'egrenage" [Vallet 93]). The evidence is largely anecdotal but it appears that children were preferred for this work for much of the first half of the twentieth century, but that later women came to play a more significant role (Sidqi 273). It is difficult to estimate the total amount of child labor in the ginning establishments but it appears that at least one child was employed at each gin. Thus at one establishment, 150 boys between the ages of 9 and 13 worked at the gins. With some 6,000 ginning machines there must have been at least that many children in the factory workforce. Children were preferred by employers because their wages were one-half to one-third of adults on whose wages they exerted downward pressure (Vallet 94). At any rate, Macara pointed out, "gins are fed by children of 13 or 14 years of age, who receive three piastres per day of sixteen hours—but it must not be thought that they work continuously during that time" (International Cotton Federation [1912] 165). This may mean that children worked in shifts, but it also may simply mean that they were not very consistent workers and required significant monitoring costs provided by "overseers, who in some cases make use of a lash [and are] present in large numbers."

By 1927, some gins had installed suction equipment to move cotton around the factory as Macara had suggested in 1911. However, "the majority of factories have declined to use [self-feeding suction], it being argued that a girl or a boy at a gin can feed it more regularly and so ensure a better flow of cotton through the knife and roller, and consequently an improved out-turn" (International Cotton Federation [1927] 139). In 1937 it was still common for the gins to be fed by hand according to standard accounts (Ahmad 51). Not until 1950 are there frequent accounts of the employment of adult women at this stage in the production process.

The failure to mechanize the ginning process intensively was overdetermined. The collective-action problem of the entrepreneurs was extremely difficult to resolve. The investment in reputation that prohibited seed imports made achievement of scale economies impossible but the same investment in reputation made it desirable to check the flow of raw materials by hand for defects. Despite the efforts of the Wafd, ginning and associated industries that were points of entry for indigenous entrepreneurs had very limited growth potential. Equally important, however, is a point to which I shall return in the conclusion: the demand for children's labor was strong and created disincentives for some families to invest in their children's education. Many more children engaged in wage labor in the cotton fields than in the gins, of course. The effect of children's labor was both directly to limit some kinds of investment in physical capital and also to limit the supply of human capital available after a lag to industrial undertakings in other sectors of the economy.

### Labor Legislation, Child Labor, and Growth

Even if the legislation of the military government had an unintended negative effect on investment in physical capital it had a positive effect on investment in human capital (probably equally unintended): it made labor in general, and child labor in particular, more expensive. The new law therefore discouraged hiring children in the large factories that made up the formal sector of the economy and increased the returns to primary education for many parents. Child labor did not disappear in urban Egypt but it appears to have diminished in precisely these sectors. The regulation of labor markets in the early 1950s worked surprisingly well to increase the levels of literacy in society, especially for males. To understand why this is so it is necessary to look briefly at education in the first half of the twentieth century in Egypt.

### Investment in Education

Education was a contentious issue in Egypt during the first half of the twentieth century because it was clear that it would affect rural labor relations directly and through its impact on women and family structures. Thus, although an economist such as Al-Gritly believed that skilled workers in Egypt exhibited productivity roughly equal to that of Europeans, he also believed that the illiteracy of 80 percent of the population made "their adaptability to machine production ... very difficult" (Gritly 531). Gritly was aware that labor regulation in the nineteenth and twentieth century usually began with limits on child labor. He observed a similar path for Egyptian legislation but noted that child labor remained common through the 1930s (Gritly 537) and understood that without enough schools and higher adult wages, it would be impossible to end child labor (Grilty 538–539).

During the period of direct British control of Egyptian finances, Egyptians (like Black Americans) faced severe supply constraints. The British were unwilling to let the government provide as much education as parents wanted. In 1910 about 3.4 percent of the state budget was spent on public education and 90 percent of the pupils in the elementary schools were boys (Matthews and Akrawi 16, 34). When Egypt gained formal independence, the 1923 Constitution made elementary education compulsory and free for boys and girls but left determination of the school structure to the legislature. The parliament turned to a private religious and a compulsory public school system to provide literacy. The private religious schools (*kuttab* or *maktab*) descended from a traditional Islamic educational system. By 1930 nearly 11 percent of the state budget, three times the proportion spent 20 years earlier, was apportioned to public education but illiteracy still decreased very slowly. This is not surprising because pupils only attended half-day sessions in order to leave them available for work (Matthews and Akrawi 24, 41) and school retention rates were so low that even those children usually only attended schools for two or three years (Matthews and Akrawi 547).

It would be easy to see the failure of the Egyptian government to eliminate literacy as a regulatory failure due to the absence of power to identify and compel social actors. The problem, as many studies have shown, is that creating a literate population requires that parents participate. Parents who see education as worth the opportunity cost of children's incomes must do most of the work of compelling attendance which is why compulsory attendance laws usually followed rather than preceded mass literacy. As long as children's contributions to family incomes whether through wages or the provision of unpaid labor were relatively high and as long as the returns to increased education were relatively low, school attendance and performance in school were not likely to be great.

Egyptian children were not in school, but neither were they out playing. They were working and they were certainly allowed to work by the existing labor legislation. Under the 1933 child labor law, children between 9 and 15 years of age were legally allowed to work in the spinning and weaving industries as well as in sugar processing, cotton ginning and pressing, and other forms of industrial production.[31] Between 1917 and 1947, nearly 14 percent of the enumerated Egyptian male workforce was between 5- and 14-years-old (table 7.2). Most of these children, like most Egyptians in the workforce, were in agriculture, but children worked in many other occupations. Boys in the same age group appear to have comprised about 10 percent of manufacturing employment and nearly that much service employment. Seen from the perspective of activity rates, nearly 16 percent of the male population between 5 and 9 years of age worked in some enumerated occupation and nearly 70 percent of boys between the age group 10 and 14 worked. These, pre-1952 proportions are considerably higher than in Egypt since 1960s but they are also far higher than the proportions of children in the workforce in the industrialized countries of Europe or Japan in the first half of the twentieth century. They are, however, somewhat similar to the proportions of children who worked in industry in the American south where most of the competition for Egyptian producers (workers and landowners) lay (Walters and James; Walters and Briggs).

That the supply of schooling in Egypt did not translate into decreasing illiteracy for the first half of the twentieth century is not surprising in the light of the comparative experience of the American South. In the South, school attendance was negatively correlated with landlessness (which increased the need for income from children) and with the availability of employment opportunities for children (Walters and James; Walters and Briggs) and positively correlated with mechanization (Guest and Tolnay). In other words, as small farmers and farm laborers became poorer in either

**Table 7.2** Percent age distribution of male labor force in industry and manufacturing

| Year | 5–9 | 10–14 | 15–19 | 20–29 | 30–39 | 40–49 | 50–59 | 60+ | 5–14 | Young and old |
|------|-----|-------|-------|-------|-------|-------|-------|-----|------|---------------|
| 1917 | 1.93 | 8.21 | 11 | 22.06 | 22.43 | 15.31 | 9.39 | 9.66 | 10.14 | 19.8 |
| 1927 | 1.77 | 9.59 | 13.02 | 23.52 | 21.91 | 14.74 | 7.98 | 7.26 | 11.36 | 19.34 |
| 1937 | 0.88 | 7.73 | 12.72 | 23.64 | 22.52 | 16.41 | 9.1 | 6.64 | 8.61 | 15.25 |
| 1947 | 0.96 | 8.24 | 16.66 | 25.13 | 20.64 | 14.43 | 8.07 | 5.72 | 9.2 | 14.92 |
| 1960 | 0.45 | 3.89 | 14.08 | 27.67 | 25.11 | 15.57 | 8.51 | 4.71 | 4.34 | 9.05 |

*Source:* Nassef, Table D 21.

income or assets or both, they were more likely to send their children to work rather than to school. Strictly speaking we have no way of knowing whether the demand for children's labor and the supply of employment for children in Egypt before 1950 resembled the powerful effects seen in the United States at the same period but the logic of the argument is so powerful and the findings so robust that they are compelling for Egypt. We have no studies of family labor budgets in Egypt for that period and none of the aggregate material allows us to look very closely at the issue.

One study designed to examine directly whether there was excess or underemployed labor in a poor agricultural country was undertaken in Egypt in 1965 and it considered the role of children at work. It found that about 15 percent of hours worked on farms were contributed by children between the ages of 6 and 15 (Hansen [1969] 312). The similarity in the proportion of labor provided by children suggests that for much of the first two-thirds of the twentieth century, Egyptian children were "overemployed" and that the opportunity costs of education were too high for many Egyptian peasant families to bear.

The positive effect of mass primary education on economic growth was intuitively understood by Egyptian economists in the middle of the twentieth century such as Charles Issawi and has been confirmed by detailed statistical and comparative historical research since then (Benavot [1989] 25; Psacharopoulos and Woodhall; Easterlin). The new government did enact legislation that changed some of the incentives for child labor and thus for increased literacy, but this does not appear to have been its primary goal. On the contrary, the new legislation was primarily oriented to resolving the problem of productivity in terms of plant-specific skills and (like land reform) to increase the income of an impoverished sector of the population.

The wholesale substitution of female for male labor was clearly not an option in a country in which nearly the entire female population was illiterate and as I showed in chapter 6 Egyptian economists generally believed that, because high-quality cotton was easily available, the government should promote the extension of relatively high-quality spinning and (to a lesser extent) weaving. Such a strategy provided a rationale for improving the stability of the adult male workforce and to the degree that the adult male labor force became more stable, its members also became more capable of foregoing the earnings of their children and allowing them to attend school.

### Conclusion

Egyptian labor law and the associated changes in corporate law had a profound effect on Egyptian society and the Egyptian economy. Rather than seeing the legislation as purely the result of interest group politics or as an attempt to contain real or potential interest groups, it is more useful to put it in the context of the sudden accession to influence of new policy makers. The new laws had a negative effect on investor confidence and probably did diminish private investment in the years immediately after the coup. Without the 1956 war with Britain, France, and Israel, it is possible that there would have been a larger role for private capital mobilized abroad (Tignor [1998]). Most observers believed that attracting foreign capital was crucial because they believed that Egyptians did not have the kind of free assets necessary to make significant investment and growth possible. Certainly El-Naggar knew that the levels of investment his plan called for were beyond the capacity of the Egyptian economy to mobilize. Such plans made the state a far more direct actor than it had previously been, important as its presence in regulation, the provision of public goods and even the promotion of investment had been.

If the labor legislation had a negative impact on physical capital investment, it probably had a positive effect on investments by families in human capital. Observers, perhaps too hopefully, noted a decrease in the role of child labor in the early 1950s and there is no doubt that the rise of literacy in the population at large dates from those years (and consequently even before the guarantee of employment to high school and college graduates). In 1960 activity rates for children between 5- and 9-years-old had dropped substantially from 1947 and for children in the 10–14 age group (who would have entered school around the time of the coup) had dropped to historic lows. To the degree that labor legislation increased the returns to seniority and allowed men and children to compete more equally in the industrial sectors of the economy, it played a role along with other social regulation in keeping urban children out of factories and in school. In other sectors of the economy, however, children appear to have retained their own labor markets down to the present (Human Rights Watch).

I will return to these issues in the concluding chapter but what must already be apparent is that along one very important dimension a significant difference exists between Egypt and the East Asian economies: the relatively widespread literacy and concomitant absence of child labor in the latter by the time of their spectacular growth in the 1970s. What is far less apparent is why the issue of child labor has so totally eluded students of comparative political economy as a causal and an ethical problem worthy of investigation.

# CHAPTER 8

## Conclusion

I n *Catch-22*, the protagonist Milo agrees to purchase the entire Egyptian cotton crop and is then faced with financial ruin because "he had never dreamed that the Nile Valley could be so fertile or that there would be no market at all for the crop he had bought" (Heller 255–256). In picaresque fiction, traders can call out air raids to restore market equilibrium, but in real life finding solutions to economic problems ranging from excessive supply to inadequate demand is exceedingly difficult.

For a long time, the Egyptian elite in the era before 1952 has been portrayed like Milo: a feckless and dangerous character from a picaresque novel. I hope that is no longer possible. Like a vessel proceeding down a coastline that suddenly turns out to have unexpected depths and surprising twists, this book has revealed new dimensions to the political economy of Egypt in the first half of the twentieth century. Some of the sure landmarks such as the ecological crisis induced by imperialism or Nasser's anti-labor policies turn out to be illusory, but many other prominent features marked by earlier voyagers remain, as they must, largely intact.

In conclusion I want to outline the implications of this for understanding trade and growth in countries with highly specialized export sectors in the first half of the twentieth century. By introducing a different theoretical approach to trade coupled with a focus on regulation, my account of Egyptian political economy has shown that members of the elite, played a far more important role as agents in shaping their own economy and its relationship to global trade than in most accounts. That they accomplished their intervention primarily through government regulation; that, although they responded to price incentives, their economic intervention was shaped by many discussions that were often only tangentially related to immediate price differences; did not spare Egypt other negative consequences including a reliance that continues into the present on child labor. Child labor was not an accidental feature left over from the past, but an active factor of production constantly, if not always fully consciously, reproduced.

Beginning with an account of theories of trade and comparative advantage enabled me to substitute the concept that countries trade combinations of productive factors (primarily labor and capital) for the idea that they trade commodities. The focus on comparative, as distinct from absolute, advantage introduced Egyptian agency through the use of regulatory mechanisms that ensured the quality of Egyptian agricultural production. This in turn made it possible to see quality and reputation as goods themselves requiring investment and a return on investment rather than as inherent qualities of commodities.

Such an approach places Egypt usefully in several different comparative frameworks rather than within the now-standard account of a country trapped in the production of a raw material indistinguishable from other similar producers. At the turn of the twentieth century, Egyptians produced a high-quality fiber (homogenous long staple cotton) for export using vast quantities of human labor, especially that of children; Japan produced another raw fiber (silk) of high quality for export of using much less labor (and fewer children) and in addition produced finished products of low quality (cotton textiles) for export. California also produced a high-quality fiber (long staple cotton) using vast quantities of capital and far less human labor, very little of which was that of children. Germany produced a similar high-quality fiber (rayon) from chemical ingredients using equally large amounts of capital and no children whatsoever.

Because buyers of these products could not observe their characteristics before using them, some producers, but not all, found it useful to invest in reputation. Such investments required producing a good of higher than average quality. Because reputations could be affected by many actions and even appropriated by competitors in some circumstances, producers preferred government regulation of production as collective or social investment in reputation to fully bearing the cost privately. Egyptian government policies for ensuring the production of a high-quality export by private firms were exceptionally sophisticated. Thus, the production of the cotton crop and its transformation from the field to the dock was far in advance of regulatory practice in California or the American South at the turn of the century.

It would be possible to write an account of the development of underdevelopment by pretending that Egypt in 1910 was an advanced country because it had sophisticated government and regulatory structures that were copied by Californians later. It would be absurd to place Egypt at the forefront of development but it is useful to show that Egyptians developed the regulatory capacity, itself largely the result of the construction of coalitions of influence, to accomplish a task similar to that of many other large-scale exporters (including Argentina) at the same period. It is nevertheless striking that in the most important case of development in the first half of the twentieth century, the relevant actors—Japanese textile manufacturers—deliberately chose not to invest in quality. Japanese cotton goods were cheap in every sense of the word and Japanese industrial goods would remain synonymous with low quality until well into the 1960s. Because this was also the case with many Korean industrial goods in the 1970s and with many Taiwanese and Hong Kong products, it suggests that firms (and by extension countries) that pursue a capital-intensive export-oriented strategy must begin with low-quality goods.

Regulation plays a role in export economies but regulation need not ensure high-quality production nor skew factor markets. What the literature on development misunderstands is that regulatory capacity only exists when the relevant factors of production (land, labor, and capital) also exist in specific form and when those who employ the factors want regulation to work. Without the cooperation of factor owners even the idea of regulation means little. Because regulation requires access to strategic information, regulatory administration always requires cooperation from those being regulated. Regulation is a joint exercise rather than a force applied externally to passive recipients.

In writing this account I have diverged from a standard Egyptian historiography that frequently employs the passive voice. It is commonplace that British authors, especially officials writing during and after the Occupation, saw Egypt as the passive recipient of British energy and culture. It is not perhaps surprising that more recent analysis, although written under the influence of left or nationalist concepts of history, echoes the older British accounts by describing Egyptians, in that period as bystanders in the making of their own history. I have investigated the rise, and I hope, decline of just such a concept of Egyptian history in the guise of the ecological crisis that is supposed to have occurred in the first two decades of the twentieth century. I am not alone in writing in such a mode and have been drawn along by more recent accounts that present elite history in a similarly active fashion (Vitalis [1995]; Tignor [1984]).

A recent and influential article about the political economy of countries like Egypt in the 1950s and 1960s explains the move toward import-substituting industrialization and ultimately state ownership in the economy as a response to regulatory weakness. "At base, government ownership is more often a response to the administrative weakness of the state in developing countries rather than a reaction to the private sector's inability to provide the skills and capital necessary for bulky investments" (Chaudhry 247). "[C]ases as diverse as India, Pakistan, Iraq and Egypt suggest that government in late developers became directly involved in the economy . . . after long and frustrating failures to tax, redistribute and regulate the behavior of private actors following decolonization or during the systemic crises of the 1930s and World War II" (Chaudhry 257).

Just as the literature on export-oriented growth confused quality with capital intensity, here we see a common failure to distinguish between quite distinct government tasks (regulation, taxation, and redistribution) and between policy formation, implementation, and outcomes. The Egyptian government was quite capable of producing regulation and implementing it, but it could not guarantee how others would react to its policy initiatives. The Egyptian government was quite successful in regulating the production of high-quality cotton and almost as successful in the transition away from the specialization in extra-long staple cotton to long-staple production. Before 1952 neither the government nor its primary constituency was interested in redistributing wealth through taxation or otherwise; yet the only way to increase the stock of human capital would have required such redistribution.

After 1952, the military government was also quite successful in regulating the labor markets, enhancing the power of the trade union organizations, and substituting legal mechanisms of control for market-oriented collective bargaining. The government did, in fact, manage to set Egypt decisively on the road to regulating labor–management conflict through "European" rather than "American" institutions. In addition, it appears that the threat posed by child labor to adult men was largely eliminated from the large industrial enterprises. What the regulatory strategy did not accomplish was to increase private investment in physical capital, which suggests that it is at least as likely that the theory on which the legislation was based was flawed rather than that the regulatory capacity of the state was insufficient or that a "pro-capitalist" state was unable to communicate its preferences to investors. Neither did the regulation of labor lead to the elimination of all child labor, but (again) that was not its purpose.

Thus, the most important problem for Egyptians in the first half of the twentieth century seems to me exactly opposite to claims of regulatory weakness. The state had the administrative capacity to regulate areas of the economy where requisite investments had been made. The failure to make investments in fixed (which I believe is what Chaudhry means by bulky) capital arose from the absence of the complementary investments in human capital that were necessary. As many investors realized and as economists such as Luhayta and El-Naggar explicitly argued, there were very few profitable investments in fixed capital to be made without enormous concessions from the state. In the late 1920s and early 1930s, it was still plausible to assert that Egypt was in a liquidity trap along the lines of Ralph Harari's argument and might escape. By 1950 incomes were low enough that very few knowledgeable observers believed there were viable investments for industry in the country.

It is instructive to compare Egyptian experience to that of early twentieth-century Japan and to that of the American South because these were the available reference points and because in both of those places a large agricultural sector producing raw fiber existed. To say that Egypt did not conform to the Southern or Japanese paths of investment in industry cannot allow us to forget how closely the Egyptian experience of regulation and investment in the creation of a high-quality agricultural good conformed to the Japanese and the Californian experience. Egypt did not differ from California in regard to regulatory strategy or regulatory capacity; it differed in the particular mix of labor and capital employed to produce such a good. In California there was a massive and early investment in capital at the level of the farm and not simply in the provision of water. California labor was in the aggregate far more skilled than that in other areas of cotton production (the American South and Egypt) and the wages of labor there were significantly higher than those obtained by African Americans in the Old Confederacy or Egyptian peasants.

Rescuing the Egyptian elite from the condescending gaze of historians does not excuse them from the human costs of their policy choices. The crucial failure of Egyptian development in the 1930s and 1940s lay in the continuation of mass illiteracy and there is little doubt that the policy choices of the state in this area reflected the desire of influential Egyptians to ensure an adequate supply of cheap labor, including but not limited to children so as to engage profitably in world trade. The failure to provide adequate education to Egyptian children is a "regulatory dilemma" that requires explanation only if it is believed that the country faced two polar opposite choices. Either Egypt had a poorly trained elite that staffed a weak state or it had powerful officials who staffed a strong state and were about to march bravely into an East Asian future *avant la lettre*. If we can be satisfied with more complex stories about countries like Egypt and with more complex stories about growth, development, trade and equity in the Third World than comparative politics has hitherto preferred, this may be acceptable. Such stories would, necessarily, have to include the ways in which producers in countries such as Egypt find markets for their goods in advanced countries.

Writing in 1995, Robert Vitalis asserted that we know very little about the politics of investment in Egypt before 1952 (Vitalis [1995] 218). Of the countries of Asia and Africa, Egypt is the one with a remarkably rich documentary record in government files in London, Paris, and Cairo as well as in an unofficial record built up of contemporary academic studies, newspaper accounts, and article-length analyses in academic journals. Our ignorance of Egypt is likely to be equaled by our ignorance of much of the rest of the world in the twentieth century. It is certainly remarkable that mine is one of the very few accounts of commodity production and export to have seriously explored the role of so basic and characteristic an institution of capitalism as the futures market.

Egyptian arguments in the first half of the twentieth century about agricultural exports and development have a peculiar sound to contemporary ears. In part this is because we have spent too much time on crises that never happened at the expense of understanding severe problems in their full magnitude. The fashions of academic discourse have something to do with this but it also intimately connected with the trajectory of Nasser's experiment in Egypt from early hopes to dashed promises. In 1947 when Charles Issawi published the first edition of an influential study on Egypt, he addressed overpopulation and poverty, two important issues that still dominate the literature on Egypt (Issawi [1947]; Mitchell [2002]). Writing before the army coup in 1952, Issawi noted that Egyptian agriculture required approximately 380 million man-days for production and about half that many woman and child-days (Issawi [1947] 201). He recognized that the slow progress of Egyptian industrialization was due to the absence of skilled (literate) labor (Issawi [1947] 199). His trenchant analysis of the failure of industrialization was intimately related to the poverty of the countryside:

> As long as the industrial labour market continues to be flooded by cheap rural labour it is futile to seek to enforce higher standards. Once the supply is cut off, however, the bargaining position of labour will be greatly enhanced and a rise in wages as well as wider social legislation may be expected to follow. (Issawi [1947] 200)

This was, I have argued, the logic developed by Luhayta and it lay behind the plans for industrialization that specialists like him had already developed when the Free Officers seized power. This is the logic that provides the conceptual coherence between land reform and labor legislation in the early days of the new regime. In the edition immediately after the 1952 coup, this fundamental insight disappeared, never to reemerge in successive versions. Issawi returned to these early themes toward the end of his life to explain Egypt's low growth. He noted that of equal importance with the Egyptian government's inability to control the tariff issue and to mobilize private savings was widespread illiteracy (Issawi [1995] 116] although he may have placed more emphasis on higher education than is warranted (Issawi [1995] 121). There is a well-known conundrum that, despite high private returns to education (in the form of higher wages), the aggregate effect of education globally appears to be neutral to negative. This finding may be due to measurement error (Blinder) or the absence of complementarities (Pritchett) but it is certain that it does not apply to the provision of primary education in impoverished countries. There are good reasons to believe that primary education makes agricultural labor significantly more productive, that it has far higher social rates of return than secondary or university education, that maternal education significantly increases the well-being of children, and that additional mean years of education increase the rates of economic growth (Dasgupta 98–99, 158). On balance, education is most productive when linked to ongoing change in technology (Pritchett).

What Issawi, and those like him, expected was a land reform that would be far more sweeping and an economy that would remain far more fully in private hands and open to free trade with the rest of the world. It was what I would consider to have been a truly Keynesian solution to poverty and injustice in Egypt and it was not, it seems to me, either premature or simply statist.

Very late in this study I realized there was a country that, in the late nineteenth century, resembled Egypt in many ways. It barely seems possible that I could have discovered a country that exported a high-quality agricultural good to a developed industrial economy for use as an input in an industrial process and that this input was not used at home despite the availability of the necessary technology. Such a product existed; was produced primarily by unskilled peasant labor (including children) to such a degree that its minimal processing employed the largest number of workers in domestic industry; was the most valuable industrial product in aggregate; and it provided the largest single source of foreign exchange. Japan was just such a country because it was Japan where until 1930 raw silk for a rapidly expanding American industry accounted for about one-third of the country's exports (Orchard [1930] 113, 120–131; Lockwood 45).[1] In the 1960s it was still possible to imagine Egypt rather than Japan as the success story of nineteenth-century industrialization (Hobsbawm 216) but it seems harder and harder to imagine that Egypt could have been Japan. Although colonial rule may account for the difference, the contrast between the two countries forces us to ponder why Japan did not remain like Egypt.

The contrast between Japan and Egypt is certainly more telling than the similarity, and the most compelling difference between Egypt and Japan throughout the first half of the twentieth century was the dramatic difference in school attendance and literacy rates, especially for girls. Using a scale in which Canadian school attendance was 100 in 1934, Japan stood at 78, not only far above Egypt, but also above Italy and Argentina (Bennett 647). If, therefore, the stock of human capital—especially the investment made in the education and well-being of girls—was significantly greater in Japan than in Egypt we would expect Japanese comparative advantage to lie more strongly in industrialization.[2] Although prewar Japan can be made to look very much like Egypt in terms of monetary indicators such as per capita real income, it looks very different when nonmonetary indicators such as health or education (forms of investment in human beings) are included in a comparison. The same kinds of arguments that I find largely spurious are often made about Egypt (or any other poor country) and Korea or Taiwan in the postwar era to explain why one state in one country has succeeded in regulating its way out of poverty and another country has failed. These kinds of arguments appear to reproduce the uncritical modernization theories of a generation ago in which rural inhabitants and farmers around the world are all the same: rude and unlettered.

Education is a crucial form of investment and it appears to be a form of investment in which parents often wish to participate as long as the costs, including the opportunity costs, are low. It is for this reason that I do not wish to rescue the prewar Egyptian elite from the condescension of the present but not its criticism. The provision of primary education, the opportunities for children to work, and the minimum paid to adults were all affected by public policy. All the policies enacted reflected the political and economic desires of members of the elite that in Egypt were landowners, who like those in the American South, did not wish to face the social, political, or economic consequences of a more literate workforce. Of course, like American and Egyptian children, Japanese children also worked and in the first decade of the century they could legally enter factories at the age of ten if they were engaged in "light work." But the legal age of entry into factories was raised and by the Depression it was higher than in Egypt (14) and younger children could be employed only after they had completed primary school (Lockwood 556–558).

Low growth in Egypt in the first half of the twentieth century was not due to insufficient state capacity or regulatory failure. On the contrary, many of

Egypt's problems arose because local elites, Egyptian and European by origin, were extremely successful in using state regulation to enter international trade as an efficient producer of a high-quality good. Egypt was primarily a rural society in the nineteenth and early twentieth centuries, most of whose producers fall under the rubric of the peasantry. Just as the theory of comprador capitalism has been discarded, it is time to do away with one of Issawi's most important contributions: the idea that Egypt was a dual economy in which a backward or traditional society produced goods for export alongside a small enclave urban society. Integration into the market did not make Egyptians less literate, less urban, and it certainly does not appear to have made them, at least between 1890 and 1912, less wealthy. The tragedy of Egypt was that rural illiteracy and poverty provided a comparative advantage for Egypt in global trade; many Egyptians and many experts in the cotton industry were well aware of this and Egyptian elites employed the relative abundance of these factors in the domestic economy remarkably well. Global trade created an increased demand for these abundant factors of production and in so doing may have made it difficult to stimulate the investments necessary to replace them with other sets of factors, especially skilled labor. If, under the British Occupation, the supply of schooling was criminally insufficient it is nonetheless true that the effective demand for education and the supply even after 1923 remained, in economic terms, far too slight to create a society abundant either in human capital or physical capital.

Perhaps the radical literature of the 1970s arguing for a concept of the "underdevelopment of underdevelopment" had a point although it misunderstood the relevant mechanisms and the depth of the problem. As long as Egypt had a comparative advantage in, for example, child labor then under free trade there would be continued demand for the abundant factor of production which would, in turn, make it economically beneficial for parents to send their children to work rather than to school. We can imagine other inhibitions to universal schooling including cultural norms that inhibited sending girls to school or the open employment of adult women that were at work. Without dismissing such explanations, however, we need to recognize that there was a powerful set of economic forces at work.

To pursue the analogy to the American South suggested by Wright, Egyptian men had largely excluded women from the industrial economy in the 1930s but found it far more difficult to exclude children from those sectors of the economy until after the seizure of power by Nasser. Children continue to make up about 12 percent of the workforce, primarily in agriculture and in smaller, privately owned enterprises. The wages of children continue to be very low and because children do not work in the public sector they do not have the benefits for which adult men fight so strongly. Researchers in the mid-twentieth century were acutely aware of the problem of child labor. In 1951 a regional conference in Teheran was explicit: "Work by young people is also a cause of disorganization of in the employment market, since cheap juvenile labor is preferred to adult labor. The employment of children at an early age is a running sore from which the Middle East still suffers acutely" (ILO 34). Early advocates of outlawing child labor in the United States understood only too well why labor markets coupled with technological change brought children into the factory:

> The causes for the growth of child labor are not difficult to discover and can be briefly indicated. Improved machinery and minute subdivision of labor has rendered their labor as effective as that of adults, though they will invariably accept lower wages for it. Again, children and women are helpless, and have, as yet, proven themselves incapable of effective organization, and seldom carry a strike to a successful conclusion. With the present friction between employer and employés, the former finds this no slight consideration in his choice of operatives. (Willoughby 11)

Seen in the light of the foregoing discussion, problems deemed regulatory are deeply political but sufficiently complex to continually require more intervention. I have argued that the regulation of Egyptian cotton production was so successful that even some of its presumed failures (such as the "ecological crisis") were actually examples of its success. I have also argued that the regulation of cotton production also made it extremely difficult to resolve another problem that is usually only very tangentially linked to it: investment in education. The regulation of the labor market was, in many ways, quite successful. The new legislation in fact evoked significantly greater use of the court and arbitration systems than had previously been the case. Coupled with other instruments the Egyptian government under the Free Officers was able to move far more rapidly in the direction of administering labor markets than had any other government before it. Egyptian governments had been moving to administer labor markets and through that administration to obtain far greater control over what happened within the formerly privileged arena of the factory walls than it had ever had before. I believe this led to lower levels of investment where regime advisers may have expected increased investment. Adverse strategic reactions to a regulatory regime do not, however, imply that it has been poorly implemented; more likely they imply the contrary. At all events, in the wake of adverse strategic reactions policy makers may need to decide how well advised the policy itself is. Egyptian policy-makers, like those elsewhere, had to balance their competing desires for control of production and distribution with increasing private investment. Increasingly during the 1950s and 1960s, they chose (in some as yet poorly described and poorly understood way) to move further away from attempting to win private investment.

I have employed a variety of Keynesian insights in this study and, as must be clear, the study of political economy of underdevelopment must become more self-consciously Keynesian if it is to prosper. In part, this requires us to pay, as did Keynes, more attention to the activities of elites. In part it also requires us to pay closer empirical attention to the problems of incentives, information, and unemployed resources than we have done in studies such as this one. In arguing, along the lines first suggested by Bent Hansen, that Egypt's children were "overemployed" even if adult men there were "underemployed" I have made what I think is the most important contribution I can to the study of labor, investment, and the role of gender in Egyptian history.

The Egyptian experience is neither unique nor completed. According to UNESCO in 2000, nine countries (Bangladesh, Brazil, China, Egypt, India, Indonesia, Mexico, Nigeria, and Pakistan) accounted for half of the world's population and nearly 70 percent of its illiterates. Illiteracy is also increasingly a condition of women. The implications of this are stark, as Myron Weiner pointed out in 1980, in a book that hardly seems to affect the discipline of comparative politics or indeed any of the area studies apart from India: "barring a conceptual change . . . and a new direction in policy by the Indian government, the number of children in the labor force will not significantly decline, conditions for working children will not significantly improve, school retention rates will not significantly increase, and literacy rates will continue to grow at a slow pace and will leave a large part of the Indian population illiterate well into the middle of the twenty-first century. With illiteracy and child labor declining world wide at a faster rate than in India, India's global share of illiterates and child laborers will continue to increase" (Weiner 207). Weiner's analysis fits Egypt as well as India for the coming century and for the previous century.

And yet why do not all of these failures and tragedies lie at the door of the bureaucracy and the weak state? Because what the materials here suggest is that governments cannot substitute policies for the existence of assets that embody factors of production and that at least until the mid-1950s the Egyptian bureaucracy accomplished most of the tasks it was set to do. It is true that Egyptian officials often did not know as much as they would have liked, for example, about cotton production and found it difficult to predict accurately the coming year's cotton acreage or production. They also understood, as it seems we often do not, that these were the same problems faced by American officials and that the solution lay in how the government worked with local landowners and associations because the relevant information lay with them. The information the state sought was not free nor did the intermittent existence of free elections—no more than a handful were held—account for it. Whatever complex links exist between taxation and representation, they did not account for the relatively high levels of information the state was able to develop about the economy. That information came because the state sought it in ways that were, to a high degree, incentive-compatible with those who had.

Egyptians often had surprisingly good information about society and the economy. Those who dealt with the peasants and cotton production obviously had a far more acute understanding of the condition of the peasants than many writers who came after them. Whether British or Egyptian, the bureaucrats did not cause an ecological disaster but effectively assisted the rapid transition from one variety of cotton to another. Their records provide acute insights into peasant responses to price and the physical difficulty of producing cotton. Later officials in other ministries had very good information about children who worked, their impact on the economy, and the difficulties that stood in the way of increasing parental investment in education or capitalist investment in physical plant. Besides their own surveys, they had a variety of other public and private institutions that allowed them to track significant parts of the economy with sufficient accuracy that some of the very important work on the econometrics was accomplished using Egyptian data. Egyptians were acutely aware that that it was not taxation but the rendering of a complementary service that rendered producers willing to cooperate by making private information public.

If we are concerned about development and the well-being of Egyptians, then the area of concern in Egypt lies elsewhere than in regulatory or other capacity of the state. The problem lies in the inability or unwillingness of Egyptian political leaders to create the kinds of coalitions that would have made the education of children incentive-compatible for parents and for employers. Without suggesting that democracy or local control of resources is a panacea, it is hard to consider the history of Egyptian regulatory experience without believing that the crucial failure was one of political vision.

# Notes

## Chapter 2    *Reputation, Regulation, and Trade*

1. Empirically, diverse and even counterintuitive institutional solutions to the problem of signaling quality are found. Sometimes doing nothing provides a signal of quality assurance because buyers prefer average quality to the risk of being given low- rather than high-quality goods (Rosenman and Wilson [1991]).
2. These are what Leamer identifies as the factor mobility and technology assumptions. In addition he identifies three other assumptions that are less relevant for my argument (Leamer [1984] 2).
3. For example, crops grown on different soils in weather conditions that vary over time can have very different tastes, something noticeable to connoisseurs of wine and tobacco; logs are of widely varying circumferences; the proportion of metal in ore varies over time and space; even oil from nearby wells can have different physical characteristics. This particular meaning of "staple" dates from the seventeenth century.
4. Shafer (1997).
5. Rueschmeyer and Evans (1985) 68.
6. Meyerson (1979) and Baron and Meyerson (1982).
7. For a formal analysis see Spulber (1989). I think the concept of coalition formation is the point that underlies what the state–society literature was aiming at (Migdal [1988]) and I believe it is the content of the argument of Timothy Mitchell's somewhat opaque critique of the unitary state idea (Mitchell [1990]).
8. Cumings (1984).
9. Durkheim announced this role of the state early on but I am grateful to Mary Ann Tetrault for reminding me that development stories are moral tales.
10. See Krugman (1994) and Rodrik (1999) regarding the relative roles of increasing volumes of physical capital and labor in the growth process rather than the statistical residual called total factor productivity.
11. In 1989, World Bank figures indicate that 45% of the exports of low-income economies were nonmineral primary goods or textiles and clothing; they were 41% of the exports of lower-middle income countries and 32% of the exports of middle-income economies.

12. International Cotton Federation [1912] 44.
13. *L'Egypt Contemporaine.*
14. El-Naggar 161–162.

## Chapter 3    Growing the World's Best Cotton: Colonial Crisis or Business as Usual

1. Of course, Great Britain's *second* most important, and fastest growing, export was itself a staple: coal.
2. English firms were also vulnerable to competition because unlike their counterparts in Japan they did not work double shifts.
3. See Temin for an overview and Garside and Greaves for a useful discussion of specific problems of postwar industry in the staples sectors of coal and textiles.
4. Strictly speaking the canal system was a renewable asset produced purely by labor but it is convenient to treat it as a capital asset.
5. None of the accounts of biological testing before 1920 appear to indicate systematic attempts to employ randomization, for example. Fisher's application of the Latin square to biological experiments still lay in the future.
6. For a concise account of the technical issues including the concept of a "norm of reaction" see Lewontin 16–30.
7. Thabit [1936] cites an opening speech given in French (on behalf of the prince by an assistant), which explicitly evoked seed selection as a method to reverse the tendency of the fiber length of the then-dominant Mit Afifi strain of cotton to shorten over time and its consequent declining market premium (49–50).
8. Sidqi (1950) on the role of the export firms in developing seed strains and marketing them abroad (40).
9. Sidqi (1950) describes a joint venture to market the seed by Sakellaridis, Fourega, and Choremi that went bankrupt after investing £E. 300,000 (57). Choremi was one of the main export traders in Alexandria.
10. In April 1949 however, 9,500 growers in California, farming nearly a million acres, switched from one strain of Acala to another (Musoke and Olmstead 390).
11. Sakellaridis himself was given several monetary awards by the Egyptian government in recognition of the importance of the type.
12. Sakel was grown until World War II, but the area yield remained on average about 3 cantars per feddan for the years 1935–1939 during which no drainage problem could possibly have obtained (Sidqi 260; International Institute of Agriculture [1926] 177 "thus in Upper Egypt, where Achmouni is the principal variety, the average yield is estimated at 450 pounds, while in Lower Egypt, where Sakellaridis is the principal variety, the average yield per acre was 300 pounds").
13. International Cotton Federation [1927], 90 notes the decrease in the number of pickings.
14. In 1936, Black (70) could still easily assert "A major reason for the increase in yields in Egypt is a shift toward upland or medium-staple cotton away from the

low-yielding long-staple varieties." This is one of the last occasions in the literature that crop shifting was understood to be related to changes in yield.

15. Mosseri was an internationally recognized expert as well as a large landowner and an extremely influential family; he was president of the Egyptian Institute, a corresponding member of the Agricultural Academy of France, and a technical adviser to the Royal Agricultural Society of Egypt (Cotton Federation [1927]; Kramer 43).

16. Nahas gives the same overall yield difference as Mosseri—15%—but splits it into two parts: crop yield and ginning out-turn.

17. It is not clear how rapidly we could expect salinity to become a problem and then subside in the wake of drainage projects. Two decades seems like a very rapid period although in Iraq in the 1970s about 14% of the land went out of tillage due to salinization over 15 years but that was also in a country in which 60% of irrigated land was already somewhat saline (Hillel 99).

## Chapter 4    Regulation for Reputation in the Egyptian Delta

1. In 1975, however, Leamer calculated that Egyptian trade was most affected by a shortage of capital (Leamer [1984] 205).

2. In the dryer words of a 1994 report "cotton has higher labor requirements than other crops" (Eisa 83).

3. Because these statistics were collected during World War II when demand for adult labor associated with the Middle East Supply Center was high, the role of child labor may be overstated relative to the preceding three decades. Or maybe not.

4. "l'Egypte était l'unique producteur des qualités superieures de coton...il faut ajouter que ses acheteurs avaient installé des broches et des metiers destinés uniquement au coton du longue fibre. Ils ne pouvaient donc ce passer...sans effectuer des transformations très couteuses" (88–89).

5. Egyptian consumers responded to reputation in choosing to buy foreign, trademarked textiles (Owen [1969] 301).

6. Islamic law has a contractual form—*salam*—for the present purchase of goods to be produced and delivered in the future. There were not then and are not now any construals of shari‹a to write contracts for the purchase of uncertain quantities of goods at unknown prices in the future nor was it legitimate to buy and sell contracts exhibiting such uncertainties. There was an important debate about whether the state could pay interest (*riba*) on postal savings accounts and relevant fatwas were issued. There do not appear to have been any fatwas or even any discussion about the selling of uncertain contracts in the future (*gharar*), which was an issue of great concern to the dominant social elite. Clearly Islamic legal concepts were deployed only when they did not negatively affect powerful domestic interests.

7. *Halaqas* provided, in return for a nominal fee, access to an official weighing machine, information (the daily opening price in Alexandria), and a place in

which to exchange cotton. They were also used to distribute seed which, as I have argued, was not simply an "improvement" (Owen 218; Ahmad and Hafiz 34–35).

8. Bay and pasha were government ranks.

9. Mosseri was one of the rapporteurs of the 1910 government Cotton Commission as well as the author of at least eight technical papers including one on drainage.

10. He understood that the Japanese could spin Indian yarn on ring spindles; he believed that the crucial innovation by the Japanese was spindle design rather than cotton blending (Abdel Wahab [1930] 13).

11. The words "mass production" appear in English, which accentuates their role as a new policy.

## Chapter 5   Economics, Development, and Egyptian Economists

1. Harari, whose grandfather came to Egypt from Beirut in the 1830s, was Jewish and English-educated (Kramer 45). It is indicative of the social complexity of the Egyptian elites and their truly cosmopolitan nature that Harari's wife, Manya, was the first translator of Boris Pasternak's *Doctor Zhivago* from Russian into English, an active Zionist, and (in the 1930s) a Catholic convert.

2. Because Bank Misr is usually seen as a nationalist enterprise, its financial singularity is largely unnoted.

3. Five of the seven men who served twice as finance minister between 1923 and 1950 later served as prime minister. One of the two who did not, Makram Ubayd, was a Copt and therefore out of contention for the role in that period. The other was Ahmad Abdel Wahab who died shortly after leaving government.

4. The particular issue was a proposal by the British-dominated government to the Legislative Assembly for a law to create agricultural cooperatives. Zaghlul asked Nahas to lend him the latest books on the subject so that he could prepare for the debate.

5. *Al-aduw al-fatak.*

6. Compare the description of peasants by the Wafd premier, Mustafa Al-Nahas (no relation to Joseph-Nahas) in *The Egyptian Upper Class* (Baraka 267–268).

7. Not to belabor the argument made in chapter 3, but no mention is made in this article of drainage.

8. Seyf al-Nasr also served as head of the Wafd trade union federation in 1936, which may be taken to mean that in the conceptual universe of Egyptian national politics trade unions were not differentiated from unions of private owners (Beinin and Lockman) but it may simply mean that both were seen as interest groups that required significant government support to maintain their viability. That Nasr remained only briefly in the trade union federation certainly suggests that for the Wafd the role of powerful agricultural interests was far more crucial than of urban trade unionists.

9. "Natural law [namus tabaʿi] and economic factors are a force that cannot be resisted or conquered" (Nahas [1954] 31).

10. He proposed "il faudrait plus de cohesion entre les producteurs…l'avenir est du côté de ces fortes organizations économiques privées, qui, liberées des parties-pris politiques, dirigées par des hommes capables, arriveraient peut-être à épargner l'humanité ces soubresauts douloureux…" (Minost 453).

11. Nahas never provided either a theoretical reason for the existence of these kinds of market power nor even connected them. It was Keynes who provided the first sustained analysis of these kinds of phenomena.

12. Between 1885 and 1925 the output of horticultural products in the United States expanded hundredfold, thereby forcing collapses in citrus and other fruit products in the Mediterranean. Tariff barriers and technical innovation allowed high-wage, capital-intensive agricultural production to succeed (Critz; Olmstead and Rhode 316, 321, 324). On the role of U.S. wheat, see Heckscher (II) 357.

13. As long as the Egyptian currency was tied to sterling there could be no independent devaluation.

14. Writing in *L'Egypte Contemporaine* in 1935 on "Cotton Policy in the United States" an official of the Crédit Lyonnais summed up the experiences by the Hoover and Roosevelt administrations in pursuing price supports, advances to farmers, and acreage restrictions for an Egyptian audience. Davezac began by noting "how far we have come in recent years from liberal theories of an automatic equilibrium between production and consumption mediated by the price mechanism…" (Davezac [1935] 693). He concluded by asserting that agriculture must inevitably, albeit slowly, decline in the United States because it could not be mechanized and therefore U.S. cotton farmers would suffer a race to the bottom with Egyptian and Indian peasants just as English textile workers were experiencing in relationship to Japan (Davezac [1936] 69).

15. Great Britain, to whose pound the Egyptian pound was tied, had gone off the gold standard in 1931.

16. By intensity, Nahas explicitly referred to the use of two shifts to ensure that the machinery was constantly running.

17. Nahas consistently opposed the idea that peasants responded to coercion rather than to economic incentives. In the section of *Le Fellah* on which this passage is based he explicitly rebukes authors like the Duc D'Harcourt for purveying "the most fantastic stories [about the peasant], such as his capacity to be hit."

18. Luhayta obtained a bachelor's degree in economics from the University of Birmingham in 1916 and a doctorate from the University of Leeds in 1926. He was a member of both the Royal Statistical Society and the Royal Economics Society.

20. Mahir could be considered an early proponent of the guided economy and Egyptian corporatism. He proposed that the 1923 Constitution include the clause "Labour is under the power of the state" thereby allowing the government to set national employment standards (Baraka 78).

21. In winter Fu'ad was said to awake at 5 a.m. and, after breakfast, to have read the Egyptian Arabic and foreign-language newspapers as well as clippings from the American and European press, then to receive visitors from 10 a.m. until

2 p.m.; after lunch he met with government officials and signed legislation until 4:30 p.m. when he received more visitors. He spent the evenings in political discussion with members of his personal administration through the evening and then retired after a light dinner (Thabit [1931], 10). In his memoirs Joseph Nahas recalls sending a memorandum to King Fuad in 1923 that elicited direct government intervention in the Bourse to support the price of cotton (Nahas [1952a] 63–64).

22. Luhayta himself uses all of these synonyms from time to time for *tawjih.*
23. He discusses trends in the Communist movement ([1946b] 156).
24. Luhayta does not use the terms dynamic and static but he sharply differentiates between, situations in which excessive inputs are used relative to marginal price for a given industry and those where macro-economic conditions such as bankruptcy or overinvestment occur.
25. "*tuwattun al-sindʿah.*"
26. "min haythu al-aʿid al-madi li-ʿaml rabbiha wa thabatuhu fi'l ʿaml."
27. It made no sense, Luhayta argued, for workers under capitalism to suggest labor-saving changes to the production process (Luhayta [1946b] 217).
28. In this he is echoing Alfred Marshall (Marshall 565); see the discussion of efficiency wages in chapter 7.
29. Sugar cane cultivation was only profitable because a state monopoly arbitrarily set prices (Issawi [1954] 119).
30. For Marshall this was the role to be played by unions (Marshall 702–708).
31. Luhayta had a more positive view of inflation that he saw—as long as it was limited—as a factor tending to make investment easier (Luhayta [1946b] 235–236).
32. Harbison and Ibrahim also spoke of "vast surpluses of unemployed or underemployed agricultural labor...[and] an almost inexhaustible pool of unemployed or partially employed labor" in the cities (Harbison and Ibrahim 135).
33. In 1931, Arno Pearse, a long-time adviser to Egyptian textile firms, writing in *L'Egypte Contemporaine* told his readers that "on a recent visit to the Missr Cotton Mill...we saw quite a number of weavers after 6 weeks training, taking care of 4 looms each, weaving a 48″ Grey Shirting, which is the number of looms looked after by a Lancashire weaver" (Pearse 397). A U.S. Department of Commerce Official, Charles K. Moser, was far more pessimistic: "aside from a lack of unity in management and unsuitable staple, Arab and Egyptian labor has not proved itself well adapted to the kind of machine and factory work found in a cotton mill" (Moser 3). Recent scholarship affirms that Egyptian production could not, as then constituted, compete with Japanese production (Tignor [1989] 61–62; Shimizu 103; Hansen [1990] 89).

## Chapter 6   Labor Regulation in Egypt After 1952

1. Dating the emergence of a formal policy "discussion" with the Report on Industry published in 1916.

2. If for no other reason than that industrial development altered the locations at which industrial goods were produced.

3. For a comprehensive review and classic statement of the distinction between inefficient allocations of factors and insufficient efforts on the part of the workers see Leibenstein.

4. So, too, the collapse of prices for high-quality cotton induced growers generally and the government in the form of the Abdel Wahab memorandum to supply cotton of lower quality.

5. At least one contemporary observer saw the macroeconomic problem of development in late nineteenth-century Japan in these terms, for in 1890 he wrote, "We have already noticed the unusually low rate of wages and long hours of labor, prevailing in new factories, and if we remind ourselves that the competition of surplus-laborers will tend to keep the rate of wages down, the necessity of regulations becomes evident" (Ono 119). Also Orchard [1930] 362–363.

6. The term "efficiency wages" is Marshall's (Marshall 549) as is the claim "high-paid labour is really cheap to those employers who are aiming at leading the race, and whose ambition it is to turn out the best work by the most advanced methods" (Marshall 565).

7. Marshall's *Elements* are cited in Luhayta's bibliography as is the work of William Beveridge.

8. "It is well known," wrote Luhayta "that trade unions in Egypt are not organizations with sufficient capacity to provide the kind of support similar organizations do in other countries" (Luhayta [1946b] 278 fn. 3).

9. The concept of efficiency wages only makes sense in terms of opportunity cost: these wages are significantly better than those gained in the next best job. I would not claim that any such wage premium is absolutely desirable and it certainly is not likely to be desirable if one thought the entire world was a single labor market.

10. Recall that if there is no threat of unemployment and wages clear the market then employees need not put in much effort because they can always find another job.

11. He "more than a legislative reform, the new regime set off a change in the climate of social and labor relations" (Tomiche 42).

12. This seems like a perfectly valid assumption, but it is possible that the disputes to which the series refers were individual concerns while the court cases were involved collective conflicts. Because the records of decisions by the Arbitration Commissions refer to an ordered set of "conflicts," however, I feel confident that this assumption is valid. For published accounts of decisions see Egypt (Ministry of Social Affairs [1954] 419–461).

13. If not all court cases are initiated by workers then some proportion of cases dismissed could represent victories for workers rather than defeat. The original legislation assumed either side could bring a court action as a result of a dispute, but later amendments are in line with the assumption followed here. There is some question about the relative weight of individual and collective grievances and which were more likely to become court actions (Posusney 262 fn. 32) but

without any reason to believe systematic differences obtain between them, I treat them as an aggregate.

14. To avoid spurious accuracy here when using these figures I round in the text to the nearest decile. The tables provide more accurate calculations.

15. With the exception of calendar 1953 (which was within months of the promulgation of the new law and I therefore take to be an outlier in this regard) and 1955, the value of the statistic is always within one standard deviation from the average.

16. The $r^2$ is 0.81; the F value is 13.6 and significant at the 0.03 level. The relevant coefficient is 2.1. With the small number of data points involved such a showing is obviously not conclusive of anything.

17. It is impossible to evaluate claims in this regard without much more knowledge than we have at present regarding the content of arbitration and conciliation decisions. However, to take one example of an agreement between workers and the Esso Standard Company signed on August 28, 1952: the workers were denied portal-to-portal pay but were granted a 15-minute paid wash-up period with the proviso that workers who left the premises before the end of the wash-up period were to be docked an hour's pay. By the classification standards that govern the data Beinin presents, such a case probably counted as a loss for the workers.

18. A convenient source for the law and some explanatory material is Egypt (Ministry of Social Affairs). I will refer to the ordinances themselves by paragraph but to additional explanatory material by page number to this source when appropriate.

19. For a fuller account of this incident see Beinin and Lockman 422–425.

20. The Arabic word *fasl* is equivalent to separation, the common umbrella term encompassing quits, firings, and layoffs until the middle of the twentieth century.

21. Parenthetically, Posusney seems to believe these are unreasonable grounds for which to fire employees, which suggests that for her there would be no reasonable grounds whatever. For a critique of implementing such regulation in the United States see Freed and Polsby who argue in favor of no limits whatsoever on the power of employers to terminate employees.

22. ʿIzz al-Din 815.

23. Article 52 that dealt with fines was rewritten to eliminate judicial discretion in the size of the fine, which was increased from the old maximum of ten pounds. The original range of fines was, of course, predicated on the assumption that workers as well as owners might have to pay.

24. The major difference between the 1953 Law and a similar one passed in 1948 appears to have been that the 1953 legislation reduced the size of the conciliation commission by eliminating a member chosen from the Ministry for Trade and Industry (thereby enhancing the power of the government labor affairs representative), provided a precise (and presumably more rapid) timetable for answers, and made the arbitration process binding and compulsory (which on balance was more likely to favor workers than owners). Under the 1948 Law

arbitration was only compulsory and binding if a previous arbitration order had provided no solution or if bakers, butchers, utilities, transport, or wholesale food consumption was involved.

25. The conciliation commissions, e.g., did not accept complaints by individual workers about arbitrary firings. These were rejected and referred back to the courts under the relevant provisions of the Civil Code. See Conflict 152, 1953 issued on October 15, 1953. Egypt (Ministry of Social Affairs 429).

26. Paragraph 695, subparagraph 2: the injured party gains "the right to compensation for what he has suffered because of the arbitrary termination of the contract."

27. See paragraph 696, subparagraphs 1 and 2.

28. In the words of a ministerial legal opinion: "The intended goal of Military Order 75 of 1945 continued by Decree 102 of 1945 was not the interest of the workers nor was this a piece of labor legislation . . . the primary goal was to guarantee the continuation of work in organizations that concerned the Ministry of National Defense . . ." (Ministry of Social Affairs 84). Despite the disclaimer, the decree was of course contained in collections of labor laws.

29. Dr. Muhammad Mandur was a well-known left Wafdist writing in *Al-Wafd al-Misri*, May 5, 1946.

30. In Chile a much more left-oriented labor movement actively and successfully pursued such an approach to labor–management relations and labor market regulations. See Drake: "Traditionally, union activity in Chile aimed more at extracting benefits through the state than at seeking them directly from individual employers. Worker appeals to labor inspectors, labor courts, labor laws, and the labor ministry were used routinely to settle grievances. Collective bargaining was frequently more effective with the government than with business. That statist orientation was reinforced by extensive government intervention in the economy and by the need to cope with chronic inflation. The state regulated not only labor disputes, but also wages, working hours, working conditions, job security, vacations, and profit sharing."

31. *Shubra*, May 14, 1942.

32. Dispute 3, 1953 decided on February 9, 1953. Egypt (Ministry of Social Affairs 420).

33. ʿAbd al-Sabbur 332, citing the preparatory materials for the Civil Code.

34. ʿAbd al-Sabbur, citing a 1959 technical report.

35. ʿAbd al-Sabbur, citing a Cairo appellate court decision of 1953.

36. Harbison and Ibrahim 164. Harbison and Ibrahim synthesized the results of interviews with employers, which I quote or summarize here. See also Ibrahim (100) for problems that involve claims of worker dissimulation and what would now be called adverse selection.

37. See also ILO 32.

38. Admittedly conflating a confusing process occurring over a protracted period of time, 1953 began not only with the accusation that Rashad Mahanna (with whom Amin's fate was linked) had plotted a coup against the regime but with the arrests of ʿAbbas Halim and Fuʾad Siraj al-Din (two former leaders of the right

wing of the Wafd generally associated as well with restraining the labor movement) and before it was over former Prime Minister Ibrahim Abd al-Hadi had been condemned to death (although the sentence was later commuted). For intimations of the effect of legislative changes limiting the rights of businessmen to serve on many boards of directors and other prerogatives see Vitalis (1995) 209.

39. I have calculated the values for this chart using a series developed by Tignor (1989) that provides profits for a large (20+ firm) sample. Tignor does not give a price deflator so all values are nominal L.E.

40. See El-Naggar 118–120 with its warning of undesirable distributional effects and inflation by using debt and proposal to use the government's tax powers to raise the major proportion of 10% of national income for financing industrialization projects (149). Knowing that such rates of accumulation were "lower than what the Russian economy was capable of attaining during the initial period of industrialisation" would have provided investors with little comfort.

41. The evidence about dividend payout rates is fragmentary. Firms went in and out of business and not all firms paid dividends in Egyptian currency. I have not been able to assemble a complete set of stock exchange yearbooks to track dividends of all companies. Because the available price series (from the yearbooks) provide only annual high and low prices, few data points are available and there is no way to control for temporal variation in investment sectors.

42. In a earlier eras investors bought stocks because they paid dividends rather than because they yielded capital gains.

43. The reported annual low price was in September, just before the edited version was sent to the printer.

## Chapter 7   *Efficiency Wages, Moral Economies, and Involution*

1. Even in the Depression, Egyptian industrial wages exhibited some rigidity (Hansen [1991] 56).

2. Posusney confuses recognizing the possibility that workers may vary their effort with character assassination: "'they pretend to pay us, and we pretend to work' attitude disparagingly ascribed to Egyptian workers by neoliberal reform advocates" (Posusney 17). Rather than wages, Posusney suggests, ideology counts as it did in the 1950s when "the regime explicitly appealed to workers' nationalist sentiments when encouraging them to increase their productive effort" (16).

3. Posusney appears to believe that Egyptian workers suffer severe information constraints but that American and European workers do not (Posusney 18). In Keynesian and neo-Keynesian theories (but not neoclassical theories) imperfect information is a structural condition; there is no reason to believe that Egyptian workers are systematically less rational or more angry than workers elsewhere.

4. Technically children were forbidden, under ministerial notice 108 of December 10, 1934, to engage in competitions at work "with the aim of increasing production" (Ministry of Social Affairs 12).

5. The origins of legally defined pay differences between children and adults first appeared in Decree 358 of December 9, 1942 which (under the 1940 martial law authority) ordered factory owners to pay cost of living allowances to their employees. Workers more than 18-years-old were to receive a minimum of 7.5 piasters a day; the minimum wage for workers less than 18 decreased by half a piaster per year to a minimum of 5 piasters day for children who were (presumably) 12-years-old.

6. At the Ahliyah spinning and weaving factory in Alexandria workers were covered by a written, collective agreement (rather than the individual contract). The 1949 contract explicitly refers to Chapter 30 of Law 41/1944 for the training period and a minimum wage for workers older than 18 years of age of 10 piasters during the six-month training period while extending the training period for those in the age group less than 18 to two years at the same wage (Sharikat Al-Ghazl Al-Ahliyyah 37–38).

7. Strictly speaking this is a feature of our knowledge rather than the Wafd, but for the countless pages written about the Wafd it is remarkable that it now appears that "not having a policy" rather than "our knowledge is slight" has now become an accepted fact of Egyptian history. For example, see Anis (1977): "After 1936 the Wafd had no progressive social program to replace its struggle for independence as its *raison d'etre*" (212).

8. See Deeb 273.

9. See Egypt *Taqrir*.

10. The cottonseed market appears to have been quite efficient with quotes not only on the Alexandria Bourse but also London quotes on Egyptian seed and oil. Thus a slight amendment to the description below of the net-back price. English users would bid the price of seed and seed products up to the next economically viable substitute, in all likelihood a level above what Egyptian consumers would pay.

11. See Robert Tignor ([1984] 40–41) for a discussion and tables A.9 and A.10 for profits and growth of reserves.

12. In the 1936–1937 harvest, world cottonseed production was almost 14 million tons with the United States obviously the largest producer (because it was the largest producer of fiber). Almost all the world's cottonseed, however, was used in the country in which it was grown. In 1932, total net world exports of cottonseed were 417,000 tons of which Egypt accounted for 199,000 tons. In 1935 total exports were 802,000 tons of which Egypt accounted for 368,000. Great Britain imported about 75% of total world exports. See Bahl 22–24.

13. The United States ceased to be a major oil exporter during the 1930s and Soviet exports also declined while those of Brazil increased. See International Institute 7–9.

14. See Egypt [1925] 184. This is the Arabic version of the 1916 report on industries and it appears to include material regarding postwar conditions. Owen (1969) indicates there was overcapacity in the 1890s in ginning as well. Husayn Hamdi, a researcher in the Ministry of Social Affairs, estimated that only half of Egypt's crushing capacity was employed during the mid-1930s, which implies

doubling production was a possible outcome. See Hamdi, 238. He indicates seed throughput doubled during the war and that 4 million ardebs of seed produced 90,000 tons of edible oil and 430,000 tons of cake for fodder, fuel, and fertilizer, which certainly meant Egypt was able to weather lessened imports of oil, soap, and fertilizer better during World War II than during World War I.

15. Tignor ([1989] 46). That same year the importation of cotton seed into the United States was outlawed and fumigation of cotton fiber required (see Brown [1938] 364).

16. The directors of the Ahliyyah textile factory in Alexandria asked that the 1916 law be changed in 1916 (Egypt, *Taqrir* 176); the directors of Kafr al-Zayyat asked at the same time to be able to import seed (Egypt, *Taqrir* 182).

17. See Owen ([1969] 274) for the accounts of the Manzalawi family in which it is apparent that the ginner is engaged in the marketing of seed at least as much as in ginning. Manzalawi paid about 9 pounds to gin his December cotton but sold the seed to the ginner for about 590 pounds.

18. The ESR had set rail tariffs so that rates for the same goods from Upper Egypt to Alexandria were cheaper than from Upper Egypt to Kafr al-Zayyat although Kafr al-Zayyat was hundreds of kilometers closer. Gritly proposes that railway tariffs "were framed with the avowed object of yielding the highest possible revenue for the state, whose freedom of indirect taxation was circumscribed by the shackles of the Capitulatory regime." See Gritly 474.

19. Owen 219.

20. INSEE (103).

21. Gritly 593–594.

22. The quality issue was that human beings pick less trash than machines and also disturb the plants less; exactly the concerns that led to the use of child labor in Egypt.

23. Egyptian Federation of Industry 193.

24. Egyptian Federation of Industry. Of course the oil could have been considered a by-product of cake production and simply given away if need be.

25. ʿAbd al-salam (160) clarifies an important point about how growers and buyers contracted over a joint product whose precise proportions could not be initially determined. It was assumed that the fiber content was 100 *ratls* out of a 315 *ratl cantar* of raw cotton and a premium was paid for higher fiber content as well as a price for the seed itself.

26. Dasuqi, tables between 214 and 215. Eleven of fifteen members of the committee on trade and industry were large landowners as were seventeen of twenty-one members of the treasury committee, which would appear to be the relevant legislative bodies.

27. Gritly 504.

28. Despite a rearrangement of his government Nahas remained in office until December 30, 1937. Jumʿah remained Minister of Trade and Commerce throughout this period. Makram ʿUbayd remained finance minister for the entire period.

29. Gritly 505.
30. Gritly 505.
31. Legally children were prohibited from such work unless they obtained a certificate certifying that they were healthy enough to perform the work for which they were hired. The certificate was delivered gratis; no particular examination was required; and even this nominal requirement was often ignored by employers.

## Chapter 8  Conclusion

1. Cotton textiles accounted for about another third.
2. As earlier in this book, to claim that Japanese girls were more educated or had greater well-being than Egyptian girls at the same time makes no claim about the absolute levels of well-being they experienced.

# Bibliography

Abaza, Fu'ad (1941) *Kitab 'an al-ma'rid al-zira'i al-khamis 'ashr* (Cairo: Matba'at 'Ali 'Inani).

Abbas, Mohamed Hosny (1946) *Essai sur l'évolution du commerce extérieure égyptien* (Cairo: Imprimerie C. Tsoumas and Co.).

Abd al-Motaal, Zaki (1930) *Les Bourses en Egypte* (Paris: Librairie générale de droit et de jurisprudence).

'Abd al-Sabbur, Fathi (1961) *Al-Wasit fi 'Aqd al-Amal al-Fardi* (Cairo: Arab Book Publishers).

'Abd al-Salam, Muhammad (1980) *Tiknuliji intaj wa tasni' al-qutn al-misri* (Giza: Cotton Research Institute).

Abdel-Khalek, Gouda and Robert Tignor (1982) *The Political Economy of Income Distribution in Egypt* (New York: Holmes and Meier).

Abdel-Malek, Anouar (1964) "Nasserism and Socialism" in Ralph Miliband (ed.) *The Socialist Register* (New York: Monthly Review Press).

Abdel Wahab, Ahmad (1930) *Memorandum on the Bases of a Stable Cotton Policy* (Cairo: Government Press).

———— (1934) "The Great Experiment in America" in *L'Egypte Contemporaine* 148–149: 169–195.

———— (1935) "L'Egypte Moderne: Problemes Economiques et Financiers" in *L'Egypte Contemporaine* 26: 147–165.

Abdel Wahab, Ahmed (1937) "Quelques Aspects de l'économie dirigée en Egypt Durant ces dernières années" in *L'Egypte Contemporaine* 28, 170: 137–153.

Ahmad, Ibrahim and Muhammad Abd al-Rahman Hafiz (1937) *Aswaq al-qutn wa tijaratihi fi misr* (Cairo: Al-Saadah Publishers).

Alchian, Armen A. and Harold Demsetz (1973) "The Property Right Paradigm" in *Journal of Economic History* 33,1: 16–27.

Akerlof, George A. (1982) "Labor Contracts as Partial Gift Exchange" in *Quarterly Journal of Economics* 97, 4: 543–569.

———— (1984) "Gift Exchange and Efficiency-Wage Theory: Four Views" in *The American Economic Review* 74, 2: 79–83.

———— and Janet L. Yellen (1990) "The Fair Wage-Effort Hypothesis and Unemployment" in *Quarterly Journal of Economics* 105, 2: 255–283.

ᶜAli, ᶜAbd al-ᶜAziz (1978) *Al-tha'ir al-samit* (Cairo: Dar al-maᶜarif ).

Amsden, Alice H. (1991) "Diffusion of Development: The Late-Industrializing Model and Greater East Asia" in *The American Economic Review* 81, 2: 282–286.

Anis, Mahmoud Amin (1950) *A Study of the National Income of Egypt* (Cairo: Société Orientale de Publicité).

Anis, Muhammad (1977) *Tatawwur al-mujtamaᶜ al-misri min al-iqtaᶜ ila thawrat 23 yulyu* (Cairo: Al-Jabalawi Press).

Antonini, Emile (1927) *Le Credit et la Banque en Egypte* (Lausanne: Imprimerie G. Vaney-Burnier).

Apter, David (1965) *The Politics of Modernization* (Chicago: University of Chicago Press).

Arab Republic of Egypt (1982) *The Parliamentary Positions of the Late Professor Muhammad Fikri Abaza* (Cairo: Al-Amiriyya Press).

Arthur D. Little, Inc. (1955) *Opportunities for Industrial Development in Egypt* (Cairo: Government Press).

Assaad, Ragui (1996) "Structural Adjustment and Labor Market Reform in Egypt" in H. Hopfinger (ed.) *Economic Liberalization and Privatization in Socialist Arab Countries* (Stuttgart: Justus Perthes Verlag).

Baer, Gabriel (1982) *Fellah and Townsman in the Middle East* (London: Frank Cass).

Bahl, J.C. (1938) *The Oilseed Trade of India* (Bombay: New Book Company).

Baker, Raymond William (1979) *Egypt's Uncertain Revolution* (Cambridge: Harvard University Press).

Balls, Lawrence (1918) "Analyses of Agricultural Yield, Part III, The Influence of Natural Environmental Factors Upon the Yield of Egyptian Cotton" in *Philosophical Transactions of the Royal Society of London, Series B*, 208: 157–223.

Balls, William Lawrence and Francis Holton (1915) "Analysis of Agricultural Yield: The Spacing Experiment With Egyptian Cotton, 1912" in *Philosophical Transactions of the Royal Society, Series B*, October: 103–180.

———— and M.A. Zaghloul (1932) "Analyses of Agricultural Yield, Part IV, Water-Table Movement on a Farm in Egypt" in *Philosophical Transactions of the Royal Society of London, Series B*, 221: 335–375.

Baraka, Magda (1998) *The Egyptian Upper Class Between Revolutions, 1919–1952* (Reading: Ithaca Press).

Baron, David P. and Roger B. Meyerson (1982) "Regulating a Monopolist with Unknown Costs" in *Econometrica* 50, 4: 911–930.

Barzel, Yoram (1989) *Economic Analysis of Property Rights* (Cambridge: Cambridge University Press).

Bates, Robert H. (1982) *Beyond the Miracle of the Market* (Cambridge: Cambridge University Press).

Robert Bates and Da-Hsien Donald Lien (1985). "A Note on Taxation, Development and Representative Government" in *Politics and Society* 14: 53–70.

———— (1997) *Open-Economy Politics* (Princeton: Princeton University Press).

Beattie, Kirk J. (1994) *Egypt During the Nasser Years* (Boulder: Westview Press).

Beatty, John (1990) "Dobzhansky and Drift: Facts, Values, and Chance in Evolutionary Biology" in (eds.) Lorenz Krüger, Gerd Gigenzerer and Mary S. Morgan *The Probabilistics Revolution* (Cambridge: MIT Press).

Beinin, Joel and Zachary Lockman (1987) *Workers on the Nile* (Princeton: Princeton University Press).

—— (1989) "Labor, Capital and the State in Nasirist Egypt, 1952–61" in *International Journal of Middle East Studies* 21 (February 1989): 71–90.

—— (1999) "Egypt: Society and Economy, 1923–1952" in M.W. Daly (ed.) *The Cambridge History of Egypt* (Cambridge: Cambridge University Press).

Bennett, M.K. (1937) "On Measurement of Relative National Standards of Living" in *Quarterly Journal of Economics* 51, 2: 317–336.

Benavot, Aaron (1983) "The Rise and Decline of Vocational Education" in *Sociology of Education* 56, 2: 63–76.

—— (1989) "Education, Gender, and Economic Development: A Cross-National Study" in *Sociology of Education* 62, 1: 14–32.

Bianchi, Robert (1989) *Unruly Corporatism* (New York: Oxford University Press).

Bishara, Ibrahim (1934) "The Cotton Worm, Prodenia litura F. in Egypt" in *Bulletin de la Societe Royale Entomologique d'Egypte* 3: 289–416.

Bishri, Tariq al- (1977) *Sa'd Zaghlul yufawid al-istiʿmar* (Cairo: Egyptian General Book Organization).

Black, J.D. (1936) "The Outlook for American Cotton" in *The Review of Economic Statistics* 17, 3: 68–78.

Blanchard, G. (1932) "La Second Phase de la Crise Égyptienne" in *L'Egypte Contemporaine* 135 (April).

Blinder, Alan (2000) "Education for Growth: Why and For Whom?" (Princeton University: International Relations Section Working Paper #429).

Bourkser, David (1925) "L'Egypte et Une Banque Centrale d'Escompte" in *L'Egypte Contemporaine* 89 (December).

Bowman, John R. (1982) *Capitalist Collective Action* (New York: Cambridge University Press).

Bresciani-Turroni, C. (1930) "Relations Entre La Recolte et le Prix du Coton Egyptien" in *L'Egypte Contemporaine* 124: 639–713.

—— (1931) "L'Influence de la speculation dur les fluctuations des prix du cotton" in *L'Egypte Contemporaine* 126: 308–341.

—— (1934) "Egypt's Balance of Trade" in *The Journal of Political Economy* 42, 3: 371–381.

—— (1938) "The 'Multiplier' in Practice: Some Results of Recent German Experience" in *The Review of Economic Statistics* 20, 2: 76–88.

Brown, Henry Bates (1938) *Cotton* (New York: McGraw Hill).

Brown, John C. (1992) "Market Organization, Protection and Vertical Integration: German Cotton Textiles Before 1914" in *Journal of Economic History* 52, 2: 339–351.

Buchanan, Paul G. (1995) *State, Labor, Capital* (Pittsburgh: University of Pittsburgh Press).

Carson, William Morris (1953) "The Mehallah Report" (Badr al-Shayn: Ford Foundation).

Casoria, Matteo M. (1922) "Chronique Agricole de l'Année 1922" in *L'Egypte Contemporaine* 70: 141–161.

Caves, Richard E. (1965) "'Vent for Surplus' Models of 3 Trade and Growth" in Robert Baldwin *et al.* (eds.) *Trade, Growth and the Balance of Payments* (Chicago: Rand McNally and Co.).

Chandler, Alfred (1977) *The Visible Hand* (Cambridge: Bellnap Press).

Chapman, S.J. and J. McFarlane (1907) "Cotton Supplies" in *The Economic Journal* 17: 57–65.

Chaudhry, Kiren Aziz (1993) "The Myths of the Market and the Common History of Late Developers" in *Politics and Society* 21, 3: 245–274.

Chiswic, Barry R. (1971) "Earnings Inequality and Economic Development" in *Quarterly Journal of Economics* 85, 1: 21–39.

Clark, Gregory (1987) "Why Isn't the Whole World Developed? Lessons From the Cotton Mills" in *Journal of Economic History* 47, 1: 141–173.

Coase, R.H. and R.F. Fowler (1935) "Bacon Production and the Pig-Cycle in Great Britian" in *Economica* 2, 6: 142–167.

——— (1937) "The Pig-Cycle in Great Britian: An Explanation" in *Economica* 4, 13: 55–82.

Cole, Taylor (1941) "National Socialism and the German Labor Courts" in *The Journal of Politics* 3, 2: 169–197.

——— (1956) "The Role of the Labor Courts in Western Germany" in *The Journal of Politics* 18, 3: 479–498.

Constantine, John H. and Julian M. Alston (1994) "Economic Impacts of the California One-Variety Cotton Law" in *Journal of Political Economy* 102, 5: 951–974.

——— and Vincent H. Smith (1994) "Economic Impacts of the California One-Variety Cotton Law" in *The Journal of Political Economy* 102, 5: 951–974.

Cooper, Mark (1982) *The Transformation of Egypt* (Baltimore: Johns Hopkins University Press).

Cornell, Drucilla "Dialogic Reciprocity and the Critique of Employment at Will" in *Cardozo Law Review* 10.

Crafts, N.F.R. and Mark Thomas (1986) "Comparative Advantage in UK Manufacturing Trade, 1910–1935" in *The Economic Journal* 96, 1: 629–645.

Craig, James I (1910) "Notes on Cotton Statistics in Egypt" in *L'Egypte Contemporaine* 166–198.

Cromer, Earl of (1908a) *Modern Egypt* Vol. one (London: Macmillan and Company).

——— (1908b) *Modern Egypt* Vol. two (London: Macmillan and Company).

Crouchley, A.E. (1938) *The Economic Development of Modern Egypt* (London: Longman, Greens and Co.).

Cumings, Bruce (1984) "The Origins and Development of the Northeast Asian Political Economy: Industrial Sectors, Product Cycles, and Political Consequences" in *International Organization* 38, 1: 1–40.

Cunningham, Hugh (2000) "The Decline of Child Labour: Labour Markets and Family Economies in Europe and North America Since 1830" in *Economic History Review* LIII, 3: 409–428.

Darwish, Muhammad (1941) AL-iqtisadiyyah al-qutniyyah *Majallat al-qanun wa al-iqtisad* 3 and 4, 11: 355–374.

Dasgupta, Partha (1993) *An Inquiry into Well-being and Destitution* (Oxford: The Clarendon Press).

Davezac, G. (1935) "La Politique Cotoniere des Etats-Unis" in *L'Egypte Contemporaine* 158–159: 693–721.

———— (1936) "La Politique Cotoniere des Etats-Unis *suite et fin*" in *L'Egypte Contemporaine* 160: 43–71.

Davis, Eric (1983) *Challenging Colonialism* (Princeton: Princeton University Press).

Davis, Horace B. (1929) "The German Labor Courts" in *Political Science Quarterly* 44, 3: 397–420.

Deeb, Marius (1979) *Party Politics in Egypt: The Wafd and Its Rivals 1919–1939* (Reading: Ithaca Press).

Dekmeijian, R. Hrair (1971) *Egypt Under Nasir* (Albany: State University of New York Press).

Dillard, Douglas (1946) "The Pragmatic Basis of Keynes's Political Economy" in *The Journal of Economic History* 6, 2: 121–152.

Disuqi, ᶜAsim (1975) *Kibar mullak al-aradi al-zira ᶜiyyah* (Cairo: New Culture Press).

Dixit, Avinash K. (1998) *The Making of Economic Policy* (Cambridge: The MIT Press).

Doeringer, Peter B. and Michael J. Piore (1971) *Internal Labor Markets and Manpower Analysis* (Lexington, Mass.: Health Lexington Books).

Dollar, David (1993) "Technological Differences as a Source of Comparative Advantage" in *The American Economic Review* 83,2: 431–435.

Ducruet, Jean (1964) *Les Capitaux europeens au proche orient* (Paris: Presses Universitaires de France).

Dudgeon, G.C. (1923) "A Brief Revue of the Cotton Conditions in Egypt During the Past Five Years" in *L'Egypte Contemporaine* 14: 517–532.

Drake, Paul M. (1996) *Labor Movements and Dictatorships* (Baltimore: Johns Hopkins University Press).

Dunn, John (1990) *Interpreting Political Responsibility* (Princeton: Princeton University Press).

Easterlin, Richard A. (1981) "Why Isn't the Whole World Developed?" in *Journal of Economic History* 41, 1: 1–19.

Egypt, Government of (1925) *Taqrir lajnat al-tijarah wa'l sinaᶜah* (Cairo: Amiriyyah Press).

Egypt, Ministry of Agriculture (1953) *The Cotton of Egypt* (Cairo: Government Press).

Egypt, Ministère des Finances (1916) *Annuaire Statisque de l'Egypte* (Cairo: Imprimerie Nationale).

Egypt, Ministère des Finances (1921) *Annuaire Statisque de l'Egypte* (Cairo: Imprimerie Nationale).

Egypt, Ministry of the Interior (1910) *Rapport Generale de la Commission du cotton* (Cairo).

Egypt, Goverment of Ministry of Social Affairs (1954) *Collected Labor Legislation of Egypt* (Cairo: Amiriyyah Press).

Egypt, Arab Republic of (1982) *Parliamentary Positions of the Late Muhammad Fikri Abaza* (Cairo: Government Printing Office).

Egyptian Federation of Industry (1948) *Livre d'Or de la Fédération Egyptienne de l'Industrie* (Cairo: Imprimerie Schindler).

Eichengreen, Barry (1996) *Globalizing Capital* (Princeton: Princeton University Press).

Eisa, Hamdy M. *et al.* (1993) *Cotton Production Prospects for the Decade to 2005* (Washington, D.C.: The World Bank).

Elgood, P.G. (1928) *The Transit of Egypt* (London: Edward Arnold and Company).

Ellis, Leonora Beck (1903) "A Study of Southern Cotton-Mill Communities, Child Labor, The Operatives in General" in *American Journal of Sociology* 8, 5: 623–630.

El-Emary, Ahmed (1936) "La Crise du Chomage en Egypte et Ailleurs, Ses Causes et Ses Remèdes" in *L'Egypte Contemporaine* 164 (May).

———(1937) "La Structure economique de l'Egypte" in *L'Egypte Contemporaine* 168–169: 187–221.

Eman, André (1943) *L'industrie du cotton en Egypte: etude d'économie politique* (Cairo: Imprimerie de l'institut français d'archéologie).

Enayat, Hamid (1988) *Modern Islamic Political Thought* (Austin: University of Texas Press).

Epstein, Richard "In Defense of Contract at Will" in *Chicago Law Review* 51: 947–982.

Evans, Peter (1979) *Dependent Development* (Princeton: Princeton University Press).

———(1997) "State Structures, Government-Business Relations and Economic Transformation" in Sylvia Maxfield and Ben Ross Schneider (eds.), *Business and the State in Developing Countries* (Cornell: Cornell University Press).

Falvey, Rodney E. (1989) "Trade, Quality Reputations and Commercial Policy" in *International Economic Review* 30, 3: 607–622.

Federazione coloniale italiane di Alessandria (1921) *Memoriale sui recente avvenimenti* (Alexandria).

Feeny, David (1979) "Competing Hypotheses of Underdevelopment: A Thai Case Study" in *Journal of Economic History* 39, 1: 113–127.

Fieldhouse, David Kenneth (1978) *Unilver Overseas: The Anatomy of a Multinational 1895–1965* (London: Croom Helm).

Freed, Mayer and Daniel Polsby (1989) "Just Cause for Termination Rules and Economic Efficiency" in *Emory Law Journal* 38: 1097–1144.

Freeman, Richard B. and James L. Medoff (1984) *What Do Unions Do?* (New York: Basic Books).

Frieden, Jeffry (1991) "Invested Interests" in *International Organization* 45, 4: 425–451.

Fuller, Bruce *et al.* (1986) "When Does Education Boost Economic Growth? School Expansion and School Quality in Mexico" in *Sociology of Education* 59, 3: 167–181.

Garside W.R. and J.L Greaves (1997) "Rationalisation and Britain's Industrial Malaise: the Interwar Years Revisted" in *Journal of European Economic History* 26: 37–68.

Gertel, Jorg (1995) *The Metropolitan Food System in Cairo* (Saabrucken: Verlag fur Entwickungspolitik).

Goirand, Leopold (1898) *A Treatise Upon French Commercial Law* (London: Stevens and Sons).

Goldberg, Ellis (1986) *Tinker, Tailor and Textile Worker* (Berkeley: University of California Press).

——— (1996) *The Social History of Labor in the Middle East* (Boulder: Westview).

Gordon, Joel (1992) *Nasser's Blessed Movement* (New York: Oxford University Press).

Gourevitch, Peter Alexis (1977) "International Trade, Domestic Coalitions, and Liberty: Comparative Responses to the Crisis of 1873–1896" in *Journal of Interdisciplinary History* 8, 2: 281–313.

——— (1984) "Breaking with Orthodoxy: The Politics of Economic Policy Responses to the Depression of the 1930s" in *International Organization* 38, 1: 95–129.

Greenwald, Bruce C. and Joseph E. Stiglitz (1995) "Labor-Market Adjustments and the Persistence of Unemployment" in *The American Economic Review* 85, 2: 219–225.

Greif, Avner (1993) "Contract Enforceability and Economic Institutions in Early Trade: The Maghribi Traders' Coalition" in *The American Economic Review* 83, 3: 525–548.

Griliches, Zvi (1957) "Hybrid Corn: An Explanation in the Economics of Technological Change" in *Econometrica* 25, 4: 501–522.

——— (1988) "Productivity Puzzles and R & D: Another Non Explanation" in *The Journal of Economic Perspectives* 2, 4: 9–21.

Al-Gritly, Ali (1948) *The Structure of Modern Industry in Egypt* (Cairo: Government Press).

Guest, Avery M. and Stewart E. Tolnay (1985) "Agricultural Organization and Educational Consumption in the U.S. in 1900" in *Sociology of Education* 58, 5: 201–212.

Habib, SaᶜdᶜAbd al-Salam (1954) *Majmuᶜat qawanin al-ᶜamal wa al-ᶜummal* (Cairo: Arab Rennaissance Bookstore).

Hafiz, ᶜAbbas (1936) *Mustafa Al-Nahhas Aw Al-Zuᶜama wa al-Zaᶜim* (Cairo: Misri Press).

Haggard, Stephan (1990) *Pathways From the Periphery* (Ithaca: Cornell University Press).

Hall, Peter (1989) *The Political Power of Economic Ideas: Keynesianism Across Nations* (Princeton: Princeton University Press).

Hamid, Ra'uf ᶜAbbas (1992) *Arbaᶜun ᶜamm ᶜala thawrat yulyu* (Cairo: Center for Political and Strategic Studies).

Hansen, Bent (1969) "Employment and Wages in Rural Egypt" in *The American Economic Review* 59, 3: 298–313.

——— and Karim Nashashibi (1975) *Foreign Trade Regimes: Egypt* (New York: National Bureau of Economic Research).

——— (1991) *Egypt and Turkey* (Oxford: Oxford University Press).

Hanafi, Muhammad (1951) *Tashriᶜ al-ᶜamal fi misr* (Alexandria: Muhammad Khalil Press).

Hanson II, John R. (1988) "Why Isn't the Whole World Developed? A Traditional View" in *Journal of Economic History* 48, 3: 668–672.

Harari, Ralph A. (1936). "Banking and Financial Business in Egypt" in *L'Egypte Contemporaine* 161 (February).

Harbison, Frederick and Ibrahim Albdelkader Ibrahim (1958) *Human Resources for Egyptian Enterprise* (New York: McGraw Hill Book Company).

Haridi, Salah Ahmad (1985) *Al-hiraf wa al-sinaᶜat fir ahd muhamad ᶜali* (Cairo: Dar al-maᶜarif).

Hart, Oliver and John Moore (1990) "Property Rights and the Nature of the Firm" in *Journal of Political Economy* 98, 6: 1119–1158.

Hasan, ᶜAli ᶜAwad (1974) *Al-Fasl al-Taᵓdibi fi Qanun al-ᶜamal* (Cairo: University of Cairo, Doctoral Dissertation in Law).

Heckscher, Eli (1955) Rev. ed E.F. Söderlund *Mercantilism* 2 vols: I and II (London: George Allen Unwin).

Heller, Peter S. (1976) "Factor Endowment Change and Comparative Advantage: The Case of Japan, 1956–1969" in *The Review of Economics and Statistics* 58, 3: 283–292.

Henderson, Hubert Douglas (1922) *The Cotton Control Board* (Oxford: The Clarendon Press).

Heriot, Gail (1993) "The New Feudalism: The Unintended Consequences of Contemporary Trends in Employment Law" in *Georgia Law Review* 28: 167–222.

Hicks, J.R. (1946) *Value and Capital* (Oxford: Clarendon Press).

Hillel, Daniel (1994) *Rivers of Eden* (New York: Oxford University Press).

Hobsbawm, Eric (1966) *The Age of Revolution* (New York: Vintage).

Hodge, M.J.S. (1990) "Natural Selection as a Causal, Empirical and Probabilistic Theory" in Lorenz Krüger, Gerd Gigenzerer, and Mary S. Morgan (eds.) *The Probabilistic Revolution* (Cambridge: MIT Press).

Horan, Patrick M. and Peggy G. Hargis (1991) "Children's Work and Schooling in the Late Nineteenth-Century Family Economy" in *American Sociological Review* 56, 5: 583–596.

Horrell, Sara and Jane Humphries (1995) " 'The Exploitation of Little Children': Child Labor and the Family Economy in the Industrial Revolution" in *Explorations in Economic History* 32, 4: 485–516.

Hubbard, G.E. and Denzil Baring (1935) *Eastern Industrialization and Its Effect on the West* (London: Oxford University Press).

Human Rights Watch (2001) "Underage and Unprotected: Child Labor in Egypt's Cotton Fields" (New York: Human Rights Watch).

Huntington, Samuel (1968) *Political Order in Changing Societies* (New Haven: Yale University Press).

Ibrahim, Ibrahim Abdelkader (1957) "The Labor Problem in Industrialization in Egypt" Dissertation, Department of Sociology, Princeton University.

Ikeda, Misako (1998) "Sociopolitical Debates in Late Parliamentary Egypt, 1944–1952" (Harvard University: Ph.D. Dissertation in Middle Eastern Studies).

International Cotton Congress (1904) *Official Report of the Proceedings of the First International Congress* (Manchester: N.P.).

———(1905) *Official Report of the Proceedings of the Second International Congress* (Manchester: N.P.).

International Federation of Master Cotton Spinners' and Manufacturers' Associations (1912) *Official Report of the Delegation to Egypt* (Manchester).

———(1927) *Official Report of the International Cotton Congress.*

———(1938) *Official Report of the XVIII International Cotton Congress* (Manchester: The Cloister Press).

International Labor Organization (1951) *Manpower Problems* (Geneva: International Labor Office).

International Institute of Agriculture (1939) *Oils and Fats: Production and International Trade* (Rome: Villa Umberto).

Irwin, Douglas (1996) *Against the Tide: An Intellectual History of Free Trade* (Princeton: Princeton University Press).

Issa, Hossam (1970) *Capitalisme et Societes anonymes en Egypte* (Paris: Librairie Generale de Droit et Jurisprudence).

Issawi, Charles (1947) *Egypt; An Economic and Social Analysis* (London: Oxford University Press).

———(1954) *Egypt at Midcentury, An Economic Survey* (London: Oxford University Press).

———(1963) *Egypt in Revolution; and Economic Analysis* (London: Oxford University Press).

———(1995) *The Middle East Economy: Decline and Recovery* (Princeton: Markus Wiener Publishers).

———(1963) "Public Control of the Natural Gas Industry" in Alfred M. Leeston, John A. Crichton, and John C. Jacobs (eds.) *The Dynamic Natural Gas Industry* (Norman: University of Oaklahoma Press).

Johnson, Leland L. (1960) "The Theory of Hedging and Speculation in Commodity Futures" in *Review of Economic Studies* 27: 139–151.

Judge, A.S. (1920) "The Production of Tea in the Empire and Its Relation to the Tea Trade of the World" in *Bulletin of the Imperial Institute* 18: 490–530.

Jullien, Leopold (1914) "Chronique cotonière de 1913" in *L'Egypte Contemporaine* 5, 18: 223–231.

Kahler, Miles (1985) "Politics and International Debt: Explaining the Crisis" in *International Organization* 39, 3: 357–382.

Kasaba, Resat (1988) "Was There A Compradore Bourgeoisie in Mid-Nineteenth Century Western Anatolia" in *Review* XI, 2: 215–228.

Katzenstein, Peter J. (1977) "Conclusion: Domestic Structures and Strategies of Foreign Economic Policy" in *International Organization* 31, 4: 879–920.

Keynes, John Maynard (1936) *The General Theory of Employment, Interest and Money* (New York: Harcourt Brace and Company).

———(1963) *Essays in Persuasion* (New York: W.W. Norton).

Kirk, George (1953) *The Middle East in the War* (London: Oxford University Press).

Klein, Benjamin and Keith B. Leffler (1981) "The Role of Market Forces in Assuring Conctractual Performance" in *The Journal of Political Economy* 89,4: 615–641.

Koo, Hagen (1987) "The Interplay of State, Social Class and World System in East Asian Development: The Cases of South Korea and Taiwan" in Frederic C. Deyo (ed.) *The Political Economy of the New Asian Industrialism* (Ithaca: Cornell University Press).

Kramer, Gudrun (1989) *The Jews in Modern Egypt 1914–1952* (Seattle: University of Washington Press).

Krugman, Paul (1994) *Peddling Prosperity* (New York: W.W. Norton and Company).

Kuran, Timur (1989a) "The Craft Guilds of Tunis and Their Amins: A Study in Institutional Atrophy" in *The Journal of Political Economy* 89,4.

———(1989b) "The Wholesale Produce Market of Tunis and Its Porters: A Tale of Market Degeneration" in Mustapha Nabli and Jeffrey Nugent (eds.) *The New Institutional Economics and Development: Theory and Applications to Tunisia* (Amsterdam: North Holland).

Krugman, Paul (1997) *Development, Geography and Economic Theory* (Cambridge: The MIT Press).

Landes, William M. and Lewis C. Solomon (1972) "Compulsory Schooling Legislation: An Economic Analysis of Law and Social Change in the Nineteenth Century" in *Journal of Economic History* 32, 1: 54–91.

Lazonick, William (1981) "Factor Costs and the Diffusion of Ring Spinning in Britain Prior to World War I" in *The Quarterly Journal of Economics* 96, 1: 89–109.

——— and William Mass (1990) "The British Cotton Industry and International Competitive Advantage: The State of the Debates" in *Business History* 32, 4: 9–66.

Leamer, Edward E. (1984) *Source of International Comparative Advantage: Theory and Evidence* (Cambridge, Mass.: MIT Press).

———(1993) "Factor-Supply Differences as a Source of Comparative Advantage" in *The American Economic Review* 83, 2: 436–439.

Leibenstein, Harvey (1980) *Beyond Economic Man* (Cambridge: Harvard University Press).

Lewis, William Arthur (1953) *Aspects of Industrialization* (Cairo: National Bank of Egypt).

Lewontin, Richard (2000) *The Triple Helix* (Cambridge: Harvard University Press).

Lindemann, Hugo (1931) "Le Coton Egyptien du Point de Vue de l'Exportateur" in *L'Egypte Contemporaine* 22, 127: 399–407.

Llewellyn, K.N. (1925) "The Effect of Legal Institutions Upon Economics" in *The American Economic Review* 15, 4: 665–683.

Lockman, Zachary (1993) *Working Classes in the Middle East: Struggles, Histories and Historiographies* (Albany: State University of New York Press).

Lockwood, William W. (1968) *The Economic Development of Japan* (Princeton: Princeton University Press).

Lloyd, Lord (1933) *Egypt Since Cromer,* Vol. One (London: Macmillan and Company).

Luhaytah, Muhammad Fahmi (1945) *Ta'rikh Fu'ad al-Awwal al-Iqtisadi*, Vol. 1 (Cairo: Maktabat Al-Nahdah al-Misriyyah).

———(1946a) *Ta'rikh Fu'ad al-Awwal al-Iqtisadi,* Vol. 2.

———(1946b) *Ta'rikh Fu'ad al-Awwal al-Iqtisadi: Al-ʿAdalah al-ijtimaʿiyah,* Vol. 3.

———(1939) *ʿIlm al-iqtisad li'l-misriyyin* (Cairo: Matbaʿat al-ʿItimad).

Macaulay, Stewart (1963) "Non-Contractual Relations in Business: A Preliminary Study" in *American Sociological Review* 28, 1: 55–67.

Maneschi, Andrea (1998) *Comparative Advantage in International Trade* (Cheltenham, UK: Edwar Elgar).

Mares, David R. (1985) "Explaining Choice of Development Strategies: Suggestions from Mexico, 1970–1982" in *International Organization* 39, 4: 667–697.

Margo, Robert A. and T. Aldrich Finegan (1993) "The Decline in Black Teenage Labor-Force Participation in the South, 1900–1970: The Role of Schooling" in *The American Economic Review* 83, 1: 234–247.

Marshall, Alfred (1961) *Principles of Economics* (London, MacMillan and Company Limited [reprint of the Eighth Edition, 1920]).

Martin, Gabriel (1910) *Bazars du Caire et les petites metiers arabes* (Cairo: Egyptian University Press).

Marsot, Afaf Lutfi Al-Sayyid (1977) *Egypt's Liberal Experiment* (Berkeley: University of California Press).

Matthews, Roderic D. and Matta Akrawi (1949) *Education in the Arab Countries of the Near East* (Washington, D.C.: American Council on Education).

Mazuel, Jean (1937) *Le Sucre en Egypte* (Cairo: E. & R. Schindler).

McCoan, J.C. (1888) *Egypt As It Is* (New York: Henry Holt).

McPherson, William H. and Frederic Meyers (1966) *The French Labor Courts: Judgment By Peers* (Urbana: Institute of Labor and Industrial Relations).

Meeker, J. Edward (1932) *Short Selling* (New York: Harper and Brothers).

Metin, Albert (1903) *La transformation de l'Egypte* (Paris: Felix Alcan).

Meyerson, Roger B. (1979) "Incentive Compatibility and the Bargaining Problem" in *Econometrica* 47, 1: 61–74.

Migdal, Joel (1974) *Peasants, Politics and Revolution: Pressures Toward Political and Social Change in the Third World* (Princeton: Princeton University Press).

———(1988) *Strong Societies and Weak States* (Princeton: Princeton University Press).

Mikesell, Raymond (1945) "Financial Problems of the Middle East East" in *The Journal of Political Economy* 53, 2: 164–176.

Miles, Caroline (1968) *Lancashire Textiles: A Case Study of Industrial Change* (Cambridge: Cambridge University Press).

Milner, Alfred (1892) *England in Egypt* (London: Edward Arnold).

Minost, E. (1931) "L'Action Contre La Crise Cotonnière en Egypte" in *L'Egypte Contemporaine* 22, 128: 409–457.

Mitchell, Timothy (1988) *Colonising Egypt* (New York: Cambridge University Press).

——— (1990) "The Limits of the State: Beyond Statist Approaches and Their Critics" in *The American Political Science Review* 85, 1: 77–96.

——— (2002) *Rule of Experts* (Berkeley: University of California Press).

Moore, Austin (1954) *Farewell Farouk* (Chicago: Scholar's Press).

Moser, Charles K. (1930) *The Cotton Textile Industry of Far Eastern Countries* (Boston: Pepperell Manufacturing Company).

Musoke, Moses S. and Alan L. Olmstead (1982) "The Rise of the Cotton Industry in California: A Comparative Perspective" in *Journal of Economic History* 42, 2: 385–412.

El-Naggar, Said (1952) *Industrialisation and Income with Special Reference to Egypt* (Cairo: Fouad I University Press).

——— (1960) "Foreign Aid to United Arab Republic" Institute of National Planning.

Nahas, Joseph (Yusuf) (1901) *Situation economique et sociale du fellah egyptien* (Paris: Librairie Nouvelle de Droit and de Jurisprudence).

——— (1927) *Al-Fallah: halah al-iqtisadiya wa'l'ijtimaʿiyyah* (Cairo: Al-Maqtataf Press).

——— (1952a) *Dhikrayat* (Cairo: Dar al-Nil).

——— (1952b) *Juhud al-Niqabah al-Zirāʿiyya al-Misriyya al-ʿAmmah fi Thalathina ʿAmm* (Cairo: Dar al-Nil).

——— (1954) *Al Qutn Fi Khamsin ʿAm* (Cairo: Dar al-Nil).

Nassef, Abdel-Fattah (1970) *The Egyptian Labor Force: Its Dimensions and Changing Structure, 1907–1960* (Philadelphia: Population Studies Center, University of Pennsylvania).

Nourse, Edwin G. (1927) *The Legal Status of Agricultural Cooperation* (New York: The MacMillan Company).

O'Donnell, Guillermo (1973) *Modernization and Bureaucratic Authoritarianism* (Berkeley: Institute for International Studies).

——— (1978) "Reflection on the Patterns of Change in the Bureaucratic-Authoritarian State" in *Latin American Research Review* 13: 3–37.

Oncu, Ayse, Caglar Keyder, and Saad Eddin Ibrahim (1994) *Developmentalism and Beyond* (Cairo: American University in Cairo Press).

Ono, Yeijiro (1890) "The Industrial Transition in Japan" in *Publications of the American Economic Association* 5, 1: 17–121.

Orchard, Dorothy (1929) "An Analysis of Japan's Cheap Labor" in *Political Science Quarterly* 44, 2: 215–258.

Orchard, John E. (1930) *Japan's Economic Position* (New York: McGraw Hill Book Company).

——— (1937) "Contrasts in the Progress of Industrialization in China and Japan" in *Political Science Quarterly* 52, 1: 18–50.

Otsuka, Keijiro, Gustav Ranis, and Gary Saxonhouse (1988) *Comparative Technology Choice in Development* (Hong Kong: MacMillan Press).

Owen, Roger (1969) *Cotton and the Egyptian Economy 1820–1914* (Oxford: The Clarendon Press).

——— (1984) "The Study of Middle Eastern Industrial History: Notes on the Interrelationship Between Factories and Small-Scale Manufacturing With Special Reference to Lebanese Silk and Egyptian Sugar, 1900–1930" in *International Journal of Middle East Studies* 16: 475–487.

——— (1989) "Economic Consequences of Suez for Egypt" in William Roger Louis and Roger Owen (eds.) *Suez 1956* (Oxford: Clarendon Press).

——— (1999) "A Long Look at Nearly Two Centuries of Staple Cotton" in Alan K. Bowman and Eugene Rogan (eds.) *Agriculture in Egypt from Pharaonic to Modern Times* (London: The British Academy).

Pagano, Ugo (1991) "Property Rights, Asset Specificity, and the Division of Labour Under Alternative Capitalist Relations" in *Cambridge Journal of Economics* 15: 15–342.

Papasian, E. (1926) *L'Egypte économique et financière* (Cairo: Imprimerie Misr).

Pashgian, B. Peter (1986) "The Political Economy of Futures Market Regulation" in *Journal of Business* 59, 2, Part 2: S55–S84.

Patton, Harald S. (1928) *Grain Growers' Cooperation in Western Canada* (Cambridge: Harvard University Press).

Payne, James L. (1965) *Labor and Politics in Peru* (New Haven: Yale University Press).

Pearse, Arno (1931) "Egyptian Cotton from the Points of View of the Spinning Industry" in *l'Egypte Contemporaine* 23,127: 388–398.

Polier, Leon (1911) "L'Organisation du credit en Egypte par les warrants commerciaux et agricoles" in *l'Egypte Contemporaine* 370–392.

——— (1914) "La question des prix du cotton et de l'approvisionnement des filatures" in *L'Egypte Contemporaine* 5, 19: 297–344.

Politi, E. (1965) *L'Egypte de 1914 à "Suez"* (Paris: Presses de la Cité).

Porter, Theodore M. (1995) *Trust in Numbers* (Princeton: Princeton University Press).

Posner, Richard (1995) *Overcoming Law* (Cambridge: Harvard University Press).

Posusney, Marsha Pripstein (1997) *Labor and the State in Egypt* (New York: Columbia University Press).

Prébisch, Raul (1950) *The Economic Development of Latin America* (New York: United Nations Department of Economic Affairs).

Pritchett, Lant (1996) "Where Has All the Education Gone?" Policy Research Working Paper 1581 (Washington, D.C.: The World Bank).

Psacharopoulos, George and Maureen Woodhall (1985) *Education for Development* (New York: Oxford University Press).

Qutb, Sayyid (1975a) *Ma'arkat al-Islam wa ra'smaliyah* (Beirut: Dar al-shuruq).

————(1975b) *Al-'Adalah al-ijtima'iyah fi al-islam* (Beirut: Dar al-shuruq).

Radi, Nawal ʿAbd al-ʿAziz (1977) *Adwa jadidah ala al-harakah al-niqabiyah* (Cairo: Dar al-nahdah).

Radwan, Samir (1974) *Capital Formation in Egyptian Industry and Agriculture 1882–1967* (London: Ithaca Press).

————and Eddy Lee (1986) *Agrarian Change in Egypt* (London: Croom Helm).

Rafeq, Abdul-Karim (1991) "Craft Organization, Work Ethics, and the Strains of Change in Ottoman Syria" in *Journal of the American Oriental Society* 111, 3: 495–511.

Rafiʿi, ʿAbd al-Rahman (1914) *Niqabat al-ta'awun al-zira'iyah* (Cairo: Nahdah Press).

Ramseyer, J. Mark (1996) *Odd Markets in Japanese History* (Cambridge: Cambridge University Press).

Royal Institute of International Affairs (1933) "Notes on the Textile Industry in Lancashire, India, China and Japan" mimeo text prepared for Fifth Bi-Annual Conference of the Institute of Pacific Relations (London: Chatham House).

Raymond, Andre (1973) *Artisans et commercants au Caire au XVIII^{ème} Siecle* (2 vols., Damascus: Institut Francais).

Reid, Donald (1980) "Fu'ad Siraj al-Din and the Egyptian Wafd" in *Journal of Contemporary History* 15: 721–744.

Reisman, David (1986) *The Economics of Alfred Marshall* (New York: St. Martin's Press).

Richards, Alan (1982) *Egypt's Agricultural Development 1800–1980* (Boulder: Westview Press).

Rizq, Yunan L. (1975) *Tarikh al-wizarat al-misriyyah 1878–1953* (Cairo: Al-Ahram Strategic Studies Center).

Rodrik, Dani (1999) *The New Global Economy and Developing Countries: Making Openness Work* (Washington, D.C.: Overseas Development Press).

Rogowski, Ronald (1989) *Commerce and Coalitions* (Princeton: Princeton University Press).

Rosenman, Robert E. and Wesley W. Wilson (1991) "Quality Differentials and Prices: Are Cherries Lemons?" in *Journal of Industrial Economics* 39,6: 649–658.

Rosenzweig, Mark R. and Robert Evenson (1977) "Fertility, Schooling and the Economic Contribution of Children of Rural India: An Econometric Analysis" in *Econometrica* 45, 5: 1065–1079.

Rowe, J.W.F. (1936) *Markets and Men* (Cambridge: The University Press).

Rubinson, Richard and John Ralph (1984) "Technical Change and the Expansion of Schooling in the United States, 1890–1970" in *Sociology of Education* 57, 3: 134–152.

Rueschmeyer, Dietrich and Peter Evans (1985) "The State and Economic Transformation: Toward an Analysis of the Conditions Underlying Effective Intervention" in Peter Evans *et al.* (eds.) *Bringing the State Back In* (Cambridge: Cambridge University Press).

Rushdi, Muhammad (1972) *Al-tatawwur al-iqtisadi fi misr* (Cairo: Dar al-maʿarif ).

Sadowski, Yahya (1991) *Political Vegetables* (Washington, D.C.: The Brookings Institution).

Saleh, Nabil A. (1986) *Unlawful Gain and Legitimate Profit in Islamic Law: Riba, Gharar, and Islamic Banking* (Cambridge: Cambridge University Press).

Samuels, Raphael (1977) "Workshop of the World: Steam Power and Hand Technology in mid-Victorian England" in *History Workshop* 3: 6–72.

Sandberg, Lars G. (1974) *Lancashire in Decline* (Columbus: Ohio State University Press).

Saqqaf, Mustafa al- (1954) *Al-raqaba ʿala al-naqd al-ajnabi fi misr* (Cairo: Egyptian Rennaissance Press).

Said, Gamal Eldin (1948) "Productivity of Labour in Egyptian Industry" in *L'Egypte Contemporaine* 41, 259–260: 493–506.

El-Sarki, Mohamed Youssef (1964) *La Monoculture du coton en Egypte et la developpement economique* (Geneva: Librairie Droz).

Saxonhouse, Gary (1974) "A Tale of Japanese Technological Diffusion in the Meiji Period" in *Journal of Economic History* 34, 1: 149–165.

———(1977) "Productivity Change and Labor Absorption in Japanese Cotton Spinning 1891–1935" in *The Quarterly Journal of Economics* 91,2: 195–220.

Schneider, Ben Ross and Sylvia Maxfield (1997) "Business, the State and Economic Performance" in Sylvia Maxfield and Ben Ross Schneider (eds.) *Business and the State in Developing Countries* (Cornell: Cornell University Press).

Schultz-Gaevernitz, Dr. G. von (1895) *The Cotton Trade in England and on the Continent* (Manchester: Marsden and Co. Ltd.).

Scott, Maurice and Deepak Lal (1990) *Public Policy and Economic Development* (Oxford: The Clarendon Press).

Shafer, D. Michael (1997) "Strong States and Business Organization in Korea and Taiwan" in Sylvia Maxfield and Ben Ross Schneider (eds.) *Business and the State in Developing Countries* (Ithaca: Cornell University Press).

Shapiro, Carl (1983) "Premiums for High Quality Products as Returns to Reputations" in *Quarterly Journal of Economics* 98, 4: 659–680.

——— and Joseph E. Stiglitz (1984) "Equilibrium Unemployment as a Worker Discipline Device" in *The American Economic Review* 74, 3: 433–444.

Sharabi, Hisham (1990) *Theory, Politics and the Arab World* (New York: Routledge).

Shibli, Ali and Mustafa Nahas Jabir (1981) *Al-inqilabat al-dusturiyah fi misr, 1923–1936* (Cairo: Egyptian General Book Organization).

Shimizu, Hiroshi (1986) *Anglo-Japanese Trade Rivalry in the Middle East in the Interwar Period* (London: Ithaca Press).

Sidki, Hasan (1950) *Al-qutn al-misri* (Cairo: Egyptian Renaissance Press).

Simmons, Beth A. (1994) *Who Adjusts?: Domestic Sources of Foreign Economic Policy During the Interwar Years* (Princeton: Princeton University Press).

Singerman, Diane (1995) *Avenues of Participation* (Princeton: Princeton University Press).

Skidelsky, Robert (1992) *John Maynard Keynes: The Economist as Saviour* (London: Macmillan Limited).

Smith, Adam (1976) ed. *Edwin Cannan An Inquiry into the Nature and Causes of the Wealth of Nations* (Chicago: University of Chicago Press).

Spulber, Daniel F. (1989) *Regulation and Markets* (Cambridge, Mass.: The MIT Press).

Stein, Jerome L. (1979) "Spot, Forward and Futures" in *Research in Finance* (Greenwich, Connecticut: JAI Press).

Stigler, George (1968) "The Division of Labor is Limited by the Extent of the Market" *The Organization of Industry* (Chicago: University of Chicago Press).

Stigler, Stephen (1986) *The History of Statistics: The Measurement of Uncertainty Before 1900* (Cambridge: Belknap Press).

Stiglitz, Joseph E. (1987) "Causes and Consequences of The Dependence of Quality on Price" in *Journal of Economic Literature* 25, 1: 1–48.

——— (1993) "Post Walrasian and Post Marxian Economics" in *The Journal of Economic Perspectives* 7, 1: 109–114.

——— (1994) *Whither Socialism?* (Cambridge: MIT Press).

Strange, Susan (1992) "States, Firms and Diplomacy" in *International Affairs* 68, 1: 1–15.

Taeuber, Irene (1951) "Family, Migration and Industrialization in Japan" in *American Sociological Review* 16, 2: 149–157.

Telser, Lester G. (1958) "Futures Trading and the Storage of Cotton and Wheat" in *The Journal of Political Economy* 66, 3: 233–255.

——— and Harlow N. Higginbotham (1977) "Organized Futures Markets: Costs and Benefits" in *The Journal of Political Economy* 85: 969–1000.

Temin, Peter (1988) "Product Quality and Vertical Integration in the Early Cotton Textile Industry" in *Journal of Economic History* 48, 4: 891–907.

Teymur, M. Hussein K. (1914) "De la nécessité d'une réforme de la bourse de commerce d'Alexandrie" in *L'Egypte Contemporaine* 21: 68–88.

Thabit, Karim (1931) *Jalalat al-malik bayna Misr wa Urubba: rihlat jalalatihi fi Almaniya wa Chikuslufakiya* (Cairo: Dar al-Hilal).

Thabit, Thabit (1936) *Al-Maʿrad al-ziraʿi al-sinaʿi* (Cairo: Al-Akhaʾ Press).

——— (1938) *Almaniya Al-Yawm* special supplement to *Al-Fallah al-Misri* September–October No. 12.

Thompson, E.P. (1966) *The Making of the English Working Class* (New York: Random House).

Tignor, Robert L. (1982) "Equity in Egypt's Recent Past: 1945–1952" in Gouda Abdel-Khalek and Robert Tignor (eds.) *The Political Economy of Income Distribution in Egypt* (New York: Holmes and Meyer).

——— (1984) *State, Private Enterprise and Economic Change in Egypt, 1918–1952* (Princeton: Princeton University Press).

——— (1989) *Egyptian Textiles and British Capital* (Cairo: American University in Cairo Press).

————(1998) *Capitalism and Nationalism at the End of Empire* (Princeton: Princeton University Press).

Tippett, L.H.C. (1969) *A Portrait of the Lancashire Textile Industry* (London: Oxford University Press).

Todd, John A. (1911) "The Market for Egyptian Cotton in 1909–1910" in *L'Egypte Contemporaine* 2, 5: 1–29.

————(1915) *The World's Cotton Crops* (London: A. & C. Black, Ltd.).

————(1927) *The Cotton World* (London: Sir Isaac Pitman and Sons).

Tomiche, F.J. (1974) *Syndicalisme et certain aspects du travail en Republique Arab Unie (Egypte), 1900–1967* (Paris: Maisonneuve).

Trimberger, Ellen Kay (1978) *Revolution From Above: Military Bureaucracy and Development in Japan, Turkey, Egypt and Peru* (New Brunswick: Transaction Books).

Turner, John R.G. (1990) "Random Genetic Drift, R.A. Fisher, and the Oxford School of Ecological Genetics" in Lorenz Krüger, Gerd Gigenzerer, and Mary S. Morgan (eds.) *The Probabilistic Revolution* (Cambridge: MIT Press).

Tussing, Arlon (1966) "The Labor Force in Meiji Growth: A Quantitative Study of Yamanashi Prefecture" in *Journal of Economic History* 26, 1: 59–92.

United States Department of Agriculture (1936) *Agricultural Adjustment 1933 to 1935* (Washington: Government Printing Office).

Unites States Bureau of Corporations (1908) *Report of the Commissioner of Corporation on Cotton Exchanges* (Washington: Government Printing Office).

United States Department of Commerce and Labor (1910 and various) *Daily and Consular Trade Reports* (Washington, D.C.: Government Printing Office).

Vallet, Jean (1911) *Contribution a l'étude de la condition de la grande industrie au Caire* (Valence: Imprimerie Valenciemne).

Vatikiotis, P.J. (1969) *The Modern History of Egypt* (New York: Frederick Praeger).

Vietor, Richard H. (1994) *Contrived Competition* (Cambridge: The Belknap Press).

Vitalis, Robert (1990) "On the Theory and Practice of Compradors: The Role of ᶜAbbud Pasha in the Egyptian Political Economy" in *International Journal of Middle East Studies* 22: 291–313.

————(1995) *When Capitalists Collide* (Berkeley: University of California Press).

————(1996) "The 'New Deal' in Egypt: The Rise of Anglo-American Commercial Competition in World War II and the Fall of Neocolonialism" in *Diplomatic History* 20,2: 211–239.

————and Steven Heydemann (2000) "War, Keynesianism and Colonialism: Explaining State-Market Relations in the Postwar Middle East" in Steven Heydeman (ed.) *War, Institutions and Social Change in the Middle East* (Berkeley: University of California Press).

Vogel, Frank E. and Samuel L. Hayes III (1998) *Islamic Law and Finance: Religion, Risk and Return* (The Hague: Kluwer Law International).

Wade, Robert (1993) "Managing Trade: Taiwan and South Korea as Challenges to Economics and Political Science" in *Comparative Politics* 25, 2: 147–167.

Wahba, Izzat (1985) *Tajribat al-dimuqratiyyah al-liberaliyyah fi misr* (Cairo: Al Ahram Strategic Studies Center).

Wahba, Mourad Magdi (1994) *The Role of the State in the Egyptian Economy: 1945–1951* (Reading: Ithaca Press).

Waldner, David (1999) *State Building and Late Development* (Ithaca: Cornell University Press).

Walters, Pamela Barnhouse and David R. James (1992) "Schooling for Some: Child Labor and School Enrollment of Black and White Children in the Early Twentieth Century South" in *American Sociological Review* 57, 5: 635–650.

———and Carl M. Briggs (1993) "The Family Economy, Child Labor, and Schooling: Evidence from the Early Twentieth Century South" in *American Sociological Review* 58, 2: 163–181.

Waterbury, John (1983) *The Egypt of Nasser and Sadat* (Princeton: Princeton University Press).

Weiner, Myron (1991) *The Child and the State in India* (Princeton: Princeton University Press).

Wellisz, Stanislaw "Regulation of Natural Gas Pipeline Companies: An Economic Analysis" in *The Journal of Political Economy* 71, 1: 30–43.

Wildavsky, Aaron (1979) *The Politics of the Budgetary Process* (Boston: Little Brown).

Wilkinson, Sir I. Gardner (1867) *A Handbook for Travellers in Egypt* (London: John Murray).

Williams, Jeffrey (1986) *The Economic Function of Futures Markets* (Cambridge: Cambridge University Press).

Willoughby, William F. (1890) "Child Labor" in *Publications of the American Economic Association* 5, 2: 5–70.

Wolcott, Susan (1994) "The Perils of Lifetime Employment Systems: Productivity Advance in the Indian and Japanese Textile Industries, 1920–1938" in *The Journal of Economic History* 54, 2: 307–324.

Working, Holbrook (1949) "The Theory of Price Storage" in *The American Economic Review* 39: 1254–1262.

Wright, Gavin (1981) "Cheap Labor and Southern Textiles, 1880–1930" in *Quarterly Journal of Economics* 96, 4: 605–629.

Wyse, R.C. (1920) "The Selling and Financing of the American Cotton Crop" in *The Economic Journal* 30: 473–483.

Yahya, Galal and Khalid Na°im (1984) *Al-Wafd al-Misri* (Alexandria: New Association Library).

Zaghlul, Sa°d (1928) *Athar al-za°im Sa°d Zaghlul* ed. Muhammad Ibrahim Al-Jaziri (Cairo: Dar al-Kutub al-Misriyya).

# Index

Abaza, Abd al-Hamid   30–31
Abaza, Osman   47
Abbud, Ahmad   57
Abbud (industrial complex)   138
ᶜAbd al-Hadi, Ibrahim   152,
   184 fn. 38
Abdel Wahab, Ahmad   69, 77–83, 94,
   100–103, 105, 108, 178 n.3
Abdel Wahab memorandum   77,
   83, 97
Adverse selection   12, 13, 24, 70,
   183 fn. 36
Alexandria   38, 68, 72, 74, 99, 153
Alexandria Cotton Pressing
   Company   140
Alexandria General Produce Association
   68, 81
Amin, ᶜAbd al-Munᶜim   131
ᶜAqqad, Mahmud ᶜAbbas al-   106
Arthur D. Little Company (report by)
   111, 114–117, 120, 128
Ashmuni (cotton)   49, 50, 51, 52, 79
Asset specificity   15, 126, 127

"bad spinning"   40, 42, 136
Balls, Lawrence   43, 56, 80
Bank Misr   92, 153, 178 fn. 2
Banks, commercial   73, 74, 83, 92,
   98, 99
Beinin, Joel   35, 43, 50, 60, 124,
   125, 128
"Big Push" industrialization   126, 148

Brazil   152, 173
Bresciani-Turroni, Costantino   81, 100
British Cotton Growers Association
   39
Bursat al-ᶜuqud   74; see also markets,
   commodities and contracts,
   futures

Cairo   3, 46, 70, 78, 80, 94, 104,
   152, 168
Cairo University   31
Cairo Water Company   140
California   21, 34, 37, 48, 84, 85,
   153, 164, 167
Camp, Wofford B.   84
Carson, William   146
Catterall, William   42
Chadbourne Accord   102
Chamber of Ginning
   Establishment   154
Chaudhry, Kiren   166
Child labor   2, 5, 171, 172, 173
   And cotton production   63–67
   And industrialization   143,
   148–149, 151, 155, 157–158,
   160–161, 164, 166
Civil code   96, 134, 136
Coalition, regulatory   10, 16, 22, 25,
   30, 32, 82, 125, 141, 175 fn. 7
Coalition, social   3, 4, 5, 9, 16,
   19, 102
Cocoa   34

Coffee 34
Comparative advantage 17, 18, 31, 39, 67, 110, 117, 126, 164, 170, 171
Conciliation committee 133, 134, 136
Contracts, forward 71, 77, 79, 177 fn. 6
Contracts, futures 71, 72, 73, 74, 75, 76, 77, 79
Contracts, labor
In Britain 40
In Egypt 131, 134, 144
Contracts, rental 103
Contracts, spot 71, 72, 75
Corn 17, 48
Cotton ginning 46, 47, 56, 64, 100, 150–156, 158
Cotton, Indian 81, 104
Cotton seed (for planting) 42, 44–48, 62, 66, 68, 80, 84–86
Cotton seed (as a commodity) 28, 35, 150–156
Cotton seed oil 150–154
Cotton staple 3, 32, 36, 40–42, 45, 47, 49–51, 55, 67, 68, 75, 77–78, 81, 83–84, 96–97, 117, 164, 166
Craig, James 55
Crisis, ecological 5, 34–36, 48–49, 57, 59–61, 163, 165, 172

Dependency theory 7, 8, 111
Dividend premium 140, 141
Drainage 43, 44, 48, 56–57, 59–61, 84
Dudgeon, Gerald 56, 80
Duss, Tawfiq 79
Dutch disease 28; see also inflation

East Asia (development model) 6, 8, 21, 121, 146
Economic development 2, 5, 6–10, 20, 21, 22, 24, 26–29, 32, 67, 90, 111, 113–114, 120, 143, 145, 153, 165, 167–168, 174

Edgeworth, Francis 44
Education 5, 32, 65–66, 102–108, 114, 126, 139, 149, 156–158, 160, 167, 169, 170–172, 174
Efficiency wages 122–123, 144–149
Egyptian Federation of Industry 131, 151, 154
Elasticity of demand 79, 126
Elasticity of supply 126
Export-oriented growth 111, 116, 119, 121, 165–166

Factor abundance (scarcity) 9, 19, 63–64, 87, 90, 120–122, 171
Factor endowments 1, 4–5, 8–9, 16, 18, 32, 65, 67, 104, 113–114, 116, 126, 143, 164–165
Fascism 92, 93, 101
Finance Ministry 101
Foaden, William 46
Free Officers 115, 125, 168, 172
Fuad (King of Egypt) 95, 105–106, 180 fn. 21
Futures 40, 62, 71–76, 79, 154, 168

Galton, Francis 44
Gasche, Robert 138
General Union of Agriculturalists 70, 79, 81–82, 95, 97–98, 100
Germany 21, 77, 89, 90, 93, 105, 106, 164
Great Britain 31, 32, 38, 84, 93, 116, 123
Great Depression 4, 28, 31–32, 75, 77, 83, 89, 91, 93–95, 98, 100–101, 103, 170
Greif, Avner 3
Gritly, Ali el- 147–148, 157

Halaqas 77
Hansen, Bent 7, 60, 173
Harari, Ralph 92, 109, 178 fn. 1
Hechscher, Eli 18, 110–111, 117

Heydemann, Stephen   90–91, 93–94
Hitler   106
Human capital   6, 13, 20–21, 29, 32,
     39, 45, 126, 156–157, 161,
     166–167, 170–171
Hussein Kamil (Sultan of Egypt)
     45, 95

Imperfect information   6, 14, 16–20
Import substitution   6, 27, 31, 93,
     110–111, 115, 119–120, 124
India   33, 34, 166, 173
Inflation   100, 115, 180 fn. 31, 183
     fn. 30, 184 fn. 40; see also Dutch
     disease
International Cotton Federation; see
     International Federation of Master
     Cotton Spinners
International Federation of Master
     Cotton Spinners   30, 31 39,
     41, 98
Issawi, Charles   160, 168–169
ʿIzz al-Din, Amin   132

Japan   21, 40, 104, 117, 122–123,
     147, 158, 164, 167, 169–170
Jumʿah, ʿAbd al-Salam   154

Kafr al-Dawwar   131
Kafr al-Zayyat Oil Company
     140, 153
Keynes, John Maynard   6, 90–92,
     94, 102, 111, 115, 117, 144,
     173, 179 fn. 11
Keynesian economic theory   6, 7, 27,
     31, 90–95, 97, 109, 115–116,
     118, 122–123, 135, 144, 146,
     169, 173
Khedivial Agricultural Society   30, 45,
     62
Kitchener, Lord   77

L'Egypte Contemporaine   59
Lewis, Sir Arthur   93, 113, 116

Literacy   4, 5, 66, 103, 113, 127, 149,
     157–158, 160–161, 170, 173
Liverpool   38, 40, 98, 99
Luhayta, Muhammad Fahmi   104–110,
     113, 121, 123, 148, 167, 168

Macara, Sir Charles   155, 156
Mahir, ʿAli   104–105, 124, 154
Manchester   40, 41, 72
Mandur, Muhammad   136
Markets
     Commodity   22, 23, 36, 37, 67, 71,
          72, 73, 87
     Future   71, 72, 74–79, 154, 168
     Labor   5, 6, 9, 40, 113, 114, 118,
          120, 123, 148, 172
     Spot   71, 74, 75, 79, 81, 82, 99
Marshall, Alfred   17, 123, 146
Mehallah al-Kubra   146
Mercantilism   18, 90, 92, 94, 109
Mina el-Bassal   74, 81, 82
Ministry of Agriculture   46, 47, 61
Ministry of Commerce   115
Ministry of Social Affairs   105,
     108, 132
Ministry of War   104
Mit Afifi (cotton)   49, 50, 51, 52,
     55, 75
Monopoly   8, 24, 47, 77, 81, 85, 106,
     107, 121, 147
Moral economy   120, 144–146, 148
Moral hazard   12, 13, 24, 70, 132
Mosseri, Victor   56, 65, 80, 177 fn. 15
Mussolini   94, 101, 106

Naggar, Said el-   31–32, 110–116,
     120–121, 126, 139, 148, 161, 167
Nagib, Muhammad   131
Nahas, Joseph (Yusuf)   3–4, 7–8, 56,
     61, 66, 70–71, 76, 79–82,
     94–101, 103–104, 108, 110, 125,
     179 fn. 11, 179 fn. 16, 179 fn. 17,
     180 fn. 21
Nahas, Mustafa al-   154

National Bank of Egypt    92, 166
Natural selection    44
Neo-classical economic model    6, 11,
    14, 91, 93, 97, 99, 104, 120–121,
    123, 144–145, 148
Nile Delta    84, 86
Nile Valley    4, 38, 48, 163

"on-call" sales    76, 77
Organization of Petroleum Exporting
    Countries    23

Posusney, Marsha    124–125, 148–149,
    182 fn. 21, 184 fn. 2
Prébisch, Raul    111
Premium (paid for quality)    1, 4, 14,
    33, 41, 45, 49, 51, 62, 67, 69, 75,
    77, 79, 85, 97, 122, 127, 146
Price
    (differential)    1, 14, 30, 36, 41, 45,
        48, 51, 55, 56, 76, 78, 85, 97
    effects of    13, 19, 40, 41, 42, 74,
        152, 174
    for Egyptian cotton    3, 42, 61, 62,
        68, 70, 79, 81, 98, 100, 153
    of inputs    44, 92, 96, 97, 109, 147,
        151, 153, 154, 155
    spot    76, 77
    supports    79, 98, 102, 151
    system    12, 26, 36, 71, 72, 73, 76,
        97, 99, 163
Productivity, labor
    In Egypt    9, 21, 28, 31, 107,
        109, 121, 144, 146–148,
        153, 157, 160
    In Japan    123
Productivity, physical    28, 43, 102,
    108, 113
Productivity, peasant    57, 115
Productivity, total factor    86

Regulation
    as a coalition    3, 74, 81, 100
    and product markets    75, 125
    and incentives    10, 23, 25, 37, 45,
        48, 63, 69, 96, 120, 150, 154,
        165, 171
    and information    12, 23, 25, 164,
        165, 166
    and institutions    3, 45
    and labor markets    107, 111,
        119–120, 123, 128, 142, 147,
        157, 172
    and rents    113
    and the state    7, 9–10, 25, 30, 63,
        94, 108
Reputation
    as an asset    5, 12, 14, 16, 21,
        22, 24, 47–48, 61, 66,
        68–69, 127, 164
    (for quality)    1, 3
    of agricultural goods    11, 14, 21, 34
    of Egyptian cotton    3, 16, 28–30,
        33, 36–37, 41, 43, 47, 62, 64,
        66–68, 83–84, 96, 97, 155
    and imperfect information    6, 11,
        12, 14, 20, 66, 164, 177 fn. 5
    an outcome of regulation    10, 22,
        23, 34, 80, 81, 86, 150, 151
    and price    1, 14, 45, 77, 122
    and trade    2, 16, 17, 21, 23, 32, 66
Ricardo, David    17, 18
Rice    35, 57, 65, 86
Richards, Alan    57, 60
Rogowski, Ronald    19
Roosevelt, President Franklin    94, 101,
    102, 179 fn. 14
Royal Entomological Society    46

Sakel see Sakellaridis
Sakellaridis (cotton)    42, 46, 48, 50,
    51, 52, 54, 55, 56, 57, 75, 77, 79,
    81, 82, 83, 96, 101, 176 fn. 12
San Joaquin valley    34, 37, 84–87
Sayf al-Nasr, Hamdi    79, 97, 98,
    178 fn. 8
Sharia    76, 77, 177 fn. 6
Shubra al-Khaima    136

Sidki, Ismail    78–79, 82, 100–101
Sirri, Hussein    57
Smith, Adam    17
South (U.S.)    34, 64, 86, 123,
    144–145, 158, 164, 167, 170–171
Soviet Union    32, 89
    Central Asia    153
Specialization    1, 17, 30, 107, 166
Speculation    72–74, 76
Spinners    3, 12, 15, 30, 36, 39–42,
    44, 47, 55, 59, 67–71, 75–76, 78,
    81–82, 87, 99, 151
Stolper-Samuelson theorem    18
Sugar    102, 107–108, 158
Sulaiman, Salim    136
Sully, Daniel    41, 76, 87

Tariff    77, 78, 93, 102, 104, 108,
    111, 112, 153, 169
Tea    34
Texas    64, 84
Thabit, Karim    106
Thabit, Thabit    106
Thailand    37, 86
Trade unions    6, 9, 108, 112, 114,
    122, 131, 141, 166
Trigger mechanism    14, 34, 122, 146

Uniformity (of cotton fiber)    40, 46,
    48, 67–68, 155
Union of Egyptian Agriculturalists
    70, 79, 81, 82, 95, 97, 98, 100
United Kingdom    105, 152

Vitalis, Robert    57, 90, 91, 93, 94,
    102, 103, 120, 168

Wafd    70, 78–79, 82, 95,
    102–103, 105–106, 151–152,
    154–156, 185 fn. 7
"Weberian" state    11, 24, 25,
    28, 67
Weiner, Myron    173
World Coffee Organization    23

Yakan, Adli    79
Yields, crop    35
Yields, cotton    43–45, 48–51, 55–59,
    61, 84–85, 96
Yields, rice    86
Yule George    44, 49

Zaghloul, Sad    8, 94, 95,
    178 fn. 4
Ziwar, Ahmad    79